The Breathless Present

Also by Carl Vigeland

The Mostly Mozart Guide to Mozart
Letters to a Young Golfer (with Bob Duval)
Jazz in the Bittersweet Blues of Life (with Wynton Marsalis)
Stalking the Shark
In Concert
Great Good Fortune

The Breathless Present

A Memoir in Four Movements

Carl Vigeland

ISBN 978-1-937146-04-7

"What you take for granted in Franklin County you can't take for granted at Aix-en-Provence and so you *see* it…But *it* isn't *there*. It's *here*."

—Archibald MacLeish

CONTENTS

I

A Spy in the House of the Gods

THE SHADOW WAS ALMOST GONE THAT DAY. It came from within, and when something "without"—as in outside of me, external—when that happened, it would dissipate, often for a time disappear. Skiing could do that, skiing fast on a spring day with few people around and while it lasted no sense of an ending, which is when the shadow usually reappeared, sometimes taking the form of a spell, under the influence of which I had been asking myself some form of the same question since I was old enough to have sensed that something in my father's life was not right. How could the person who taught me what was beautiful and most important in the world have tried seemingly to destroy everything in his life that he loved?

Last one down the mountain, I took the back way home, turning off Route 2 in the old milltown of Shelburne Falls, Massachusetts, and then driving south several miles to the sanctuary of Conway on a road that is called the Conway Road if you begin in Shelburne Falls and the Shelburne Falls Road if you start out in Conway. It was late March, the first day of spring and the end of the ski season at Berkshire East, a mom and pop area in Charlemont, northwest of Conway, where I had made eight solo runs in the warm afternoon sun.

Years ago, I often went there with friends or family, occasionally bumping into an acquaintance who was a member of the ski patrol. Once married to a former colleague of my wife's when she taught school, he was the real estate agent who despite my efforts to delay the process had sold our Conway farmhouse be-fore we moved half an hour's drive away to  Amherst. On the day of the closing, a hot day in mid summer, with our three kids waiting in the minivan in the driveway and my wife Bonnie out of town, I had walked a last time through the empty house, hollow like the chambers of my heart, silent save for the music playing in my head.

Before my final run at Berkshire East I stopped after the chair lift left me off to ask a man whose red jacket signified he was a cur-rent member of the ski patrol if he'd known my friend, who had re-cently and suddenly died. A brief silence preceded his answer. I looked out over the terrain, white-topped only here, because they made snow all winter. Otherwise the landscape was sere, with splashes of green in some of the hills, hinting of the coming season.

"Yes," the man finally replied, as if some personal awkwardness prevented him from saying much else.

"It was a stroke?" I said, hoping to learn a little about a death that was as mysterious to me as it was troubling. But what I heard only made it more disturbing.

"He was alone," the man said. "Someone found him in his apartment. He had been dead for several days."

Unable to forget the urgency in my conversations when he was our realtor nearly twenty years ago, I wondered guiltily what could have mattered so much that I even called once to berate him for putting a For Sale sign in the front yard.

"It's what happens when you sell your house," he had replied laconically, but also with some justifiable annoyance.

"Okay," I remember saying, "but does it have to be such a big sign?" In fact there was nothing large about it, except for what it signified to me then, its sale the symbolic manifestation of my failure to become a real writer.

My lost Eden still looked pretty much like it used to, though a little more snow had melted since earlier in the week, when I'd come into town from a different direction, stopping after I'd bought some kielbasa at Pekarski's in South Deerfield and impulsively continued up the winding state highway as far as Boyden Road—so named after an old Conway family of many generations whose farm was the only major dairy operation in town to have survived the enroachment of suburbia. I'd turned there and driven as far as Potter's Garage, an anomalous structure in the woods where the owner, my friend David Potter, lived with his wife Betsy and one of their three grown sons. David was just walking back from his house toward his shop, where he fixes cars in the morning before heading down into the Connecticut River valley town of Hadley to his other job, taking care of the local power company's vehicles.

About fifty years old, I am guessing, David grew up in Amherst and South Deerfield. He married one of the Winter daughters, a family who bought an old Conway farm in the late 1960s. Gerry, the father, was dead, but Mrs. Winter still lived in the farmhouse. Their youngest child, Melanie, was a student at the Conway Grammar School when I subbed there long ago. David has a beard and long hair, is even tempered, smart, always working, owns some real estate now, I learned. His nearby neighbor when he first built here was Jamie Bryce, someone whose family I had known growing up in Buffalo. One of Jamie's brothers was killed in a car accident when Jamie was still young, and his first wife Dana, a very beautiful woman who took photographs for a living and rode horses and collected antiques for pleasure, died in the 1980s of breast cancer, an indescribably sad death. Jamie, I knew, had remarried and has a new family and lives on Cape Cod.

"He stopped by a few months ago," David said in the soft voice, almost a drawl, that I remembered from days when I'd bring a car by to be repaired and hang out for an hour talking while David figured out the mechanical problem. He never rushed and he always got things right.

"I saw him, too," I said, "a few years ago. My daughter was in a skating competition in Hyannis and he came over to watch."

At first as we talked, David stood by the window on the driver's side of my car while I remained seated inside. I hadn't planned to stay, but we kept talking and finally I got out and stood up and looked around.

"We could be in northern Vermont," I said.

"I know," David said. "It's why we've stayed. I can start walking out the back of my house and not see anything or anyone for several miles."

We talked about other neighbors. Did I remember Jimmy Antes, whose family's farm was next door? I had to think for a minute, remembering the farm well—we bought fresh eggs there on the honor system, from an old refrigerator on the front porch of the main farmhouse, and I once took Deidre Antes's photograph for the local newspaper, because she delivered the newspapers on her Boyden Road route by horseback—but I couldn't place Jimmy.

"Jimmy and I used to drive our dune buggies all over," David said. "We raised some hell." And then he paused, looked at the ground for a moment, said something to his son who passed us on the way from the garage to the house—for lunch, I supposed—and finally continued. "Jimmy's wife was killed in a car accident."

Nothing to say but how sorry I was. Hadn't old man Antes died, too? And David said you must mean Merrill, since Merrill's brother Hosmer has been dead for decades, and yes, Merrill was dead now, too. But did I remember Norm French, who had owned the small company in Conway's lone mill that made equipment for cider presses? Of course, in fact I wrote a short magazine piece about the company. Well, Norm's wife Thelma died a while back

but Norm was still living, and he's 90. "How great," I said. "I re-member when I was subbing at the school and Norm was chair-man of the school committee, he would look out the window of his shop, across the river and the road to the school, counting cars in the parking lot to see if anyone were late."

"Actually, I'm going to be late," David said, meaning to his job at the power company. "That ice storm this winter, I never made it home for like two weeks. Slept in my truck."

Now, as I approached the Harris farm where we had first lived in Conway in an apartment in the rear of the Harris farmhouse, something seemed missing, and with a sudden shock I realized that the huge old Harris barn was being torn down.

The cupola with the large H was gone, and all of the roof. I pulled over to the side of the road and got out of my car and took a few photos with the camera in my phone, drove a little farther and stopped again and walked up between the barn and the house and took some more photos. Snow was melting. The fields on the hill behind the barn had grown in almost completely, and what was once open was now mostly forest.

Archie's house was up that hill. The man who owned it now, who had also bought the Harris farm a few years ago, used to take a helicopter to work in New York City, starting out from a helipad he installed in Ada MacLeish's former flower garden. You'd hear it overhead, coming in to get him early in the morning or bringing him home late at night. By then we'd bought our own house on the other side of town, but that was much later, long after the beginning of the time when I was supposed to be looking for a job, and we never had any money.

I had left grad school after just a year, when Bonnie and I would drive down into the Connecticut River valley together in our 1963 Volvo 122S that we bought from the boyfriend of one of Bonnie's college suitemates, who had lived in the apartment on the floor below ours in Providence after we were married. We were there two years. Our Karmann Ghia convertible died just before we moved to Conway, so we bought the Volvo for $175. Bonnie's classmate visited us once afterwards, and we went skinny dipping with her at the same bend in the South River I had just passed on my way home from skiing.

Bonnie was there, too, and I remember how everyone laughed a little nervously when we decided to go swimming without our clothes. We must have walked back to the farm. It was maybe a mile, and we probably took the river path that I loved, crossing back where the tractor crossed the river below the huge field that looked out at the river and verdant expanse of the farm. It was summer, when our bedroom window was open, and in the morning as Bonnie and I lay in bed we would hear this loud trampling which was the cows after they had been milked going out for the day. I can still hear in my memory our landlord's voice.

"Bossy!" he would yell at a cow that was out of line.

The first time in the spring when the cows went out like this after being in the barn all winter was a major event. Entrances to the barnyard would be blocked so cows wouldn't go the wrong way and Dottie, a daughter-in-law who lived just down the road, would come over to help. What a commotion! Once we had settled in after that first year I went out and helped, too, or pretended to.

Our second-floor apartment in the back of the farmhouse was set over a dirt driveway that went around the back of the house, in between the woodshed under our bedroom and a stonewall that buttressed a growth of bushes with some blackberries, bordered on one side by the barway to the lower pastures, and on the other by a small lawn where Mr. Harris had placed a picnic table near an outdoor stone barbecue that was large enough to burn wood, not charcoal. We often used to cook out there in the warm weather, and when another of Bonnie's college friends came with her boyfriend, a medical school student who was an early informational help to me during the period of my father's first hospitalization, in Boston, he and I played chess on the picnic table. An old snapshot shows us playing on what must have been a chilly fall day because I have on a lumber jacket. I am smoking a pipe. Had a moustache then, too.

I have no idea how we survived financially. Our rent was $150 a month, an amount that increased by $10 when we added an unheated, second-floor bedroom in the main farmhouse as a place for me to write. You reached this room through a door in the large closet that had a hookup for a washer and dryer and that I also used for a time as a darkroom. That was one way we saved money, my darkroom. All our presents for birthdays and Christmas were mounted black and white photos that I had shot of the farm or other places in Conway, especially Cricket Hill on the other side of town, an area of abandoned farms and stone walls where the forest had taken over again, trees of second or third growth even in the cellar holes, including one across a dirt road from an old family cemetery that became the setting of my first published magazine story and the inspiration for a sestina I wrote.

I was always writing poems for occasions and commemorations—family holiday gatherings, birthdays, the death of our first dog, my brother's wedding. It was on a hike with our landlord's wife that I had learned that the poet, Archibald MacLeish, was our immediate neighbor. He lived on an estate at the top of the hill, above the pastures and beyond two ponds in the woods that were bordered on our farm's side by an abandoned apple orchard. I had spotted him a few times in town, usually at the post office, where he pulled up in his black Mercedes, wearing a white tee shirt, carpenter's overalls, and a straw hat, and retrieved an entire bushel basket of mail that the postmaster, Syd St. Peters, had been holding for him.

Mr. St. Peters had been responsible for our being able to rent the Harris apartment. In our 20s, married for two years, we were among many people who moved to the area for its rural beauty and proximity to the main campus of the state university and several excellent colleges. A week before our lease had run out in Providence, where Bonnie had graduated from Pembroke and I had taught school in a nearby town, I had contacted Mr. St. Peters, whom I'd met on an earlier, unsuccessful apartment-hunting expedition, and he had given me the number for the Harrises, whom I called immediately.

"When can you come and look?" they asked us.

"Right now," I said.

It was about a two-and-a-half hour drive from Providence. A mile from the center of town, as we came around a bend in the road that followed the course of the South River, ahead of us rose a white farmhouse, prominently standing above the road, and with the roof and cupola of a large barn partially visible beyond it.

"I think this must be the place," I said to Bonnie, barely able to catch my breath, my only worry that our prospective landlord would change his mind about renting the apartment when he saw my long hair, which came down almost to my shoulders. I'm still not sure why this didn't bother him or if, as I imagine it did, what prompted him to overlook it. Perhaps they needed the money, but that thought seemed improbable; Mr. Harris, I soon discovered, would for months at a time leave in the barn's milkhouse uncashed checks from the company that picked up his milk. And every two years he bought a new Chevrolet, trading in the old one that could not have had more than few a thousand miles on it—the longest trips he ever took were on Sunday, when he and Mrs. Harris went out to dinner—and paying the difference, I was certain, in cash.

We'd been living in Conway for several months when I overheard Syd say, "Mr. MacLeish should be back next week." In June I finally introduced myself to him. I'm not sure what I expected to happen, but I wrote him a short note saying that my wife and I had moved in at the end of the previous summer. My work was in a state of flux, I announced, as I set out to become a poet myself, or perhaps the next great stylist in American literature, once I had mastered the short-story form, which I expected—though I did not say this—to lead to the writing of novels that would solidify my rapidly growing literary reputation. Perhaps, I suggested, I could hike up the hill, where I knew by then I would come to the first pond. We could meet there and then walk together through the woods and along his road, talking about Conway, our work, the relationship of life and art.

I waited anxiously for an answer. From the large window in our living room, I looked repeatedly down the driveway and across the road, where Mr. Harris had secured a metal mailbox to the flattened top of a tree trunk. Painted red and fastened to one side of the zinc-colored box with a rivet, a metal flag, upraised, indicated to Larry, the rural route carrier, that outgoing mail awaited his pickup. When the flag was down, I knew that the mail had finally come. I would stop writing and walk outside to get it.

A week passed and no answer. Perhaps I should not have written. What could I have been thinking?

Sometimes Mr. Harris, a white-haired, stoop-shouldered Yankee in his mid 60s, got the mail instead. He might have been weeding in the huge garden on the other side of the gravel driveway from the house. Or, the lord of his domain, he could have been coming up that dirt tractor path leading from the immense sweep of his mowings and corn fields across the South River to the road, where he nodded in the direction of Larry, who had stopped next to the mailbox in his beaten-up sedan. As it idled, Larry, with a cigarette dangling from his lips, sat midway between the driver's and passenger seats so he could keep a foot on the brake and a hand on the steering wheel, while he reached through the open passenger-side window to the mailbox.

I decided I wasn't going to receive a response. But I kept on hoping.

At the bottom of the stairs that led from a door in our dining room to the entrance of his garage and woodshed, Mr. Harris when he picked up the mail put what was ours in a second, smaller mailbox nailed to the wooden wall above the stairway railing. Magazines and oversize envelopes he placed together, bent or folded at their midpoint, in a space between the railing and the wall; boxes he left below, on a stairstep. Then he continued in a kind of shuffle past enormous stacks of cordwood and opened the door to his kitchen, where the woodstove was kept going every day of the year next to the vinyl-covered lounger where he sat, manure-covered boots propped up on the chair's footrest, and read the latest issue of *Hoard's Dairyman,* to which he subscribed. While he rested there, his wife Dorothy, a large, still gregarious woman, a few years younger than her husband and not yet showing the first signs of the apparent Alzheimer's that would soon begin to change her life forever, finished cooking the noonday meal.

Had I said something in my letter to Mr. MacLeish that I shouldn't have? Was the tone right? The length? I was still pondering such profound questions when a small white envelope arrived one morning, with my name and our address written in cursive in a firm hand and a return address that consisted only of his last name, abbreviated, and that of the town's zip code. With trembling fingers, I tore it open.

"Nice letter: nice neighbors," began the short note on a small sheet of yellow, lined paper. "But the answer has to be no. In my business a man needs a private wilderness of his own where he can go without risk of meeting anyone but a duck or a deer. The pond is that to me and has been for almost fifty years. I am sure you will understand." Having greeted me as, "Mr.," in the salutation, he signed the note, "Faithfully," with his full name.

I wrote him back immediately, obsequiously apologizing for my intrusion and then asking him what I didn't realize was a bigger favor, but one that it turned out he could accommodate somewhat. Except for my wife, there was no one I knew in Conway with whom I could really share what I did. Might we somehow talk?

This time he responded right away.

"Not only learning to write but writing itself is a lonely job. I understand your letter very well. The problem is the one you suggest—time. I have to guard mine jealously and so do you. Why don't we do this—you send me the one piece, whatever it may be, you think most characteristic and I'll read it as soon as I can & reply. I may have to wait for a week or two but I'll get at it."

I froze.

The entire summer passed before I finally sent Mr. MacLeish a short poem, which I have lost. He wrote me back the following: "Two suggestions. First the rhythm. Your metrics are marching *you* instead of the other way around. Get hold of a copy of Yeats' *Collected Poems* (the 1952 collection) and read chronologically, observing his development of his own rhythms inside the rule of metrics. Second, your images are only rarely realized ("Black water in the river's bend"). They should always be specific and vivid—but managed with the fewest possible words. When you are in a library again look at Waley's translation of Chinese poems."

The next letter did not come until the following May and, like the first few, was addressed to me as, "Mr. Vigeland." In response to a short story I had sent him, based on an experience the previous fall at the nearby Totman farm, where I had worked during corn harvest, he wrote: "Forgive the delay—not forgetfulness.

"Your letter has a 'fine feel of place'—more, I think, than the 'story.' The trouble with the story is not, I think, there is 'too much farm detail' but that the images, good in themselves, are unfocussed. Is it the father's story or the boy's or the calf's? From page to page it shifts around and the result is that the images scatter. The narrating consciousness is the boy's—but at one point the father's. And *the* calf does not identify itself until the end when it takes over. Having raised calves myself I have a sense of the loss but it comes too late and in terms, not of calf or boy, but of the turkey buzzards. All this sounds very sweeping but it isn't. Your problem is the relatively simple one of construction—giving the story a center and then respecting that center. If I may presume (and it *is* presumptive) I think the story begins not with the boy in the barn at morning milking but with the calf born in the autumn cold—

the boy's sense of that simple but troubling event in the world of his life, the world of the farm."

Inspired, I revised the story right away and sent it back, and he wrote me about the revision at the end of June, for the first time adding my first name to the salutation: "Sorry to have been so slow but I want *really* to read your story and time is hard to come by these days. You'll be hearing from me. Incidentally, your title is *Autumn Calf.* That came to me in a dream. Or, better, *October Calf* if it *was* October. (November wouldn't do)."

A few days later, in response to yet another revision, he wrote me a longer letter: "If I were your age I'd use this story as a point of departure—a sort of firing exercise as they say in the field artillery. The problem, as you know, is focus. What are we to *see*? Which is another way of asking what the story is 'about.' There are times when it seems to be 'about' dairy-farming. Then again it seems to be 'about' the late-born calf. *Or* the boy. My guess is that it *ought* to be about the relation of the boy *to* the late-born calf—his discovery of error in the universe (to put it pompously). Error in nature being what we call evil—though the buzzards would disagree of course. But whatever the *discovery* of the story we should see it obliquely, see it for ourselves, not be told.

"What to do next? Well, you might go back to D. H. Lawrence's short stories—see how *he* would use the dairy farm or its equivalent—how he would use the fault in nature—the boy—the vultures. Then work out your own way of seeing."

I had also sent him a new poem called *May*, and he closed with these comments: "'Baby pea green latticed leaves' is a lot of words (which lose their image because there are too many of them). The 'cow dung' is dragged in to figure where it plays no part. The end rhythm is good."

Again, I revised the story about the calf and sent it off with what I am sure was much too long a letter. In early August he wrote back: "I'll read the story when I can find an open afternoon …Your reaction to D.H.L. is sensitive and perceptive and you have touched the nerve when you say 'his use of nature imagery is almost too good.' Why 'almost too good?' Because, I assume, every facet of the scene *works*. It's not there for *décor*. It's not there for its *own* sake. It's there for the *story's* sake. That alone is a wonderful lesson to learn. About your question (the weight of all literature on the back of your neck)—one only feels that when he thinks of himself as *competing* with the past. How '*compete*' with John Donne? You can't. And as for Shakespeare—…! The answer is that new generations of writers aren't competitive with the past. They are the continuation of the past—the latest brood of coral insects building on the shoulders of their predecessors. Get hold of Keats' *Letters* and remind yourself of his attitude toward Shakespeare. The *delight*! As though he had discovered something that was *his*: *part* of him. But indeed it was!"

Through all this time, I held a series of odd jobs, beginning with the gig at the Totman farm. I was a longterm substitute teacher at the grammar school and for two summers ran the school's Title I enrichment program, during which we went on frequent field trips that included a show at the Jacob's Pillow dance festival featuring Twyla Tharp. I worked as an assistant to a brick and stone mason, who was also my friend, a dead ringer for Frank Zappa, son of a Cambridge, Massachusetts florist and my co-Little League coach one year. For a brief, shining but extremely unprofitable moment I served as the business manager of a children's theater troupe, headed by a free spirit who later became an investment banker or lawyer.

After I had started freelancing for regional magazines, I became the town correspondent for the *Greenfield Recorder* newspaper for the sum of $50 per month, with a $10 bonus for every feature story I wrote. At that time the *Recorder*—affectionately known locally as the Distorter—was an afternoon paper, except on Saturday, when it came out in the morning (there was no paper on Sunday). That Saturday edition was essentially a copy of Friday afternoon's, with the layout, photos, and headlines changed a bit— and for good reason. After the Friday paper had been put to bed, late Friday morning, most of the editorial staff adjourned to the taproom at Famous Bill's, a restaurant a block away, so termed because its recipe for lobster pie had once been featured in…the *Ford Times* (the newsletter of the Ford Motor Company).

I never tried that lobster pie, but the beer was cold and there was lots of it, though I think the city editor preferred Manhattans. Whatever, we had a gregarious time, gathered around one large table, and somehow by mid-afternoon we all made it back to the newsroom, with its glorious smell of glue pots and ink and newsprint and cigarette smoke. The city editor was a Pall Malls guy and I a Marlboro Man, though sometimes I treated myself to Luckies, which I considered an essential tool of the writer's craft.

Another editor, dark-haired and humorously profane, had started his career in New York City as a reporter for Al Goldstein's notorious *Screw*. Years later, this man found God—in print—and became the *Recorder's* weekly religion columnist, writing profiles of local clergymen and historic churches. Like most of the other males, he also reported high school football in the fall, competing with the rest of us for the chance to cover away games because the mileage reimbursement was often more than the standard story payment. With the newspaper's longtime staff photographer, Chuck Blake, I learned to cover traffic accidents and fires with feigned dispassion. And when Archibald MacLeish was awarded the National Medal of Freedom, I was dispatched to interview him, even though I told my editor he was in Antigua, where his wife Ada had written me he was.

Leaving town after my stop to see the destruction of the Harris barn, I saw David Potter again, the same friend I had just visited earlier in the week after buying kielbasa in South Deerfield. On his way into the Conway Inn for pizza, he invited me to join him for a beer, but I was already late for dinner. The Conway Inn on Main Street in the center of town was next door to the house where I once rented an office, long after we had left the Harrises and bought the old Parker place. I would walk down Academy Hill, and Ora Hines, a sweet, gravelly-voiced older woman who had lived her whole life in Conway and whose small house was on the other side of the inn, would be smoking a cigarette in the kitchen and making coffee. The Conway Inn back then was run by two sisters, Bercia and Emily, and if the light bulb on the outside front wall was lit that meant it was open. Like eggs at the Antes, payment for the use of the pool table upstairs was your personal responsibility: you played as long as you wanted and then told the sisters how many games and they would tell you what you owed. The only food they served was burgers. We once went to a New Year's Eve party there, the place packed, people we knew only in the context of the farm they ran or the town hall office where they worked, all getting blasted.

"Next time," I said to David, who was telling me what great pizza the inn made. Who knew?

On my way back out of town I saw smoke coming from Boyden's sugar house. I had not seen Howard Boyden in twenty years, and here he was coming out of the sugarhouse. He must be the age—fifty or so—his father Raymond was when his father died, I calculated. He greeted me with great friendliness, and it was very wonderful to me, that smile. In a hurry to check some trees because the sap was really running this day, he told me to come by again when things weren't so hectic.

"Thanks, Howard," I said. "Can I ask you one question?"

"Of course," he said, maybe a little puzzled, as he fussed with something in the back of his pickup.

And so I asked him how long he had been married, and he said 27 years, why was I wondering? And I said because I have been trying to figure out when that bachelor party was, and it must have been 1982, I said, and he said yes, we have pictures, you are probably in one of them, he added, laughing now, and I told him about seeing his father the next morning, when some nails had spilled from his pickup truck onto the highway and I'd stopped to help him pick them up. How Howard smiled when I got to the punchline, which was his father saying what a great time the party had been, and yes Howard added in reply to another of my questions, yes it was in June, yes it was raining that night.

Thought about this as I headed home, thought about my drive down Shelburne Falls road just past the mill just before the Harris barn with the cupola gone, the roof too…how I had stood very still and tried to hear in my head the sweet voice of old Mr. Harris, who survived his wife but when his only daughter Pat died of an aneurysm at about the age of sixty he failed very quickly, and I had listened also for her, one of whose sons I took fishing all these years ago, and I had listened for Raymond Boyden and for Dana Bryce whom I could hear in my mind riding by the Harris farm one summer morning on her horse, clip-clop, clip-clop; how I had loved the skiing that afternoon, skied fast and never fell and there was practically no one there, no lines. I remembered taking Anna once when she was four or five and Christian when he was very little and how he wailed when I put him between my legs and we went down the wide intermediate slope that once formed a border on the west side of the area, since expanded. I always loved that drive afterwards, the turnoff to Shelburne Falls where we used to go for pizza, once when Christian was still a baby and he shat his pants at the pizza place—I knew every house on the road, every family, the turn near the famous swimming spot that is now the site of a miso business. And then that barn, gone, ripped apart, its guts spilled, old hay, tools, cow dung, horse dung, cobwebs, dirt, old timber, gone with the open fields that I hiked with our first dog, Leo, run over by an almost neighbor whose wife baked stupendous pies, gone with my youth, gone with the famous poet up on that hill.

And against the March wind and the water running around the bend in the river I heard in my head as I did every day my mother's voice on the phone calling me just a few days after we had moved in, calling to say my father had locked himself in the bathroom and that he said he had a gun, which he did not have but he said he did, and he had indeed locked himself in the bathroom, and would I please come home, which I did—my father who just a few years before had performed Poulenc's organ concerto with the Buffalo Philharmonic at Kleinhans Music Hall, my father who had called me halfway through my sophomore year in college, right after the holidays, to tell me my closest childhood friend had shot himself in the head, my father whose only sibling, a younger brother, had two years before that, again in January, died of a heart attack, my father who brought us all back to the Berkshires one summer, the back roads and meadows and the Green River where I came around a bend and there were all these beautiful young men and women swimming naked and I joined them, and that night I slept with my wife. We had been married one year, we were staying with my whole family in the home of one of my father's old girlfriends from before World War II, and the next day we went to a Boston Symphony Orchestra rehearsal at Tanglewood of Prokofiev's *Romeo and Juliet*, not an open rehearsal but my father was able to get us in because he knew the manager, and the conductor was a very young Seiji Ozawa, about whom I would write fifteen, sixteen years later in my second book. And I can see so clearly the swaying of the leafed branches outside the Tanglewood Shed everytime I hear that music, see those branches and the memory of my wife's sleeping body as she lay in the bed we shared that summer off the road to nearby South Egremont and the smile on my father's face as he won another poker hand. And I can sense the anxious joy in my mother's heart, joy because we were together—for what turned out to be the last extended time—anxious because my father was already drinking too much.

And I wondered then, that March day by the river, if only a decade later as he lived alone in a small apartment in Tryon, North Carolina, had he known he was going to die, sensed each day that it might be his last, the last time he would smell the flowers in his landlady's yard, the last time he would hear rain on the summer leaves or a car's echo down the quiet street where he lived, the last time he would walk with his cane over to the little church where he played the organ and perhaps practiced again the Bach Toccata and Fugue in D Minor that he had learned in Great Barrington,

Massachusetts, in 1939, the last time he would write his oldest son, the last time he would fall asleep thinking about the woman he had loved first as a boy practically, they were still in high school when they met, the woman he would marry before he went overseas in the war, my mother Ruth.

How happy they once were, the parties at our house, the night the legendary English counter-tenor Alfred Deller sang an old English lullaby to my baby sister, Astrid, as he rocked her in his arms—"lullay, lullay," the refrain went—or the imprompu visits of my dad's Buffalo friend who owned a plumbing company and drove an MG and smoked Phillip Morrises and carried a sketch pad in a pocket of his hunting jacket and wanted to be a singer and whose wife raced cars, all these people who used to come to our modest, shingled house across from the maternity wing of the Children's Hospital, and they all came because of my father, the spell he cast, his joy, his love of the world and of music and back then of Ruth and always his children and the hundreds of friends, none of whom finally could help him when it became too much for him, living, and how could that be I still wondered, and the question ate into me until more than one time in my life I thought "it" would get to me, too, the dark shadow, which is always there in the music, what Wynton would call the sword, and I heard it again—that sword—as I left and walked back to my car parked by the forsaken barn, heard it even though not a note was being played, "lullay, lullay."

II

Ricochet

1

"IF I WERE GOING TO READ A STORY," Maren said as we walked
Jack on a cold, gray November afternoon, "I wouldn't want to read it
if you could explain the story in a couple of sentences. I would only
want to read a story if you had to read all of it to understand it."
Maren had been sick much of the fall, with mono her doctor
thought, but the test results kept coming back negative. She'd
missed a lot of school. We had just been to her school to get work
she was supposed to make up. Now we were walking Jack in the
gathering dusk, with a brisk wind whipping the chilly air against our
faces. The soccer field next to the football stadium was littered with
cups and food wrappings from a football function the previous
weekend. Jack sniffed at the stuff as he looked for a place to pee.

What would I need to say if I were going to write the story my
daughter described, a story you could read late at night in a quiet
corner of the city somewhere? What words would find the feeling
of that summer day when I took off—went on the road—certain
this was something I had to do as I kissed my children goodbye,
Maren the youngest still sleeping with the calendar I'd bought her
on the wall by her bed, the days I would be gone marked off so she
could see? Little did I imagine then how many more days, weeks,
months…years until the Boston performances later the next
month of a piece called *All Rise*: the accelerating energy of those

men and women as they came on stage for the final rehearsal, their different lives, where they might have been the night before and with whom they had made love. And then, slowly making his way across the stage, the architect of that day's musical activity, Wynton Marsalis, whom I first met more than a decade earlier, the year Maren was born, and who repeatedly said his ambition was "to be part of something great," by which he meant jazz, Wynton who once told me that if he had to he could live happily in his old Louisiana neighborhood, passing the time on the stoop of his house, listening to the music of his neighbors' voices while watching the passage of an old couple and a pretty girl down a dusty, unpaved street.

I was four or five years old then and my father— "a keyboard musician, just like my daddy," Wynton would sometimes say by way of explaining to others one of the things he said we had in common—long tormented by competing forces of guilt and pleasure

and dead now more than twenty years, played the hall's new pipe organ on a sunlit day I would remember more for the ride we took later on one of Boston's famous swan boats and the smile I can still sense on my father's deeply expressive face because his family was young, his career ascendant.

What would Maren make of my memory of a man who died seven years before her birth, the grandfather she never knew?

And what would she think about the old lady from the audience in Lincoln, Nebraska who accepted Wynton's invitation there to sit on stage with the band and when Wynton named the musicians at the end of the gig he introduced her as well and she proudly stood and accepting the applause took a bow. Or Harold Russell in his tee shirt with the Marlboros in a tucked sleeve and Darleen sitting in the seat behind the driver's, behind Harold, when she came out one week—we were in Colorado and Wyoming that week—it was her vacation, and also her birthday, and one quiet morning in Laramie, the air still as an arrow ready to be pulled, we walked the town, along Main Street over to the deserted old train station, Darleen and Harold holding hands and talking animatedly, "Look at that, Harold, that store selling cowboy hats. Wouldn't you look handsome in one."

Wyoming was vast and made me feel small, fearful that I might never understand the complex of relationships that bound me by then to a trumpet player from New Orleans and a chain-smoking pit bull—Wynton's words—from Tennessee who used to drive for Guns N' Roses and wore a John Mellencamp leather jacket that girls, he said, had propositioned him for, Harold who spoke to me with tears in his eyes after the road life caught up to him, a doctor told him he had to quit driving, and I asked Harold following lunch in a barbecue place as we talked in his rented retirement condo—he and Darleen had moved to Colorado Springs—what was it about music that mattered?

"The people," he said, and Darleen, looking up from the coffee she was making us, shook her head and softly said, "Harold." His treasure, he called her, with the cute smile and the Harlequin romance in her lap when  she used to come out on the road and in her eyes a deep longing that Harold returned after parking the bus and locking it for the night and started talking about the petite woman who worked in Tennessee back when Harold was on the road, so that they often went weeks without seeing one another. How did Harold sleep I sometimes wondered, alone, with his cigarette cough and the hours on the road, often driving all night and then through much of the next day, crisscrossing America so many times he knew the whole country like a map— "After three million miles," he wrote me, "I was the best damn driver I have ever met! During that three million I kept looking for him. I was it all along!"—knew every shortcut around every downtown and where the cops were waiting to ticket and how the weather changed in the mountains, knew the way from Laramie to Cheyenne, which is where we were headed that time on Darleen's birthday, buffalo grazing in a pasture and the sky low over the hills with clouds and an ominous sense of enclosure, like a curtain coming down, that whole vast place a stage.

And there's Wess Anderson in the bus putting on some music, getting his horn out too, Wess with the sweet voice and the sweeter sound, and in those days still the cigarettes, so he always sat in the front of the bus as if that made a difference with his smoking, Wess with the very dark oval face with its soft features and the way his eyebrows furrowed as he listened and you felt underneath the cheerfulness the hollow hurt of his sister's death—he was in a nightclub playing when his wife Desi came in to tell him she had been shot— and also the little catch in his voice when he was maybe sitting at a bar, laughing, listening to you, how he always asked me by name how each person in my family was and when I said the same to him he always said *Des is fine, Quad is fine,* but as we looked one another in our eyes I sometimes wondered, "Should you really trust me, do I deserve your affection?" And how might I answer my own question, by what right could I answer, *the noble Norseman,* Wynton jokingly referred to me once from the stage at a club in Monterrey, California, *Mass,* as in *Massa,* he often called me when he had his plantation vibe going in the bus or on the ride from hotel to venue, and afterwards I might think, as I stood off to the side in the dressing room: *the token cracker.*

In this story I would put how the April air smells on the Dakota plains, how I once walked down a dirt road to the edge of a huge manmade reservoir there on the Missouri River and placed my hand in the water which was cold because winter lasts so long on the prairie, the ground was still frozen in places, the grass brown, and in my head I heard a Wyntonian tune, *Superb Starling,* which I felt certain could be played at either a wedding or a funeral, same song, because it was both happy and sad, not just one emotion but many, integrated in their improvisation. How I loved the prairie grass in summer, with the music a kind of backdrop, or maybe literally a soundtrack, just as it was in Boston for that December *All Rise*.

Over Thanksgiving, we had just visited with my mother, sick since summer with one ailment leading to another, now bedridden in a Bronxville, New York hospital. Would I put that in my story, too? In her hospital room she and I had watched part of *American Beauty* on DVD and I'd given her some jazz I knew she probably would not listen to ("Why can't he just stick with the melody?" she would ask when I played her one of Wynton's many versions of his favorite song, Gershwin's *Embraceable You*). She was frail but alert. As I left her in the hospital the day after Thanksgiving, the late afternoon light already disappearing into dusk, I had bumped into her doctor, a woman not much younger than my mother. Reviewing my mother's charts in the hallway near my mother's room, she had removed her glasses before speaking to me in a highly inflected English with the trace of an Austrian or German accent, shaking her head as if to emphasize the element of mystery in any prognosis, and then without any prompting on my part had said, looking directly into my eyes, "You have to seize life."

Walking outside then in the chilly, leaf-scented November air, I had looked for the café we'd all been to on an earlier visit, when my mom had still been able to walk. Couldn't find it so I'd continued past the stucco train station and down a block where the lights were on in the marquee of the old movie theater near Bronxville's Starbucks.

The traffic that had made it difficult to park in Bronxville before visiting my mother had subsided, but the sidewalk by Starbucks was still bustling. An old man walking his poodle reminded me of Jack; it was just a week since Maren and I had stopped with Jack that afternoon at the football field and talked about books while he peed. Maren had asked on this visit to go into the city to see Wynton but had happily settled for an afternoon of food shopping in the Bronx's Little Italy with my brother, who knew many of the shopkeepers, greeting them by name as he bought bread at a bakery that sold only bread and ravioli at a pasta shop that had been run by the same family since the 1930s and carried only ravioli made in the back room.

Not knowing if I would find my mother alive the next morning, I had looked for her room's window in the hospital as I walked from Starbucks to my car. Breathing quietly, she had been asleep already when I kissed her forehead and departed. I pictured that breathing as I stared momentarily at her window, a sense of the space she still occupied on the earth, everywhere people breathing, all the while the earth spinning, and then I left.

Gazing out at the post-Thanksgiving, early winter light in Boston as I waited after the rehearsal for the van that would take us back to the hotel, I remembered that it was almost the exact time of year that Wynton had invited me more than a decade ago to come to Boston with him and his septet after I'd heard them play a second time at the Iron Horse Music Hall in Northampton, Massachusetts.

"Ride with us on our bus," Wynton had suggested then, during a post-gig, midnight game of basketball, outdoors, in a parking lot located between his Northampton motel and the interstate. It was less an invitation than a command.

"Thanks," I had replied, feigning a relaxed tone. "I have family stuff in the morning," I continued. "I'll drive."

The next afternoon, a few minutes after I arrived in Boston, we had gone to a sound check at Berklee College of Music, my first ride in a limousine, and on the way back we were accompanied by Matt Dillon—"Monyure," a bastardized form of Monsieur, he was called within the band—a short, wiry-haired, sharp-tongued energetic man, a New Orleans childhood friend of Wynton's who was Wynton's road manager at that time. This was before he became a Baskin and Robbins ice cream impresario at the airport in his hometown, while living alone across the Mississippi Rivers in Algiers (where Buddy Bolden a century ago was reputed to blow his horn so loud you could hear it on Canal Street), in a small, trim house filled with memorabilia from his road days—days when he thought the touring life would always continue, the nice hotels and good crowds, adoring fans, meals like the one in Monterrey at a Mexican restaurant where they opened early for the band and prepared a few special dishes…days like that in Boston when in the limo Matt had told jokes and reminisced rhapsodically with Wynton about the beauty and sexual attraction of different New Orleans women.

Back at the hotel then, Wynton felt the top of his head, looked in a mirror, and announced that he needed a haircut. So I had accompanied him and a large white guy from Buffalo named Wes, one 's', who was hanging with the band that tour, gone along with them to a barbershop a few blocks from the hotel in what was still a mostly black neighborhood in Boston's South End.

On a table at the barbershop was a copy of a recent *Time* Magazine with Wynton on the cover. Though I would learn he shunned such terms as creations of "the media," Wynton was then at a kind of crossroads in his young career, something the *Time* article worked around. Already at the age of 29 world famous, the recipient of numerous awards including eight Grammys, he had only just a few years earlier gone through a personal and musical crisis when his brother Branford left his band. Just a year apart at birth, they had grown up together, and played music together at home with their father Ellis, a pianist, at the school, the New Orleans Center for the Creative Arts, that Ellis had helped found, and in the funk band, the Creators, they formed as teenagers. Branford's defection had been a rebuke, made worse in Wynton's eyes because his older brother had departed to play with a British pop star, Sting. It was something Wynton rarely discussed; we would have only one extended conversation about it, in Shreveport, Louisiana, the first fall after I began touring with him, when the initial hurt seemed to be softening into the realization that perhaps the brothers were better off playing on their own. Emerging from the loss, which also included that of two other players in his old quintet, Wynton had gradually formed a new band which, with the addition of trombonist Wycliffe Gordon, had in 1989 become a septet. This was the group which I would hear that same year when I first encountered Wynton and his music in person in Northampton's Iron Horse, and it was the septet that had just appeared again a year later at the Iron Horse.

The barber in Boston fussed over Wynton, and didn't want to take any money, but Wynton insisted on paying. Then he reached into his pocket and discovered he had only a few singles on him. He almost never carried more in those days, money being something he did not think about in the sense of what a gallon of milk or loaf of bread cost.

I was standing too far from them to hear what Wynton said, but I could imagine it was something like, "Hey, bruh, can you take care of my man here."

Returning from his haircut to his hotel suite, which overlooked the Boston Common, Wynton talked on the phone with his two young sons, Wynton Jr. and Simeon, who were with their mother, Candace Stanley, in New York. Wynton lived there, too, with them still, in a lower Manhattan brownstone, during the rare weeks when he wasn't traveling.

I had taken a seat at a baby grand piano that had been placed in a corner of the suite's living room; there was usually a piano wherever Wynton stayed, even if the band were in a hotel that had to arrange a rental. Waiting for Wynton, I watched the holiday lights on the Common and studied the neatly penciled manuscript for the beginning of what I was later certain was his Pulitzer Prize-winning slavery oratorio *Blood on the Fields*, though he would always insist otherwise. The music looked at once familiar and foreign to me, just as hearing the band the night before had seemed on the one hand the kind of musical event I had experienced countless times and on the other hand something very different, even exotic.

Somewhat self-consciously, I studied the manuscript, but it felt comfortable to be sitting there at the piano. My own piano studies had started when I was five, and I added the trumpet at the age of nine. Growing up in Buffalo, New York, where for several years my father managed the orchestra, I had always been surrounded by music and musicians. The eccentric pianist Glenn Gould came to a reception in his honor at our home, standing on a heating grate in our living room, where for a time there were two concert grand pianos, and, wearing gloves, refused to shake anyone's hand lest he pick up germs. A few blocks from our house was a club called the Royal Arms, where I once listened to pianist Ramsey Lewis while I stood outside, peering through the window, since I wasn't old enough to enter the club legally. I heard Louis Armstrong play in person shortly before he died, at an outdoor theater under a tent on a gig that ended with numerous encores. I did not understand who Armstrong was, and there were many jazz musicians whose music I did not know, but I never forgot that night, how at the age of seventy, "Pops" came out again and again for encores.

Long before it became fashionable in conservatories and music festivals to acknowledge this, my father—the son of Norwegian immigrants, raised in a strict, socially closed, fundamentalist environment by parents who called the Negroes living in Harlem *the chocolata*—taught me by example that Duke Ellington was an important musical figure. My dad, who studied at Juilliard when he was in high school and was only seventeen or eighteen when he left home for the Berkshires, had a stained glass window of Duke put in at the Buffalo church where he was organist. I can still remember the excitement in my father's voice when, on a visit to me in college, he said while we were having breakfast in the dining room at his hotel, "Look behind you! That's Duke Ellington at the table in the alcove."

Except for rock and roll and most atonal and serial compositions, even music my father didn't particularly like still merited a certain respect. And music he loved—all of Bach, most of Mozart, Debussy, Vaughn Williams (whose *Fantasy on a Theme of Thomas Tallis*, we were told, he wanted to be played at his funeral), and Mahler—aroused in him a kind of passionate fervor bordering on religious. How often had I come home late at night when I was still in high school to find my father in a trance listening to Mahler's *Rückert Lieder* or one of his favorite Bach chorales. It was only in such music that my father seemed able, albeit temporarily, to abate or assuage the angers and griefs of a life that included not only the early death of his only brother but constant worries about money, as if the music's struggles mirrored his own, his very salvation dependent on its triumph, however seemingly tenuous at times, over his terrors. Music for my father at those moments when he was truly hearing it *was* life—just as I imagined it was for my new friend from New Orleans, except in his case the words seemed reversible, or interchangeable. His life, this amazing combination of constant travel and performance, the rhythm of its movement and the counterpoint of its interactions with others, was a kind of music.

After Wynton had said goodnight to his sons on the phone at the Park Plaza he came over to the piano bench and played the music I had been staring at, just the first few chords, lush, taut, evocative. Years afterwards, when I told someone this story in Wynton's presence, he was annoyed that I repeated a misidentification of the music he played then, the way he once told me his mother would sometimes ask him a question he'd already answered or tell him something he already knew or she'd already said. Where were we during that conversation? West Virginia? Texas?

"I explained to you it was something else," I can hear him saying impatiently.

It was a long time before I learned to let these complaints go. They invariably meant nothing, or were said only to provoke for the fun of the provocation. Once he told me a woman he knew I thought was cute, who was also my friend, had come to see him one night in New York and…he looked at me with a wild grin, his eyes brightening, before breaking into laughter, no longer able to maintain the pose. Months later when I quizzed him he insisted they had never even kissed.

So, Skain, what are you really trying to tell me? It was a question that, after years of traveling with his bands, I would ask myself often. Reading a mood, Wynton anticipated how someone else might react to what he said. In a debate (and what conversation with Wynton was not a debate?), he was artful at keeping an oppo-

nent off balance, just like a good athlete in his favorite sport, box-
ing. He knew how to needle. But he also understood the power of
a seemingly offhand remark. One time—this was in New York—
we were walking to a Lincoln Center gig and I told him I had
been listening to the outtakes from his *In This House, On This
Morning*, one of the first extended pieces he had written, and of all
his compositions the one I still love the best.

"The second half, right from the moment Veal starts to sing, is
so beautiful," I said. "The whole thing, right to the end."

"You didn't like the first half?" Wynton responded.

His apparent refusal to accept my compliment threw me off
balance, and I was left to backtrack, which made me sound foolish.
But I was also struck by the transparency of his remark. Was this
man who came across as so sure of everything he felt exposing a
momentary uncertainty? Or was he just playing with me again?

"Yeah, Squazene, that first half was truly sad. When are you
going to write some music that has some real feeling to it?"

Boston in December these many years afterwards was cold outside
and crowded with shoppers. Returning to the hotel following the
rehearsal, the van stopped to let off baritone saxophonist Joe
Temperley at a restaurant, Legal Seafood. Glancing out the window at people with their coat collars turned up, I laughed quietly
at a joke someone made about the name of the restaurant. You
never laughed—or cried, or for that matter spoke—loudly in the
company of the band, a lesson I'd learned from another of my road
tutors, soundman David Robinson, who used to mock my high-
pitched laugh and who, like Monyure Dillon (or erstwhile road
managers Brother Elie and Billy Banks, or their present successor
Boss Murphy), did not actually play an instrument in any of
Wynton's bands but was still accorded full status as a member of
whichever of his groups Wynton was touring with: the septet that
had formed after the departure of Branford; Wynton's big band,
officially the Lincoln Center Jazz Orchestra, which was started in
the early 1990s and included many of the septet's musicians; or a
third group, a quintet comprised of Wynton and three younger

players which appeared later, following the diminution of a recon-
stituted septet. Even people who had no formal association with
Wynton were made to feel part of the ensemble while they were
on the road; there were no outsiders in this world. I had certainly
come to know that.

As we left Joe off, the darkening day mirrored my mood, melancholy over the cessation of the music and always vaguely uneasy
over the prospect of something happening in my absence at home,
and I strained to hear in my memory snippets of the chorus at the
rehearsal singing in great intervals, and then a place in *All Rise* that
dissolved with the wail of the saxophone, except I wasn't thinking in
sections, it was as if I were listening to the entire hundred-minute
piece at once. I imagined a movie and it would be the piece as written but performed both on stage and where the music had taken
me. It would be a kind of music video, but large scale, with lots of
people in it, including the performers, and also all sorts of people on
the road, the people you meet on the road through music.

The beginning was in the mountains somewhere, and then
that first part continued in some cities; the section for strings in
the west, or Appalachia; the moment I was listening to played
against the Golden Gate at dawn, the sunlit morning several years
ago when Wynton and photographer Frank Stewart and I crossed
it on our way from Santa Rosa to the airport, the night after Frank
and I drank cognac we found in a little store in the strip mall by
our motel, while Wynton in the next room dealt with the heartbreak of a pianist he was sending home, and that morning we were
flying to New Mexico, where after performing and being honored
at a native American Gathering of Nations Wynton would finish
writing the recessional of *In This House, On This Morning* in the
shadow of the mountains that guarded Albuquerque. I remembered his playing on a miniature piano in his hotel room a refrain
in the unusual, technically difficult rhythm of 7/4 (seven beats to a
measure, a quarter note gets a beat), so when I left for home the
next morning the refrain was still in my head as I looked out at the
same mountains, their tops covered in clouds, and ever after when
I have heard the harmonics of that figure over that mesmerizing

rhythm I have seen that vista, felt the clear desert air as if it were soothing my life.

Like chord changes in the music, one memory now triggered another as we waited in Boston for a traffic light to turn: little more than a month before, on a cool, cloudy early autumn day in nearby New Hampshire, Wynton announced matter-of-factly during a pre-concert dinner that his grandmother had just died. We were eating in a pine-paneled basement room of the Hanover Inn, a space with a WASPy vibe reminiscent of other Dartmouth places in the black and white movie of Budd Shulberg's novel *Winter Carnival*. At the gig that night, the hall packed with elderly blue hairs, many of the men wearing jackets and ties and most of the women in dresses, Wynton was unusually reserved backstage during intermission, but then played a highly charged duet, a spontaneous performance of *St. James Infirmary* with Wess Anderson on the piano, the instrument Wess had learned from his father before Wess became a saxophonist. Though Wynton said nothing about his grandmother from the stage, and would have denied any connection—"I play the same," he always said—it was difficult not to hear the duet as a tribute to her.

I'd driven to that gig at the last minute, meeting the band at the Hanover Inn just as everyone was walking next door to the venue for a sound check followed by supper, the kind of serendipitous timing that tended to occur frequently in my road life, and not until we returned to the hotel did I notice I had come all this way wearing my bedroom slippers. Without comment or question, but shaking his head as if to chastise a child, Wynton loaned me a pair of perfectly polished shoes. When I returned them after the gig I mentioned my response to the duet with Wess. At first Wynton feigned the kind of ignorance of a performance's impact that he often assumed.

"Did we sound like shit?" he asked.

"Yeah, right," I said, though I rarely knew what to reply in such instances, since criticism for its own sake was gratuitous and the truth often came across as cheesy. What you "thought" about a particular piece seemed far less important than understanding why what you heard made you feel. It was the same being on the road, except there the initial question turned on experience, what actually happened in a particular instance, and then once again what was the relationship to how you felt?

At Dartmouth that night, I changed the subject to a student named Kabir Sehgal who earlier had presented Wynton and the rest of the band with medals that a group Kabir was a part of had designed to commemorate this concert. Wynton publicly acknowledged Kabir, who was also a bass player, by inviting him to join the septet on the last tune. The house had emptied quickly afterwards, finally leaving only a family that had driven two hours from northern New Hampshire so their very young son, a trumpeter himself, could meet Wynton. Though it was getting late, for half an hour Wynton had played some blues on the piano while encouraging the boy, who was quite talented, to solo on the horn he had brought along with him. In more than one similar exchange that I had witnessed over the years the upshot was a call from whomever Wynton had just helped to Wynton's longtime manager, Ed Arrendell, whom Wynton would have told a student or student's parents to contact because a boy or girl could not afford music lessons, or in at least one especially notable instance because financial aid at a particular music camp was unavailable. Wynton, who had grown up in an economically struggling black family in the South and whose only real indulgence were his musicians (much of what he made he spent on his band) and his elegant clothes, would pay.

Money was only a means to an end for Wynton. In his apartment there were relatively few possessions: some paintings, a stereo one of his brothers gave him, his piano. Music. Books. Children's toys, when his sons were little. He didn't have many trumpets either, just the one he was currently playing, a decorated horn, a piccolo trumpet for baroque music, and a cornet. He gave his old trumpets away, to students and friends. Nicholas Payton from New Orleans had one, the same Nicholas for whose high school graduation Wynton flew all the way from New York to attend, the kind of gesture he made for his sons whenever it was even remotely possible, such as the time after a gig in Cleveland when he drove all night to be in New York for an event at his son Simeon's junior high.

More chord changes: I had been rereading Ralph Ellison, and as I listened to the boy in New Hampshire play his blues I remembered the place, central Florida, when Wynton introduced me to Ellison's *Little Man at Chehaw Station*. We were on the bus, Wynton, I, and Matt Dillon's replacement Lolis Elie, another New Orleans childhood friend of Wynton's, a writer between gigs, variously called Brother Elie or, by me, Reverend—because he had preached a mock sermon, which concluded with a baptismal invocation for my unlikely deliverance on Judgment Day, at a dinner party in North Carolina. On the bus in Florida as we came into Orlando, Wynton had read aloud some of the Ellison essay, which expounded on the proposition that you never knew who might be listening (or watching, or wondering).

Before the New Hampshire gig I had gone back to the Ellison because I had just seen the Little Man, except that he was a she: a young woman I knew through her father, a college classmate of mine, who had been living abroad since her own graduation from college a few years ago. Early that past summer she was badly hurt after a fire triggered an explosion in the house where she was sleeping and she was unable to escape immediately. She almost died then, and later she almost died a second time, of an embolism, in an airplane en route to a hospital in Boston. Now she was continuing her treatment but she had her life back, and despite the scars a radiance that was breathtaking. While she was still in the hospital I learned from her father that she had discovered jazz, and when she came home finally I gave her a few of Wynton's CDs, *Majesty of the Blues* and a couple of others. Some time passed, and then one day I received a note from her, illustrated by a drawing of Wynton she had done based on the photo in the *Majesty* liner notes.

"Throughout my recovery I have found music and art to be an incredibly powerful form of therapeutic healing," she wrote in a hand so striking it resembled calligraphy, "a creative expression which (as Marsalis notes) is a testament to the strength of the human spirit." Soon afterwards I saw her by chance in town, and then again a few days later at the local HMO, and all she could talk about was music. I arranged to get tickets for her to attend a gig Wynton was giving the following spring.

She came backstage to meet Wynton then but had to leave almost immediately because her parents were waiting to give her a ride. Though he had earlier listened to my reading of her heartfelt note without external reaction, Wynton asked me afterwards in the hotel where she was. The room smelled of cleaning spray, and a fan made a loud whirring noise, but Wynton seemed not to notice. Tired, he was already lying in his bed, almost nodding off.

"She had to go," I replied. "She gets tired. She's still recovering."

"She was sweet," Wynton said. "I think she wanted to stay," he continued.

Because I had known this young woman since she was a girl, I felt protective about her, and Wynton's remark struck me as self-centered. And yet, as I imagined the moment after the explosion when the woman was trapped in the burning building and the pain of that seared flesh, the agony of her long recovery and the gradual realization of what she had lost, I was less certain. Perhaps her beauty had inspired him to speak a truth my reticence had kept me from admitting.

Though it was rare that Wynton ever truly forgot something, especially a name (especially the name of a beautiful woman), he pleaded ignorance about what he'd said that night when I mentioned it to him a few months later. He was appearing in the same Northampton club where I had first met him, this time with a small group of much younger musicians who were to form his new quintet. On the first date of a double engagement an especially youthful-looking musician had shown up between sets with a piccolo trumpet to play the Second Brandenburg Concerto of Bach. After Wynton with a kind voice bluntly asked this earnest student if he knew the meaning of the word nuance, Wynton wiped off the piccolo trumpet's mouthpiece to clean it a little and then, adjusting his embouchure, launched into the Bach right there, an impromptu, hair-raising performance of a piece that had helped propel him years ago to prominence but that he no longer played in public.

On the second night of the same gig, again between sets, a petite young woman named Sally appeared to sing. Sally had driven two hours to the club, having apparently called ahead to say she was coming. I didn't know where they had met, and Wynton certainly didn't say. He rarely provided such information spontaneously, and never when asked. Sally was studying voice and she'd prepared *Autumn Leaves* for Wynton, which for some reason she sang in French. She had a sweet if tentative voice; she was clearly nervous.

"Sing some blues," Wynton requested.

Taken aback, Sally tried to recall a song that would satisfy Wynton's request. There was an awkward silence that Wynton broke with his tenor, no words, just the mimicked sounds of a bass fiddle being plucked. He was showing Sally what he meant, singing in the form of a blues. Relieved, she got the idea and began when he paused. Her singing was somewhat self-conscious but she kept the form. Pianist Eric Lewis, who had been listening to this unofficial audition from a corner of the room, now came over and, standing, facing Sally, with his own voice picked up the bass part from Wynton, who then grabbed his trumpet and provided an accompaniment. The singing and playing continued like this uninterrupted for a full fifteen or twenty minutes, until someone stuck his head in the door and said, "House is ready." Wynton smiled at Sally, took her hand, said with a pronounced pause between each word, "Practice…the…blues," and walked upstairs to play his second set.

It was raining hard by the time he left the club two hours later. The hotel was only a couple of blocks away, but Boss Murphy had brought the tour bus around, so we wouldn't get wet. At the hotel I walked Wynton to his room, where we talked for a little while—he asked about my kids, particularly Maren, whom he had known since she was an infant. Then there was a knock on the door and in came Sally. She was carrying a small bag.

I got up, but Wynton said, "Don't leave, Swig. It's not what you think." Sally had told him she was driving home in the rain, Wynton declared, and he had invited her to sleep here, in his room, and leave in the morning when the driving would be safer. He wouldn't even be there by then; the tour bus was going at four.

While Sally disappeared into the bathroom, I stayed a few more minutes, and then, having changed into some tights and a top, she reappeared, smiled, said something about the gig and the rain and, hearing part of our conversation, picked up on my daughter's name, and quickly climbed onto the double bed. She got under the covers, thanked Wynton for his hospitality, and was soon apparently fast asleep.

While an air of heightened expectation almost always animated a scene in which Wynton encountered a woman, what struck me most was the ease with which he moved in and out of most relationships, whether brief encounters such as this one with Sally or long-lasting ones. Just about a year before, Wynton's first New Orleans girlfriend, Melanie Marchand, had celebrated her fortieth birthday with him at a hotel bar in Harrisburg, Pennsylvania, where Wynton jokingly shared memories of their meeting. Melanie, now a fitness trainer and women's empowerment leader, smiled as Wynton turned the talk to an evocation of her anatomy, continuing a monologue that was also a satire of so-called street talk. Their lasting affection for one another was palpable and the happiness of the brief occasion stayed with me long afterwards, the way you remember a song you first heard long ago.

Now, back in Boston, as the van pulled into the side entrance of the Copley Plaza Hotel, where the doormen had their coat collars buttoned and were wearing gloves, I thought about driving home that June night after meeting Sally, raindrops wetting the road, the music fresh in my mind, and I remembered thinking then that it was just three months since my mother had moved from Northampton, where she had settled after my father died. And what, I thought, had Wynton's friend D.J. said to me the last time I visited with him in

Los Angeles? D.J. Riley, suffering from a disease called Morquios Syndrome, who spent most of his life now in a kind of bubble, supported by tubes and devices to help him breathe, eat, digest, whose legs long ago had failed him, whose body except for his head had shriveled to half an adult's normal size.

D.J. had first come to a gig when Wynton and Branford were playing at U. C. Berkeley many years ago, where D.J. was a law student then. When I met him, he came backstage in his wheelchair. His body was small, and his small legs just dangled there. His head seemed enormous in comparison to the rest of his body. Wynton and D.J. started talking about music and it was very apparent that D.J. knew all sorts of jazz. Coltrane. Miles. Monk. And he knew about lots of other things too. He and Wynton talked about politics and books.

"Hey, man," D.J. would say in his fast musical voice. D.J. talked very fast. "Check this out, Wynton."

And he'd tell Wynton another story. Even then he knew many people; it seemed to Wynton he knew everybody. He got sick sometimes—he had pneumonia one year—but he always recovered and got around again. He traveled all over. Home to New Jersey. And he turned up wherever Wynton was playing in California; he came to all Wynton's California gigs. He'd fly up from LA to San Francisco and a friend would meet him and bring him straight to the gig.

D.J. once called to wish me a happy Father's Day because, he said, in his high-pitched voice, he knew from his own life how important it was to have a father, so he could imagine the feeling of being one. And so, then, on that last Los Angeles reunion D.J. had reminded me that no one ever *knew*, wasn't it *odd* he added that Wynton so hated to fly that he instead drove, or, rather, was driven, everywhere he could, even though being in a car was more dangerous statistically than flying, and therefore *who knew*, Wynton's life could be wiped out in an instant, or he could develop an illness like Muhammad Ali, any of us could, *look at me*, D.J. whispered, *I could walk when I was a kid*.

Like music, like life: experience and memory merged, June and December, rain and snow, Northampton and Los Angeles and Boston, as if I were witness through music to a kind of miracle, participant in my own improvisation, second trumpet in a septet that had only one trumpet (*No, I'm not the manager*, I learned to say when club owners and promoters came up to me, the white guy, wondering if I was the person who should get the band's paycheck, *I play second trumpet*). Walking finally into the lobby of the Copley Plaza, brightly lit by recently restored chandeliers, I bumped into Wess Anderson, *How you doin', Swig, you have plans for dinner?*; pictured D.J. at that first meeting more than a decade ago on a mountaintop in Saratoga, California, at the original Paul Masson winery that was now a concert venue, D.J. being pushed in his wheelchair that starlit night by an Oakland friend of his, Charles Douglas, dead now, and the next day we had seen Charles and D.J. again, backstage, at an outdoor jazz festival in Concord, California, where David Robinson, *Sugar Rob*, after setting up the soundboard in the center of the mammoth covered pavilion danced during the entire gig with his future wife Reni; and listened again in my mind to the voice of a young woman singing near the end of the *All Rise* rehearsal that afternoon in Boston, right after a break during which I had called my mother on my cell phone in the red-carpeted hallway outside the swinging leather doors of Symphony Hall's first balcony, the hall empty and dark except for the brightly lit, crowded stage.

My mother was once a singer herself, a soprano with a clear tone and a striking ability to convey great depth of feeling in the smallest phrase in her favorite repertoire, the songs of Schubert and Ravel. How I wished she could have been with me, I told

her on the phone, to hear that triumphant voice in the hall that afternoon singing: *I say All Rise, All Rise, All Rise, All Rise, All Rise, All Rise, and be heard.*

And in my mind I had said a prayer for her, which took the form of a song for all my family and friends, for days long past when we'd drive down into the Connecticut River valley from the Harris farm and I used to get up very early in the morning, often to the accompaniment of Mr. Harris's milking machine, and while in the next room Bonnie, pregnant with our first child, slept I would sit by an open window at the dining room table and write another story.

Once, after writing through the night, I heard music from the barn radio early in the morning. I walked outside in the dawn light, where over the sound of the cows and the milking machine the radio brought in a signal first from Nova Scotia and then as the morning wore on Maine and then, finally, the sun shining brightly over the meadow by the brook across the road from the barn, Massachusetts.

"Can I help?" I asked Mr. Harris, stooped over a milk pan, his arms shaking from what I thought might have been the early signs of Parkinson's disease, and without stopping the motion of his hands he looked over a shoulder and answered in a high-pitched, hard-to-hear voice, "When have you ever done any real work in your life?"

He almost sounded like Wynton, years later, upbraiding me or someone in the band for bullshitting. Wynton was particularly critical of what he termed "Negroidal bullshitting," which he defined as promising to do a task and then never even getting started on it. You didn't have to be black to be accused of being this kind of slacker.

And then, in an instant, Wynton would change the tone, the content, the import of a conversation with a direct question or observation.

"How's our girl?" he asked, meaning Maren. And he would listen intently to my reply.

"How's your old lady?"

"Where's your son living at? He still in California?"

Some of these questions I answered completely and sometimes I just nodded or replied with only a word or two, or I'd ask similar questions in return.

"What are you working on?" I might say, a question invariably answered with a nod or a shrug, never a word, and then sometimes followed by, "Check this out," and if I were with him he would start playing whatever it was at the piano. On the phone he often did that without provocation, in fact answering the phone he might not even say hello but immediately begin playing part of a new piece, and then he might say, "Hold on," while he took a call on another line, and minutes would pass before he returned, maybe to talk or maybe to play something more, though sometimes he'd forget you were waiting and I would figure out what had happened and hang up.

Wynton never volunteered anything about his extended family or his lady friends. We were talking in the living room of his apartment a few years ago when Wynton, composing at the piano, looked up as I said something about his mother and father when he was very young.

"You must have been very lonely when your father was out playing at clubs," I said. "'Where is Daddy? When is he coming home?' I can imagine you asking your mother. Maybe she even sang you a lullaby. And rocked you in her arms."

"No," Wynton replied sternly. "It wasn't like that. She never sang no lullabies."

He was upset at my perceived presumption. But he didn't contradict me about being lonely.

The next morning he took his sons to the park to play ball, and the day afterwards he left on a fall tour.

I wondered how his sons felt when he left, and another time asked him.

"They know their father is Wynton Marsalis," he replied.

Work was a refuge. If he were about to perform he might pick up his horn rather than say something about himself. For Wynton, the exchange of information that a conversation offered was always secondary to the shared sense of the fleeting, permanent, breathless present that his music affirmed. Though he would listen to another person's problems at length, he kept his own counsel on many of his most personal matters, and he was invariably close-lipped in response to questioning that probed. He would change the subject or just ignore the person who raised it. You had to divine what he meant at such moments and then make judgments, weigh and compare different passing revelations, pickup on an off-hand comment, let it drop while he returned to the manuscript of some music he was writing at the piano while you talked, and then later, perhaps, put two and two together.

Two and two; one-two-three-four; a one, a two, a one, two, three, four: Could I write that so Maren had to read all of it…what took me away…what brought me back?

2

Years ago, when I was plotting and sketching one of my many un-published stories during the lengthy period when I was learning to write and taking care, near and from afar, of my dad, for whom the pains of his life were finally more than he could bear, and recognizing the responsibilities of being married, and taking long walks along the South River and through the fields Mr. Harris hayed and up into the woods behind the farm to the border of Archie's estate and then across through the woods to a mowing hidden high up in the hills (how I would love to show you that magic spot, Maren, there was an old apple orchard near it, too, back when the land was open enough so you could see the whole verdant valley where we lived)…anyway, one of those unborn literary efforts, something I kept coming back to again and again, stayed in my mind as a phrase: *the dance of my friends* was the phrase, which in my mind encapsulated an ambition to circumscribe a collective sense of the lives of certain other people as I understood them, their loves, their losses, all held within a consciousness that first formed itself on summer walks long before, in Vermont, where as a boy I used to hike alone across a meadow whose top looked out in every direction, with the lake we stayed by spread below me, back when our family was still more or less intact, my uncle still living…there was a girl, too, who was more interested in some older guy I of course therefore hated. No one, I thought, knew then what I knew, I mean knew within me what I already was sure that I knew about the grandeur of the world, the seasons, the sky at night, music heard over the lake in the evening, the fragrance of that meadow and the sounds there, crickets and birdsong, the immense expanse of sky. Once or twice, hiking that hilltop meadow, I took my clothes off and walked bare-assed through the field, the hay and juniper scratchy. The dance of my friends mixed in my mind with the wildflowers and pools in the brook years later where I'd stop to spot trout and the paths through the woods that I knew by heart, when we lived so happily at that Conway farm, and there would come these moments when it would all soar, when I thought I could fly.

All my life, Maren, there has been in my mind a sense of these two worlds, that mountaintop and my core, two places, what I will call for the moment the outer and the inner. Trying to resolve the tension between these two worlds has been my private preoccupation for as long as I can remember, going back to my Buffalo childhood when my room was in the rear of the second story of our brown-shingled house, with a window that looked out on the driveway and the neighbor's adjacent yard, and another yard beyond that, lit at night by a hooded lamp suspended from a corner of that family's house about twenty feet above the ground. During the long Buffalo winters, I used to get up in the night and look out my window at the snow, thick flakes falling steadily and quietly. Wondering if there would be enough for school to be called off the next morning, I would watch the flakes falling in the light from that neighbor's lamp. I loved the silence then, our house quiet except for the furnace clicking on every so often. We had no storm windows, and so with the window open a crack some of the snowflakes would blow into the room and land on the sill, where they would quickly melt. I liked to take a little snow on my hand and lick it, trying to imagine where those particular flakes had commenced their brief winter journey…from how high in the winter night sky, formed I supposed somewhere far out on Lake Erie, beyond its forbidding winter shores, windswept I was certain and forlorn, out past the beaches where we swam in the summer, where I was in love with a girl whose family moved to Toledo, Ohio, at the far other end of the lake. Maybe this snowstorm had started there. Who knew? Who ever knew? We live our daily lives, of course, in the outer world, the world of jobs and family responsibilities and school and mowing the lawn and doing the laundry and going shopping and talking on the phone, all those things that if we are lucky and have our health are a form of grace if you will let yourself think about them that way, be open to them that is, and thankful. And I love that outer world, love the sense of speed driving on the open road or the smell of woods on a walk after rain, the icy chill of the wind on a chairlift in winter. I love the responsive action of the piano keys when my finger tips touch them and the shock of cold metal on my warm lips when I pick up my trumpet and blow through the mouthpiece. I love the pure *sound* of all the instruments on stage or on the bandstand. That isn't music, of course, I mean just those instrumental sounds: the outer world. Not until you're at the other place, *within*, can there be music, which at the beginning of my travels struck me as a paradox. Something had pulled Wynton and still did, compelled him to *go*, even as he had confessed when I asked after we met that he didn't "know" where exactly he was *going*…and so I wondered, what was it, and I wanted myself to "go," to experience, understand…just as I'd read that he, too, at the age of seventeen, seeing an announcement about tryouts for musical study at Tanglewood had auditioned, been accepted, and *gone*, never come back really, on the road forevermore, so even that year right after Tanglewood at Juilliard in New York City was only another way-stop to…where? And how could I get *there*, too?

But to go back again to the beginning: you were just a baby, Maren, born a few months earlier, when your brother and mom went with me to hear Wynton that first time at the Iron Horse

Music Hall in Northampton. So your age parallels the chronology of my friendship with him. You weren't yet two late the following year when Wynton returned to the Horse, continuing to come back to the small, cozy club long after he was so popular that he could have filled a much larger area hall, because he liked the crowded space, with the audience sitting at tables right next to the stage and squeezed onto the stairs to the balcony, and because he remembered that its visionary founder, Jordi Herold, had first booked him before he was well known.

At about that time, our farmhouse was for sale, the old place on the ridge of the hill where the town's school once was that we'd bought after living at the Harrises. We'd lived there since just after your brother was born, fixing it up room by room, doing much of the work ourselves and planting a gigantic garden with asparagus and strawberry beds, near the maple by the corner of the huge barn that we'd finally had taken down because it was more than we could handle. But the whole place was; your bedroom at the front corner above the stairs never had heat, in fact the entire second floor was without heat or electricity when we moved in. The outside of the house hadn't been painted in more than fifty years, so the clapboards on the sunny side of the house were not only completely bare but curled from exposure to the weather. We'd replaced them, and fixed the shutters, wired the upstairs and gotten heat in most of the rooms, and downstairs the kitchen had been transformed from a small room with a linoleum floor with pipes that sometimes froze in the winter to a much larger area with new counters and cupboards and a hearth for the stove which burned wood that I split and stacked.

You were too young when we moved to remember it, but I can still see the path in the valley below our hill that we took to the swimming hole and the dirt road up the next hill that your mother liked to hike with our second retriever Molly and the fields across the valley where I went on my cross-country skis after a storm, once with my brother in a deep snow when we had to make tracks and we ended up on the far crest in a clearing where, looking back,

I could see our house with its lights sparkling as evening came on and I tried to imagine the lives within it at that moment, my children, my wife, my sister-in-law, my mother who'd come out from Northampton for dinner: human lights.

The first time I returned home from my job and saw the For Sale sign in the front yard, next to the tall maple where we'd hung your sister's tire swing, I stopped my car in the road and stared, then opened the door, got out, and pulled the stakes of the sign from the ground. But I knew we had to sell, and the following morning the sign went back in. I was doing some ghostwriting for a businessman just then and office work for a small, early-music outfit with offices near Northampton in an old mill building where the main tenant was an organization that employed the physically disabled and mentally challenged. Seeing some of those people every day made it difficult for me to feel sorry for myself, but I was restless. A book I'd recently published, with the naïve expectation it was going to make me famous, had yet to go into a second printing. Each day at noon I would escape from work into town, walking the gray streets, or to a nearby 9-hole golf course. There, though the golf season was officially over, I hiked the deserted, frozen fairways and hit a ball around the small layout with a 7- or 8-iron. Squeezed between a small, wooded mountain and the four-lane pavement of an interstate highway, the course's location beckoned me to light out for some still undefined territory.

Bundled up on a late autumn day, with the wind blowing near the base of the mountain where the course bordered the woods, I let my thoughts swirl with the oak leaves, always the last to fall, brittle on the ground so they made a crackling sound when you stepped on them. How beautifully their light brown blended with the faded orange and red of the maples. That afternoon I returned to my small, stark office in the old mill building, with its view of a 7-11 across the street and a Mobil station beyond, and late in the day as I watched the sky grow dim and the streetlights come on snow started to fall. By the time I left for the half-hour drive home it was snowing harder, big wind-driven flakes making the sidewalk slippery and the visibility poor. The cold wind felt like a slap on my face, as if someone or something were trying to wake me out of a deep, protracted sleep.

Wynton had left me with a phone number for his road manager that first time we met, the year before, and the next day, still chilly but with the snow gone, I called it. Matt Dillon, "Monyure," answered, and after I reintroduced myself and briefly made small talk about the *Time* Magazine piece I'd recently read and asked about the tour, how was it going—I think they were in Ohio just then, or Ontario—I said I see you're coming to Northampton again soon, and before I was able to say anything more Matt asked, "Do you need tickets?"

And that is actually how my road life began, Maren, with that call, though I was pretty clueless when I made it. I certainly had no expectation that I would eventually visit every state but Idaho and the Dakotas with Wynton, travel to Europe and the Caribbean with him, and spend so much time at Lincoln Center in New York City that as you know it became a kind of second home to me. During one stretch of nearly a year when you were little I was away from you and the rest of our family three weeks at a stretch, then home for a week or so, and then gone again…searching for something, the bridge between my outer and inner worlds, certain I was about to find it at the next gig or town in a chance encounter with a stranger, a surprising conversation with Wynton or someone else in the band, a solitary moment standing to the side of the curtain, backstage, or by the stage door, staring down a quiet street or from a window high in some hotel overlooking the city or the mountains or the sea. By the time you were a teenager I was still on the road, not as often in fact but still in feeling.

Matt had remembered to leave my name on a pass list at the Iron Horse, and afterwards, back at the band's hotel, Wynton invited me to come to Boston the next day. Like my decision to go, the clear, November air on my drive to Boston the following morning was bracing. Though I would be coming home that night, I had an immediate, deep sense of a future that I was determined to reach.

Less clear, and at what cost, was the realization that doing so meant I would miss part of your childhood, and your sister's, and the end of your brother's, though in my mind the tradeoff if I can use that word was the expectation that when I was home I would really be *home*. And what times we had, especially when you were little and I rented that office in town after we had moved from Conway to Amherst; you have probably forgotten all the afternoons I would pick you up at school and we'd stop at the bakery and then walk back to my office where you had your own desk by the window that faced the town common, but I remember—your high voice, the way you grabbed my hand when we walked somewhere, the notes you used to write me, with illustrations, and leave on my desk in a homemade envelope, with instructions to read the next morning or, if I were going on another trip, in my plane.

At the benefit concert that night in Boston I listened to the voices around me, to the interplay among the musicians in the band and between them and their entourage and audience as intently as I did to the actual music. Who were these seven men in the band— Wess, who like several others had first played for Wynton when he was still in school; the other saxophonist then, Todd Williams, so serious, with that deep serious sound in his horn; Wycliffe, enormous, and his sound was, too, strong and profound, and how he also let loose with his voice sometimes; Herlin the drummer, New Orleans born, father of five, not counting his dead sister's kids, took care of them too, steady, rock solid; bassist Reginald Veal, Swing Doom everyone called him, also from New Orleans, married at that time to Kim who joined him whenever she could on the road, she worked for Delta Airlines and so could fly for free if she weren't working, *oh I'm going to see my baby tonight*, Reginald would sing when he knew she was coming; and pianist Eric Reed, a preacher's son, irreverent about life in the band and religious about the spirituality of his sound—what prompted their joy and élan, the depth of good feeling their playing invariably inspired? They were all younger than I, and except for their bus driver, black. What must they have made of me in my button-down shirt, regimental tie, tweed jacket, and Weejans? Certainly if I were going to fit in, it was very clear to me that given the gold standard of couture set by Wynton it would not be on the basis of dress (just about everyone in the band would at some point counsel me on this tricky subject, though the only advice on it that I took completely to heart was Wess Anderson's: "tops and bottoms, Swig," he said, by which he explained to me he meant ties and sox; they were the "key").

Shortly after reaching my destination that first day, as I stood in the lobby of the Park Plaza Hotel where the band was staying in Boston, someone reminded Wynton that they were heading to Maine the next morning.

"Why don't you come along," he said to me. He had just returned from Cambridge, where he'd given a workshop for some elementary school kids and the mayor of that nearby city had presented him with its keys.

"Thank you, but I can't," I said, though there was nothing at that moment that I could imagine wanting to do more. "My oldest is just twelve. I need to plan these things."

And then we were off to join the rest of the septet who were already at the Berklee sound check, and who would remain at Berklee afterwards for a pre-gig supper while Wynton went to get his hair cut before he and I talked at the piano bench after he said goodnight to his kids on the phone.

As we sat together on that bench in his hotel room, I sensed an important moment in my life had come, but I had to find the voice within me to articulate it. I remembered the very first time I played the trumpet in public, at a chapel service for kids; I was about ten or eleven years old, and my father's assistant organist was going to accompany me in a short prelude my father had arranged for organ and trumpet. I knew my part well, but I was so nervous when it was time to play that my mouth became dry and I could not wet my lips before taking my embouchure. Not a note came out of my trumpet!

"The terror of the trumpet," another musician friend of mine termed this years later. The slightest problem in articulation produced a large mistake in pitch, projection, tone, timbre: all the qualities that, together, made a musical sound. Though by then I had only heard him perform twice, Wynton was the only trumpet player in my experience who seemed not in the least little bit fazed by the possibility, or for that matter probability, that the next train wreck, as many players called it, could occur at any moment. I'd heard a story that Wynton had told about performing Haydn's Trumpet Concerto, back at the beginning of his career when Wynton still played classical music in the concert hall, and after a few bars of the first movement Wynton stopped the conductor and asked him to start the piece again because of a mistake Wynton had made in his entrance. If this were true, it was the only such account I'd come across, and when I'd been around Wynton at the Iron Horse I'd been struck by how calm he was before the gig and between sets. There seemed no separation in his life between being off stage and on.

The same thing was immediately apparent as we sat at the piano in his Boston hotel suite, less than an hour before he was to play this benefit at Berklee. We might as well have been in a café somewhere having coffee (or tea, Wynton did not drink coffee— nor at that time alcohol for that matter, though he later developed a fondness for Armagnac after one of his trips to France, in fact the nicest gift you could present him was a bottle of fine Armagnac, which he would imbibe slowly, late at night after a gig, nursing a single glass).

"I want to write something that explains how a musician goes from there," I said, pointing to his heart, "to here," I continued, placing my hand on the piano keys, and then touching with the same hand my own heart, which was beating at what seemed to me its normal rate, my pulse normal, too: no stage fright, no fear. What I said seemed as natural to me as breathing.

Silence in the room, save for the traffic sounds outside by the Boston Common, brightly lit with Christmas decorations. For a second I wondered if perhaps I had said more than I should. It was like one of those places in a piece of music where no one plays a note, everything is suspended, you even hold your breath, and then as suddenly as the music stopped it starts again, but with a different energy and clearer purpose.

"Let's rap," Wynton said, standing. "But I've got to get ready for the gig," he continued.

He was wearing sweat pants and sweater, and it was already past 7:30 p.m. The performance was to begin at eight.

"Talk to me while I get ready," he said, and I followed him into the next room where an ironing board was already set up, and we talked while he pressed his shirt, his suit, and even his tie, and we continued talking in the elevator and out through the lobby to the waiting limo. Once in the car, however, Wynton's focus changed abruptly as he extricated his trumpet mouthpiece from the instrument's leather case that Wes had been carrying for him and played several warm-up exercises on it while kibitzing with the driver about Boston traffic.

The streets of the city passed quietly by, headlights in the window. Wynton laughed at one of Wes's jokes and told a variation of one he said he had just heard in Japan. Sometimes jokes and stories segued so seamlessly that it could be hard to tell which were what.

"I went to this concert at Lincoln Center, heard this young dude, this Russian, playing the piano," Wynton said to me. "He was playing Mozart and Shostakovich.

"I was sitting next to these newspaper critics. They were writing this stuff, it was a strange vibe to see it while this kid was playing the Mozart. I talked to them afterwards, and they were saying, 'Well, the Shostakovich will be his own territory,' you know, all that Russians-can't-play-Mozart bullshit. And I saw this critic, can't remember his name. And he asked me what I thought.

"'You think you could be up there playing Mozart with the Philadelphia Orchestra when you were twenty?' I said. 'I thought the cat was killing.'"

When the Berklee gig ended there was a reception for benefactors back at the hotel, so Wynton left the hall sooner than he might otherwise have, and I continued to tag along, though it was now late enough that I would be getting home long after midnight. At the reception I made small talk with a few guests and then told Wynton I had to go.

"I'll walk you to the elevator," he said, and despite my protestation that such a gesture was unnecessary he did, leaving the reception for a few minutes.

"How will I get in touch with you?" I asked.

"You'll find me," was Wynton's gnomic reply.

Maren, you were still shy of your second birthday a few weeks after that first Boston visit with him, when I called Wynton on New Year's Eve as he was leaving to perform at the Blue Note in New York.

"When are you coming out on the road with us?" he said, in a voice so low I could barely hear him.

"Soon," I equivocated, as if this were a summons that would be retracted if I didn't act on it immediately. It was a pointless anxiety, but I did not know that yet, hadn't realized Wynton responded to whatever people were around him at a given time, betraying little concern about those who weren't, but never forgetting them either. Partly, I supposed, this was how he dealt with a ridiculously crammed schedule, but it was also the outward sign of an inner focus that could be both inspiring and intimidating. In all the years I have known him since, he has never taken an entire day off; never gone to the movies or a show, unless with his kids; maintained a funny loathing for anything resembling the ocean, a beach, or a pool (when his manager once convinced Wynton to visit Hawaii for a kind of working vacation, Wynton left the day after he arrived); continued on the road to go out to small clubs to play after a regular gig ends, and then be up early the next morning to do a master class; worked steadily and purposefully on *something* every day, despite his procrastination on major projects, staying with his concentration to the very last minute before he has to break for some other obligation (a gig, a rehearsal, a meeting) and then returning to the work immediately upon its completion, alone in his hotel room—or at the piano by the corner windows in the living room of his 29th-floor apartment looking out at Lincoln Center and downtown Manhattan and west across the Hudson River to New Jersey, with a sense of the country opening up beyond that western horizon, the country and its towns and cities and all the people he had visited, the memories and energy of which and of whom it was his ambition to put in his music.

That same focus could become an enveloping curiosity about others when they were in his company: no part of another person's life was off limits for discussion with Wynton. He was strikingly open about the physical phenomena, the wonder and elation, of being alive, indeed he reveled in it. He was affectionately demonstrative, touching a shoulder or a head, and often working at home alone in nothing but a pair of boxer shorts, falling asleep in the middle of a conversation or in a hotel, lying on his bed as he talked on the phone.

Once, several years after I started traveling with the band, he was taking a break on the tour bus during the filming of some music videos at Tanglewood, where Wynton studied for a summer after he graduated from high school. He had returned there often to perform and endowed a student scholarship, having himself won the summer of his own residency the award for best brass student, this despite being refused a lesson by one of the Boston orchestra's former trumpet players, because of his race, Wynton told me (though when I brought the subject up again he declined to say anything further about it, as if he had thought better about saying anything in the first place).

The music videos he filmed with the BSO's music director, Seiji Ozawa, were part of a PBS series for kids. There was an audience of children in the barn building where most of the filming took place, but none in the bus where Wynton had retreated to use the john. It was a hot summer day, and the bus's air conditioner was on while the bus idled under some trees. After using the tiny bus bathroom, which anyone on the road knew by silent decree was for peeing only, he emerged, fastening his belt, and warned whoever was in earshot not to enter it for a while.

"Whew!" he exclaimed, smiling broadly. "Nasty."

Wynton entertained band members and close friends while shaving or ironing before a gig—he always pressed his own clothes—often at the last minute, while in the hotel lobby his driver and one of his road managers nervously checked their watches. Even with strangers, Wynton probed the people he was with for information about subjects from the mundane to the sacred. In a single sentence he might go from a joke about farts (for a time he used to extend an index finger in lieu of a handshake, and when the unlucky person grabbed it he would gleefully fart) to a question about the death of a loved one.

"How is your mother?" Wynton asked during that post-Boston, New Year's Eve call before he left to play at the Blue Note. He'd met her the month before at the Iron Horse, where at her request, relayed through me, he had played one of her favorite songs, *For All We Know*, and then acknowledged her by name from the stage, something she never forgot.

"OK, thanks," I said, surprised that someone who was about to perform at a fabled New York City night club could be this laid back, oblivious to the time. "So," I continued, "where are you going next?"

"I have no idea," he replied, which I was beginning to recognize as not only his standard answer to this question but the truth.

A few months after that call I saw him in New York, where he played at Carnegie Hall in an April benefit featuring a host of older, legendary musicians: Dizzy Gillespie, Gerry Mulligan, Freddie Hubbard, all on the same stage. Wynton was comfortable in their company, though he was less than half the age of all but a few of his fellow performers. I think they also included Doc Cheatham, who was in his 80s then, except I may be confusing my memory with a Town Hall gig, also in New York, at which Wynton and Doc played repeated encores to a packed house on a warm, late June night. By the date of that concert I'd already made my first, brief trip with Wynton to his hometown of New Orleans, with a run-out to San Antonio before a return flight from Houston...sorry, Maren, I'm getting ahead of myself again.

After the Carnegie Hall gig I returned to New York often that spring. Once I spent part of a day with Frank Stewart, the photographer, who took me up to Harlem to see an exhibition of collages by Romare Bearden, whose assistant Frank had been near the end of Bearden's life. Frank was married at the time to a strikingly beautiful woman named Helima, who worked at the museum where the collages were on display, and who had been seated next to me at Carnegie Hall. We'd struck up a conversation at intermission, and she'd introduced me to her husband after the gig. Frank and I would become friends—High Point and Swig—but when we met that night there was a mutual, startled moment of wariness and confusion over our respective reasons for being at the gig; we were both, it turned out, planning projects with Wynton. The next time I was in the city Frank invited me to go to the gallery with him, partly, I sensed, as a kind of test.

"There's black people living there, you know," Frank confided, his eyes sparkling, his manner mock serious.

"I think I can handle that," I said, and Frank seemed pleased by my answer, not so much its content as its tone. We wouldn't see one another again until the summer, when Frank brought his two daughters along on a run-out from the city to a gig on Long Island, and after that not until the following fall, when we found ourselves sitting in adjacent seats on a connecting flight from Chicago to Lincoln, Nebraska, where the septet was beginning a tour that took us also to Kansas, St. Louis, Kentucky, and Louisiana, and during breakfast in a downtown Lincoln hotel on a very cold, winter-like day Frank explained the foundation of his view of Wynton's musical world.

"He is the sun," Frank said, taking me aback. "Everything else revolves around him."

Frank, who'd grown up in Chicago and studied photograph at Pratt, was a street-wise intellectual who did not make wild claims. He was also pretty unflappable, one of the reasons Wynton eventually asked him to assist as a driver several years later when after a near-disaster on a plane Wynton decided to avoid flying whenever possible, even if that decision meant as it often did a lengthy van or car ride. Talking, Frank might crack a slight smile to let on when he was kidding about something, but he was dead serious about his work, and his photographs had an edge to them, a depth, making them at once a document of a particular moment and an insight into a meaning. Frank's photographs—of musicians, of Bearden, of everyday folk—weren't so much "about" their subject as they actually "were" the thing they depicted: the essence of an experience, whether musical or romantic or political.

The afternoon of the Bearden exhibit was gray and chilly, and I was cold walking from the subway station to my next stop, Lincoln Center. Wynton had started to perform there in a summer series called Classical Jazz that would soon develop into a program called Jazz at Lincoln Center, of which Wynton would become the artistic director. Jazz at Lincoln Center would in a few years boast of its equal status with the New York Philharmonic, the Metropolitan Opera, and the New York City Ballet as a full-fledged Lincoln Center constituent, and yet in stark contrast to those other organizations, which would become engaged in squabbling over Lincoln Center finances and renovations, Jazz at Lincoln Center would one day move into its own headquarters in the huge new Time Warner building at Columbus Circle, where Wynton and his bands started playing in performance spaces that cost well over 100 million dollars, much of the money personally raised by Wynton, who charmed donors with an irresistible combination of humor, self-deprecation, idealism, and chutzpah.

Wynton did have a way of creating attention, negative or positive, despite his constant disavowals of seeking publicity. To judge from what had been written about him Wynton was not only the "enigmatic," "visionary," "charismatic" heir to an entire artistic tradition, an iconic standard bearer, but also, according to some observers, close-minded, interested in only one kind of jazz, and thus...a polarizer.

"Why is it," he would ask rhetorically, "that someone else finds it so threatening when a black man has something to say *and* says it *and*—this is truly crazy—can also *play*?

"I don't know why these people call me," he continued, referring to an interview he'd just done.

"Did you see the piece in the *Voice*?" I might ask.

"What did it say?" he would reply.

But he knew.

One of my closest friends, a screenwriter who'd moved in his early 40s from Hollywood to Israel, grilled me soon after I went on the road about an incident he'd heard of second-hand that suggested, he said, Wynton might be anti-Semitic. Later, after my friend had been diagnosed with a rare form of lymphoma, he left his hospital room one day in California to meet me at a workshop Wynton was giving in a West Oakland housing project.

Working with kids seemed in some respects not so much a byproduct of Wynton's relentless touring but one of its primary purposes, as if Wynton were on a kind of mission if not to save the world with jazz at least to make jazz a more important part of its future. Some of the claims he made could come across as grandiloquent, and far removed from the wellsprings of an art form that began in smoky night clubs and old-time dance joints, but few who listened to him in person could resist responding to his importunings and cajolings. He had a way of being heard, not just with his music but with his words.

Geographically, the housing project where the Oakland workshop took place was only a short distance from a neighboring community called Emeryville, where at a club called Kimberly East, I once sat in for Wynton at a rehearsal, an experience that helped me realize, as Wynton cheerfully pointed out to me later, when he heard reports of my difficulties, that I was not a trumpet player (I could not keep up with the sheer velocity of the music with my eye, let alone my lip). Instead of the boutiques and restaurants of Emeryville, here in West Oakland the most prominent landmark was the collapsed expanse of Martin Luther King Jr. Boulevard, badly damaged in the 1989 California earthquake.

Workshop was also something of a misnomer. None of the kids in this gathering seemed musical, or particularly interested in music for that matter. They were all attending a summer program designed to improve their scholastic skills and, at the same time, feed them if they were hungry and take care of them if, as seemed to be the case for many, no one was at home to do so. We were staying in the tony San Jose suburb of Los Gatos, where the septet was performing that night at a mountaintop winery. Voluntarily participating with Wynton in that Oakland workshop was trombonist Wycliffe Gordon, who had grown up in Augusta, Georgia, and whom the other members of the septet had taken to calling Pine Cone, or just Cone for short, because the nickname expressed something about his personality and background, the country aspect of an outlook that was mixed so explosively with musical wizardry (he could play half a dozen different instruments well) and a style of improvising that was both technically sophisticated and intuitive.

Before the workshop, which lasted about an hour, I introduced Wynton to my friend, whose illness I had mentioned to Wynton on the long ride over from Los Gatos that morning. Sitting in the back seat of a limousine, working on the score for the *Citi Movement* ballet commission he was months late completing, Wynton had looked up, holding his pencil in mid-air, as we exchanged rapid-fire questions and answers about my friend:

   — Why was he in a Berkeley hospital if he lived in Israel?
   — Because this is where his Boston-based doctor had recommended, and it was relatively near his wife's family in Sacramento.
   — What was the prognosis?
   — Much better now, but still uncertain; he could have died.

And then, without further comment, Wynton had returned to his manuscript, despite his agitated distress that day over the news, delivered to him in person in his hotel room the night before, that his tenor saxophonist, Todd Williams, had decided to leave the band, for reasons having to do with his religion and being away from home so much.

"How am I ever going to replace Todd?" Wynton asked rhetorically as we waited for our host outside the building where the workshop was to take place. That's when my friend showed up.

"Wynton, this is…" I began.

"I know," he interrupted me, and then, in the same breath but to my friend, "How you doing, man? Thanks for checking us out today. But tell me something, please"—and he nodded in my direction as he finished his question—"how could you be knowing this man all these years without going crazy over all his bull"— brief pause, drawing out the vowel before the double consonant— "shitting?" Then, quickly following, came loud laughter, a smile, and a hand on my fascinated friend's shoulder.

Afterwards, still at the housing project, Wynton spied an out-door basketball game and asked if he could play. Right off he tried a few outside shots, his specialty, and missed. Driving to the hoop, he reversed the ball as he dribbled behind his back and made the layup. He clapped his hands and bounced on the balls of his feet as he ran for his position on the next play. Again, he missed a jumper from foul-line distance.

On the other side of the court, a young man about 15 or 16 edged toward the basketball players, oblivious to their proximity. The look on his face was vacant. He was wearing two pairs of pants, one over the other. The outer pair had suspenders, which were undone. This pair of pants had fallen down to his ankles, making it almost impossible for him to move. But he did not reach down to pull them up. Instead he had slowed his walk to a shuffle, even as he moved into the midst of Wynton and the other basket-ball players, who continued their game and tried to ignore him.

On the ground at one end of the court, near some little kids who were hitting a volleyball, lay a dead pigeon. No one apparently knew how it had gotten there, or why it had not been taken away. But as Wynton retrieved the basketball from out of bounds, he watched as the man wearing two pairs of pants shuffled toward the pigeon, stopped, bent over, and picked it up. Holding the pigeon in his hands, the man then resumed his shuffle.

Those nearest the man stood back, giving him all the room they thought necessary; they'd seen this behavior before. The man appeared to be going toward a loudspeaker from which was boom-ing hip-hop, but changed his mind before he got there. He headed back toward the area on the other side of the basketball court, where a little grass was growing in the space before the buildings. A few small trees had been planted in the courtyard, too.

Driving back to Los Gatos later I made what I immediately realized was a gratuitous comment on the plight of this man and the bleakness of where he lived.

"That's an opinion," Wynton shot back, looking up from the music he was again working on. He was visibly engrossed in this process, but betrayed none of the excitement he felt when he had finished something, like the afternoon several years later before the premiere of *Blood on the Fields*, when he was talking with several friends who had gathered in his sons' bedroom, and as he bounced a basketball on the apartment floor said, "I really got to something here."

Back in the car from West Oakland to Los Gatos, Wynton continued, "My mother grew up in a housing project. Never judge. You never know."

By the time of that conversation, my evolving career as second trumpet had been consecrated with Wynton's agreement to collaborate on a book with me. During a springtime visit to New York we had made a presentation before a dozen or so people gathered around a table in a conference room at the offices of one of New York's largest trade publishers. Though we had not prepared for this meeting, our impromptu give and take provided me with my first chance to practice improvisation, albeit verbal rather than musical, with Wynton. When Wynton replied to a question about Duke Ellington's memoir, *Music is My Mistress*, I added a comment about his answer, even though I hadn't read that book, and we were soon inventing the dialogue format we eventually used for our book. There would be many more chances to practice in New York, where Wynton often entertained guests after a gig with improvised, usually profane lyrics he called the Hoghead Blues (accompanying himself on the piano as he sang, except one time backstage at Tanglewood when he was waiting to perform with pianist Marcus Roberts and the two of them serenaded an amused Seiji Ozawa with a lyric about an imaginary girlfriend of Seiji's who'd supposedly left him).

After our presentation we had gone out to a celebratory lunch at which Wynton made such prolonged eye contact with our literary agent that she had finally looked up from her food and asked Wynton if he wasn't going to eat his. Was it okay, what he had ordered, or was he not really hungry?

"It gives me greater pleasure to watch you enjoying yours," Wynton had replied, in the first and only exchange I remember his having with this woman.

A few days later I drove down to New York again for a Lincoln Center gig at which he was making a solo classical appearance. An older musician friend of Wynton's was present at the gig, a white-haired man who had known Wynton at least since his single year at Juilliard and who called him not completely in jest, Mozart, a nickname Wynton said was disrespectful of Mozart but that over the years I would hear others use, including his longtime producer when he was with Sony Classical, Steve Epstein, a man who by temperament and training was not given to hyperbole.

"Just tell what really happened," Wynton would say to me in response to such excessive praise. Labels, whether positive or negative, avoided imaginative engagement with the subject, which required a different kind of thought and observation. Now that I reflect on it, Maren, the distinction he had in mind was a little like what I called outer and inner, don't you think? I mean, the analogy may break down but what else could he have been referring to as we talked about our book in his Alice Tully Hall dressing room after that guest appearance and I mentioned that his search for a new pianist to replace Marcus Roberts, who had recently left the septet to start a solo career, was the kind of event that could set in motion a good... "magazine story," he completed the sentence disparigingly.

It was a shame, Wynton continued, that in all the commentary about such musicians as Duke Ellington and Miles Davis, there was really no documentation about something as basic as "what it was like to be in a room with one of them.

"What they left for me, what Duke left, and Trane," he continued. "When something is great, it echoes, and each echo is bigger than what it came from. Think of the sound of a bagpipe in a battle. Or go to the edge of a canyon and shout, *HELLO!* The major function of your existence is to do something that will ricochet, like the echo of your voice from that cliff."

Wynton himself would remind me many times about his heritage. How often in my travels, commenting to him about his lack of sleep or some kink in his schedule had he replied: "I could be picking cotton." Or we might be in a car together, going to a gig, and his mood animated he would start in with the driver, like he had in a limousine on the way back from another gig many years later, when he announced he was really a black Dick Cheney planning a war for oil in Africa and the driver started laughing so hard—Wynton had observed that in the car there were two black men, a white man, and an Indian-American woman, "perfect criteria to apply for a grant"—that I thought we were going to crash.

In New York that night after the Lincoln Center gig our conversation continued outside after the Mozart-calling friend had left. It was a nice night, warm enough that you didn't need a jacket. Wynton was headed home, which was a brownstone in the Village that was either for sale or had already been sold; he was moving out, soon to be living in a condominium next to Juilliard (where, with the addition of space from the adjacent condo, he still lives—the place you've visited, Maren, and where Anna stayed overnight one Christmas, when we'd seen Wynton at a Boston gig where he was playing as a sideman to help out drummer Ali Jackson, and when he, Wynton, learned that Anna was flying out to California from New York very early the morning after Christmas, and we didn't know how we were going to get her to the airport, said, "she can stay at my place the night before, one of Herlin's sons will be there and two of mine, and I'll have a car pick her up for the ride to the airport").

"Let's walk," Wynton said, starting purposefully, and without waiting for a reply from me, down Broadway. He ignored something I said about his performance, seemed not to hear my question about

Mozart, and started telling me about his sons, who were one and three years old at that time. He had witnessed both births, he told me, and then described the scene of those *miracles*, his word.

"This will be my ninth New York City move," he said, but when I asked him for details, such as the actual date or how his sons felt (they were going to be living with their mother, eventually outside the city in Westchester), he clammed up, except to confess the difficulty he had dealing with the kind of day-to-day details that defined raising a family, "you know, going to the park with the kids for two hours." We kept walking, quite quickly, and gradually the rhythm of that walk helped set a rhythm for our conversation, and I began to feel more at ease, less like a visitor and more like someone on a walk.

We passed the Sheraton, near Carnegie Hall, and I mentioned staying there when I'd come down to the city with the Boston Symphony Orchestra for a performance of Mahler's Second Symphony. Wynton did not have anything to say just then about Mahler, whose music I gathered he had played in a youth orchestra in New Orleans, though we would later hear the BSO in Mahler Three at a concert that Wynton would leave, after the first movement, to take his sons who were with him back home to his apartment, where he put them to bed before returning to Carnegie Hall on time for the symphony's climactic finale. I asked him about Mahler Two as we walked, but he had a way of changing the subject by simply going, "uh-huh," if he thought he was being interviewed, instead of having a conversation, and he took the talk elsewhere.

"My grandfather used to run a segregated hotel," he said. "In New Orleans. This was before Civil Rights, when my mama had to sit in the back of the bus. I can remember sitting back there with her.

"The hotel closed after integration," Wynton concluded. I could not tell if he was wistful about the end of that period in his family history or encouraged by the change in society it represented. Many times when he said something there was no value judgment implied or to be made; it was just a statement of fact.

"Fact is," he would say.

"Yes?" I responded quizzically.

"Take a flower pot, someone's favorite flower pot," he continued. "The wind blows it off its stand and it breaks into many pieces. What happened?"

Before I could reply he answered his own question.

"The flower pot broke," he said. "But that is all. If the person whose favorite flower pot said it was too bad, what happened, that is not a fact but a feeling. A feeling is not a fact. A fact just is."

Fact is.

He had another word for that, too.

Isness.

Wynton's grandfather ran a segregated hotel: *fact.*

It's revealing that Wynton's grandfather ran a segregated hotel: *feeling.*

Wynton is moving out, his sons are going to live just with their mother: *fact.*

That's too bad, that Wynton won't see his sons as much anymore: *feeling.*

We were making our way downtown. As we neared Wynton's street, 18th, we passed an outdoor basketball court.

"Yo, fawly!" Wynton hollered to someone shooting baskets.

"Play here whenever I can," Wynton said, making me wonder if we were going to stop and do so now. But we continued to his brownstone, which was locked, the lights out, everyone asleep.

We went into the kitchen, where Candy had left a note saying there was some left over chicken in the refrigerator.

"You hungry?" Wynton asked me.

"I'm okay," I replied. "I had something earlier."

"So, where you staying tonight?" he said as he stood in front of the opened refrigerator door and ate a piece of the chicken.

"I was going to take the train to my brother's. He lives north of Yonkers."

"What time is the train?"

"I don't know, I think the last one is at one, or maybe two."

Wynton looked in the direction of the mantle, where there once must have been a clock but now, with most of the stuff already packed for the upcoming move, the only item on the mantle was a miniature statue of Louis Armstrong.

"Why don't you just stay here," he said, more as a statement than a question. "I'll get you some sheets and a towel."

I followed him down some stairs to a closet, where he rummaged around for the linens he had promised, which he then handed to me and said, without any further conversation, "Good night."

By my next visit to New York, Wynton had completed his move to the apartment by Lincoln Center. Some days the boys were with him, Wynton Jr. (who also went by his father's nickname, Skain) and his little brother Simeon. They had toys that they kept at the apartment, and extra clothes. "We go out someplace to eat and then we hang out," Wynton said. "I give them a bath, together. We make it a long bath. I mean, when I give them a bath they get *clean*. Shampoo. Everything." The boys both slept in Wynton's bed with their father, the three of them together. His bedroom then, before the apartment was expanded, was off the hallway, separate from the living room around the corner and the little kitchen and the other, smaller bedroom where he had his books and that became a study when an extra bedroom was added for the boys as they got older. Wynton's CDs were in the bedroom, and there was usually one playing; Wynton would leave it on, too, when he went out. After he gave the boys their baths and read them stories he returned to his piano to work until long after midnight. Friends often came by, young musicians who were in town or studying next door at Juilliard, people he'd met on the road whom he'd invited to call him when they were in New York, lady friends.

Wynton dressed the boys in the morning, once in matching outfits, even the caps matched. Then they'd take a few toys and ride the elevator downstairs. Simeon liked to push the buttons. Sometimes they'd go out for breakfast, and they might get a cab if it was a day when no one was picking Wynton up for a meeting or recording session, and they would drive downtown where they still lived with their mother.

"There's the old house," Wynton Jr. once said as they passed the last street where they all lived together. It wasn't much farther to Candy's. They'd get off at the corner.

Wynton Jr. might run ahead and ring the bell, and Candy might already be outside with him when Wynton and Simeon caught up.

Candy would greet Wynton, who said little in reply. He might tell her what the boys had eaten, who had a sniffles or whatever. Then they would all go inside, where Candy began fixing them breakfast.

At gigs in New York Candy would bring the boys. "If I can't see them from the stage I can hear them," Wynton liked to say. "Then I can see them because the people around them get upset and I can see those people moving in their seats. Squirming. 'Who are these boys making all this noise at this concert I paid all this money for?' My daddy always took me and Branford to gigs when we were young. And we'd be sitting just like Skain and Simeon, wondering why we had to be there. But you got to take them. You never know when one day they are going to hear something."

As I fell asleep that night after our first long walk, I could hear his voice and Candy's from down the hallway, but the house was quiet in the morning when I awoke, and no one stirred as I let myself out, still wearing my clothes from the day before, and took the subway up to Grand Central where I got the train to my brother's and retrieved my car. I did not see Wynton again until June, which is when he actually played that gig with Doc Cheatham (I checked!), but I called him once in May, after we'd received a formal offer from the same publisher we'd visited together that April day we adlibbed our plan for a book, an offer that meant with its promise of an advance that I could finally afford to join Wynton and his band on the road.

He was in Japan the day I called him, and with my miscalculation of the time difference I managed to wake him in his hotel room with the ringing of the phone. But he took the call, which he kept short, and he mostly listened without asking questions to my news. And then, thanking me for calling and admitting he was a little sleepy, he added three words before hanging up: "Great days ahead."

O'Hare Airport, Chicago

Dear Family,

It's almost nine a.m., Central Time, and I just arrived in Chicago (where it's sixteen degrees outside). The flight from Hartford was smooth, and we went right over Buffalo. I could see the Peace Bridge. It looked like one of those bridges at a toy store. And the mist from Niagara Falls looked like smoke coming out of our electric train engine. I had a cholesterol-rich doughnut at the Hartford airport, so I skipped breakfast on the plane and slept after reading the newspaper. We came into Chicago from the north, but I was snoozing before remembering I could have seen Wrigley Field. Now I'm waiting at the gate for the flight to Lincoln. Wynton and Frank are due in from New York in a few minutes, and we're sitting a row apart on the Lincoln flight, which is supposed to take about ninety minutes (we leave at nine-thirty). After checking into the Cornhusker Hotel we have a sound check at three and the gig is at seven, I think. We leave for Kansas City early tomorrow morning.

I love you all very much and miss you very much. Take care of each other and be happy.

Maren, you've probably figured out that was a note I sent from the road, soon after my travels began. It gives me a funny feeling to read it now, I mean to imagine exactly what I was thinking when I wrote it, and what was happening in all of our lives. I'm also struck by the semblance of a chronology it begins to lay out, like all my notebooks but different, too, because of its intention. This is more like a document to me, a kind of "proof" that I did whatever I did, but what I'm describing seems in some ways more distant, I mean the time that is evoked is distant. Maybe that's because I was writing more of a long postcard to all of you: *fact*. And it makes me a little sad, within the joy of what I was doing, all these references to things at home I missed: *feeling*.

Mayfair Suites, St. Louis

Dear Family,

It's just after one, and this has been the first stretch of a few hours since I left in that crazy blur on Friday that there hasn't been something to do right away. In other words, we finally got a little sleep on a real bed, after an all-night trip from Kansas City (actually three-thirty a.m. to just after noon Monday), which was followed at three by a rehearsal in the hotel's restaurant and then dinner last night for the whole band and a lot of other people at Todd Williams' parents' house. In another hour now, we go to the hall here (the same hall the orchestra uses) for a sound check that will also be recorded, so Garth Fagan will have more of the music for the ballet (he's choreographing it as the band learns it, the process made more difficult by the fact that the copyist who was writing out parts last month in New York, when the score was being faxed each day from Europe, made so many mistakes that we have another copyist named Ronnie Carbo with us who is virtually redoing all the parts as Wynton corrects them).

I'm eager for news. Christian, hockey results? Anna, how was Sunday's rehearsal? Maren, tomorrow morning we're going to Kentucky!

B., I still don't know my arrival time Tuesday in Hartford. Also, could you send any good mail care of the Meridian, if you can mail it conveniently now, or otherwise fax me ___'s letter and anything else nice. The Meridian is the New Orleans hotel where we'll be by Sunday. Or fax right here, tonight. Thank you!

St. Louis is an old, large city that has the look of Chicago but not the feel in the streets. I walked yesterday down to the Mississippi, just to get a little exercise, and saw the arch, which is kind of hokey, I think, but amazing nonetheless, that it stands. And the ballpark is nearby. The hotel we're in your grandfather would've loved; lots of old wood paneling in the bar and restaurant, and elevators that are still hand operated, and chandeliers hanging everywhere. What's missing is all of you, whom I love very much, and think about always, and talk about, too—Maren, I told Todd Williams about your toy saxophone, and

Christian, the photographer Frank Stewart has a daughter almost your age, and Anna, Garth Fagan is the same Garth Fagan you saw at Jacob's Pillow.

Much love,
Dad/Carl

Bowling Green, KY

Dear Family,

We're just arriving in Bowling Green, after an all-morning drive from St. Louis of about 300 miles. We've been eating chocolate chip cookies that someone gave Wynton, a shoebox-full; he doesn't like that kind, so there were more for us. Yesterday, after the rehearsal for New York City, Wynton, Wycliffe, and Wess went to a high school in East St. Louis, where the band director is a friend of Wynton's. We stayed almost three hours, with the guys sitting in with the kids in their band. I was supposed to go out later that evening with Wynton to visit a friend of his who collects records, but we had our signals crossed and I got some sleep instead; now, as soon as we reach the hotel, Wynton has a work-shop at Bowling Green University, then a sound check at three that will be recorded to send to Garth Fagan, and then tonight the concert is at eight, I think. Tomorrow we leave pretty early for Tennessee.

It's fall here; the landscape looks a lot like home. We crossed the Ohio River a while ago; it's about the width of the Connecticut but deeper. The weather's warmer now than yesterday in St. Louis when the temperature was in the 60s. I walked by the ballpark, where I could see in by the bleachers. Workmen were installing the new carpet in the out-field. There was a sign outside that said: Cardinals-Mets April 6.

I want some news! Send a note to the hotel here, give me some hockey scores, the weather report. Anna, I hope your cold is getting bet-ter and no one else gets it. When I called yesterday, Christian, sorry I missed you. What fun it was to hear your voice, Maren!

We just pulled into the parking lot. Nothing like where we just were; a highway strip with a pizza place next door, etc. I love you all and miss you and think of you with each place we pass, which brings me closer to when I will see you all again.

Bowling Green

Yo, Tintin,

It was great to hear from you! And everyone in the band loved your drawing. Was that me or Wynton?! Actually, I was playing his horn last night after the concert here (in an old movie theater). Earlier, he led a workshop for some college and high school students who were nervous playing with him but it all worked out. Wynton talked with them about some of the things you're learning on the piano, like those chord progressions, and he also answered questions about practicing and other things. He said he used to practice four to five hours a day when he was a kid, and when someone asked him what was his "first break" he said it was all that practicing, "which is still giving me my break."

Right now we just had breakfast at a Howard Johnson's and are about to bus it to the Smoky Mountains in Tennessee, where it is supposed to be very beautiful. Congratulations on your team's first victory! Good luck tonight against the Caps. Give my love to everyone, and I hope Anna is feeling better and can skate tomorrow. Isn't today that surprise party of her friend's? I wish you all were here right now. My window looks out on a courtyard and an indoor swimming pool in which I wish I were watching you swimming. Also, there is a pool table and a putting green. I wish you could see our bus, which has purple trim on the outside and small letters on the back that say, "Star Trax Celebrity Coaches."

Lafayette, Louisiana

Dear Family Whom I Will See Soon,

I'm writing this in a conference room at the hotel. We've been out all day at workshops (three of them), after a drive yesterday through the bayou from New Orleans (and we had crayfish for lunch, pronounced "crawfish"), then a rehearsal at the hall, concert, recording session until midnight, party at a local politician's fancy house with outdoor hot tub (it was raining, though), then tomorrow we leave for the last stop, Shreveport, which is up towards Oklahoma. Lots of gumbo, not much sleep. The concert Monday in New Orleans was actually something of a letdown, not well promoted and many empty seats, but I did get a chance to see a little more of the city, and saw Wynton's father Ellis again when we stopped at his house on the way to the concert hall at Tulane so Wynton could leave off his laundry!

I loved getting your letter, Anna, before we left New Orleans. Let's see, if this is Wednesday you must have been at gymnastics. Any new tricks? I imagine there must be a hockey game soon; Brattleboro Sunday? I'll be there!

Shreveport, Louisiana

Dear A., B., C., and M.—

It's a lovely day in Louisiana, sunny and warm, most of all nice because tomorrow at this time I will be counting the hours rather than days (or weeks) until I see you. This has been a good trip, but I missed you all very much. Will you remember me?!

Christian, good luck against Bay State and Windsor Locks.

Morgans Hotel, NYC

Dear Family,

It's nine-thirty and we're about to walk over to the recording studio, near where we were on Friday. I arrived last night after a very long drive, because of holiday traffic, and watched TV while I unpacked and then slept a little restlessly in this very nice hotel, which is also very dark: windows look out on brick, so the shades stay closed, and the lighting in the hallways is subdued (took the elevator down a floor this morning for a free continental breakfast, including fresh squeezed OJ, and all the croissants you could eat, Anna!).

The schedule today is pretty horrific, with rehearsals this afternoon and evening, but exciting, too. So I will probably not have much free time, or fax time. But I'm thinking of you, wishing you good luck in the hockey tryouts, Christian, and good dancing this afternoon, Anna, and I love you all very much. Maren, are you decorating your room for Christmas? XXXX, OOOO Dad/Carl

Morgans Hotel

Dear Family,

Are you still iced in? Here it's clear but very cold, and of course I forgot my coat. I'm just on my way to the recording studio for a ten a.m., one-hour session, then a rehearsal at the Brooklyn Academy of Music this afternoon. My sister was planning to come to the premiere but just called to say she has a stomach bug.

Leave tomorrow after meeting with our editor, who is also coming this morning to the recording session. I miss all of you and will see you tomorrow by suppertime.

Wilmington, DE

Dear Bonnie, Christian, Anna, and Maren,

It's about 3:15 and we're in Wilmington, Delaware, after a two-and-one-half hour drive from New York, after last night's Carnegie Hall concert, which was a big audience hit (if you watch on TV, Wynton plays at the beginning, in a piece that was redone after the audience left, and then before and right after intermission, and at the end). My train trip yesterday was uneventful; Maren, thanks for helping me get on the big train. Anna, you must be getting ready for ballet as I write this; and Christian, how was yesterday's hockey? Did you hear about the fight between the Sabres and Flames?

I'm about to walk across the street for sound check. Not a lot of other news. Oh yes, Bill Cosby came last night. I thought of you, Anna, eating my muffin on the bus this morning—wish I could have figured out the way to bring some home, they were homemade. Tomorrow we will we will be in Washington. See you Thursday.

Morgans

Dear Family,

I just returned from breakfast after a very short sleep, because the recording session ended at five a.m. In a few minutes we go downtown for a noontime Christmas program.

It's very cold here, and must be in Amherst, too. Let's get those skis out! Anna, you were terrific in the Nutcracker.

Hope you're all well. I love you very much—Daddy/Carl

Naples, FL

Dear Family,

It's late, after eleven, and I just got back to my hotel room from tonight's gig, held in a new hall here in "prestigious" Naples. We're staying at the "prestigious" Registry Hotel, a boardwalk to the mangoes by the Gulf where Frank and I went this afternoon, after sound check and dinner (which we ate around four). Trip was smooth, as I reported to Anna. Wynton has the flu we've all had, so he didn't make an appearance until the concert. Naples seems mostly a retirement community for rich white folks. Some medium high-rises along the water, but nothing like Miami, and there are long stretches with no building. The water is "cold" (63 degrees), but the outdoor pool, by which I walked on my way to the beach, is 78! There are not the activities we had at Amelia; even the golf course is eleven miles away.

I gather that most of the Northeast is snowed in today; someone on my plane connection from Baltimore said it was already snowing there earlier, presumably the same storm that was heading north. The air here seems to smell of orange blossoms, but I have seen no orange trees, so the fragrance, which I remember from our trip to Amelia, must be something else. Tomorrow we leave early for Kissimmee, which is near Orlando. I think of our weekend in Vermont, that run we took Sunday morning, Anna, and skiing the bumps with you, Christian, and yesterday's skate, Maren, and I send you all much love this Valentines.

Lexington, Virginia

Dear Family,

It's a chilly gray afternoon in Virginia, where we just arrived around one and are now at sound check at the university down the road from our hotel. I'm going to write this quickly so I can hopefully get it off before Anna's show tonight because, Anna, I want to wish you good luck! I wish I were going to be there to see it in person. Please be sure to order that video for me. And while we're talking about ice, how did you do against Greenfield on Thursday, CPV? Wasn't that last night in Holyoke? And did Amherst win its title?

Maren, I was so happy that you went to the airport with me. Thank you. I missed our skating and cuddling. Are you keeping your calendar? I still don't know whether I'm coming home on Monday or Tuesday, but I'll tell you as soon as I know. This morning I was in Baltimore. As we were leaving our hotel to fly down here, I daydreamed about all of you at home on Saturday morning and thought about going out for doughnuts!

I love you all and miss you very much.

Fort Collins, CO
Dear Family,

A quick note to tell you I arrived safely after a long day of traveling. I was up at 4:30, before my alarm (I was afraid of sleeping through and missing my ride to the airport), and then the man who was to pick me up was late, but we got to the airport with plenty of time. Snow in Cleveland. Sat next to a pilot from there to Denver—lots of stories from an inside perspective about flying. We were at the Denver Airport another two hours, waiting for everyone's flight to come in and locating Reginald's bass, which had been shipped separately. It's now almost 3:30, Mountain Time, and we have a twenty-minute break before leaving for sound check. It's a funny feeling going through this routine. I know it so well now, the arrival at the hotel, unpacking, searching for the concert hall. My presence is unremarked upon by the band, and no one changes the subject talking because I am there. Wynton was still quite pleased with his voice disguise a few days ago when he called. Complaining about New York press coverage of Harry Connick this week, called it another excuse for Wynton bashing. Anna, I told everyone about your May visit and they are all looking forward to seeing you!

I miss you all terribly. Be well and remember I love you very very much.

Daddy

Hi, again. This is me, now, I mean not in one of those faxes you were too little to be able to read when I first sent them. By the time of the last couple of notes here I had bought my first laptop and was converting to email as a way of staying in touch, plus of course the phone, though believe it or not there were no cell phones then. So calls were relatively expensive, and email was often iffy.

One thing reading these letters has reminded me of is the tradition you and I established that first winter I was away of going to the skating rink when I was home for a few days, and I'd put you in a chair and push you around the ice as I skated, and then you would stand in your own skates and hold onto the front of the chair's seat and push yourself, maybe with a little help from me. By the end of the skating season, which almost coincided with the end of that long sequence of trips, you could stand up on your skates without the chair and kind of shuffle your feet in a semblance of movement. Now of course you can beat me around the rink skating blindfolded, backwards.

I know you kept asking when that last trip was going to end, because I have a fax I saved that Anna sent me in California, I believe from the time when we stayed overnight in Santa Rosa, just me and Frank and Wynton, before we flew to New Mexico for that weekend when Wynton was finishing the 7/4 section of *In This House, On This Morning*. Anna's fax is of a map she drew of the western United States, and instead of stars showing just the state capitols she has put a star where I was visiting with the band. The star in California also references a note in Anna's cursive (she was almost nine when she wrote this): *"Where's Daddy?" asked Maren. Here,* the note says, repeating the same word written on the California section of the map, *After California Home!!!*

This was just before Anna went with me to New York for the premiere of *In This House,* still my favorite Wyntonian piece with its synthesis of nearly a century of different jazz styles, all combined with a forward-moving energy that sounds like the feeling of the places we visited, not just New Mexico but all over the country, and the people we met, old, young, white, black, Hispanic. When we attended that first performance Anna wanted to stay in a "fancy hotel," and so I got a deal through someone associated with the band at a midtown place called the Renaissance. It turned out to be right next to Times Square, which only added to the allure for Anna. We hadn't been in our room five minutes before she had taken all the towels off the rack and arranged them around the sides of the bathroom sink to make an indoor version of the pretend house she used to create among the pine trees that bordered our neighbor's when we lived in the Conway farmhouse. At the concert Anna became restless and spent much of the time with Lesley, an assistant of Wynton's manager who'd come up from Washington, D.C., where the business office was located back then. She rallied afterwards to go with me backstage, where Wynton presented each member of the septet with a watch to commemorate the occasion and thank them for their commitment in rehearsals, learning the piece as he wrote it each day on the bus and in hotels while we were on tour. Wynton spoke for several minutes in that closed dressing room, in a way that reminded me of the private ceremonies that took place whenever someone left the band, except in this case only Wynton spoke.

"We've all made sacrifices to be out here," he said. "You've left your families for weeks at a time. You've stayed after gigs when I called a rehearsal. It's not something that we found when we came out on the road, this life; we had to create it, a group of men working something out. So I just want to tell you all that I love you. Thank you."

The next morning a press conference took place outside, under a tent adjacent to the Metropolitan Opera building, where Wynton and Peter Martins, director of the New York City Ballet, announced plans to collaborate on the ballet that became *Six Syncopated Movements*, the first collaboration for Wynton with the company made famous by Balanchine, who had worked with such composers as Copland and Stravinsky. And so Anna, whose dancing then would lead to her trapeze work now, was able to meet one of her artistic idols, though as I recall she was—not surprisingly—a little shy when Mr. Martins smiled and offered her his outstretched hand.

Along with that map Anna made me there is a poster she designed that, unrolled, depicts in a sequence of scenes an imagined version of my travels, as well as a few notes from her that I saved. I'm guessing these notes were written around the same time as when she made the map. Her notes were always decorated with artwork, too. In one, framed with what appear to be the stems of a purple flower, are  the words, *Welcome Home Daddy!* This note unfolds, like a card, and there is another message inside, without artwork: *To: Daddy. We missed you! We're so glad you're back!*

3

For almost a year after my father's death, we didn't have his piano tuned. The man who had owned this piano played the *Art of Fugue* by memory. It was my son who seemed comfortable hitting its keys, and his curiosity led naturally to a search for a local piano teacher, with whom he began studying at the age of seven; his sisters followed in turn, with Maren the last to start…and quit.

 The piano books my son used when he was still taking piano lessons were illustrated with four-color caricatures of monsters and clowns and eighth-notes with faces and fingers. At his teacher's request, instead of dropping him off at her house I used to take a seat in the room adjacent to the one that functioned as her studio. I rarely said anything as he learned chord inversions, played a piece we had practiced at home during the week (would he remember the pedal in the coda?), and fidgeted as his teacher explained the week's assignment—understanding the minor mode or the difference between a note marked staccato and a slur that ended with a

staccato. He was a good pupil, and for a time he worked harder at the piano than I ever did; later he learned a little jazz piano, too, before becoming obsessed with recorded techno.

During his lesson, I occasionally stared out the window at the maples in the yard, which bordered the road and a brook beyond. Eventually the sound of my son's playing became associated in my mind with the vision of afternoon light in the leaves.

We usually stopped for a snack afterwards, or I rewarded him with a pack of bubble-gum cards.

"Gary Carter!" he shouted.

I loved the way his voice rose at such moments. We talked about the Mets, his favorite team in those days (though his favorite player was a Yankee—Reggie Jackson, whose name for a time he substituted for his). We discussed his playing and the new pieces he had to learn. Sometimes I practiced with him, sitting in a chair by the piano bench, and I frequently used sports analogies to explain how he should concentrate before he began playing or how he should approach what his teacher had assigned.

"Think of that fingering like you were getting ready to bunt," I would say. Or, repeating advice my father had given me, "Get the rhythm right."

My own lessons ended when I was thirteen. My final repertoire consisted of two works, a Bach prelude and the Adagio of Beethoven's *Pathétique* Sonata. I was still studying the trumpet then, and sometimes I broke the monotony of my warm-up by humming part of the Beethoven. The warm-up consisted of slurred intervals that sounded in my head to a repeated sequence of vowel sounds, "Ouu, eee, ahh, eee, ouu." Relaxing my lips as I moistened them before beginning a breath, I wondered at my decision to quit the piano. Then I remembered that learning Beethoven had been no different. Music was work.

Less taxing were the mornings at home when I was very young, and the radio station that played classical music was turned on in my parents' bedroom. The programming always ended with the chorale theme from the final movement of Brahms' First Symphony, so that when I hear that piece now I immediately think of my mother making the beds. Late afternoon, my father came home while I was playing Schmidt exercises or John Thompson little pieces. He took the pipe out of his mouth before walking over to the piano to pat my shoulder. I wished I were outside, throwing a baseball. If my father were a lawyer or a doctor, I could tell him now how much I hated to practice.

"The melody is not the song," Wynton will often say, and perhaps his listening sessions with Branford when they were growing up were preparation for that insight. Even now, when he is trying out a singer or instrumentalist, Wynton will ask a musician to play the bass part or sing, say, the alto harmony, just as, during a perhaps partly apocryphal high school moment, Wynton once asked Branford, "What was that note just then in the tenor part?"

"E flat," replied Branford offhandedly.

Then they stopped the recording and checked the precise place in the music. And the note was, in fact, E flat.

"How'd you know?" said Wynton.

"It had to be," replied Branford.

When I first heard Wynton tell this story, I was reminded again of my own childhood, when I would be practicing on one of the two grand pianos in what was the largest room in my family's house. Playing the piano was not a choice; it was simply something you did, like eating and sleeping, and when after graduating from eighth grade I exercised my choice to opt-out, as it were, my parents correctly predicted this was a decision I would regret all my adult life.

But when I was young the piano could feel like torture, especially when I made a mistake that was corrected by my father, in the nearby kitchen, where he was talking about his day with my mother as she prepared dinner.

"That's a G in the left hand," he might say in a loud voice.

It had to be.

By that time in my life my father had given up his position as artistic manager of the Buffalo Philharmonic Orchestra to devote himself to teaching and to playing the instrument he loved, the pipe organ. Serving as choirmaster and organist at one of the city's largest, most prosperous churches enabled him to perform every Sunday and practice throughout the rest of the week. Nothing gave him greater pleasure than to be at the console of the magnificent Aeolian-Skinner organ he had designed, with its twin pipe chambers, facing one another from each side of the rear balcony that served as the choir loft, and with a division of trumpet-sounding pipes on the wall between and an antiphonal register of other pipes hidden at the opposite end of the church, behind the nave.

As a boy, I often kept my father company on his early Sunday morning walk from our house to church, and then I would sit by him on the organ bench as he reviewed a last time the music for that day's service. He would nod when I was to turn a page, but he said very little other than a brief hello to choir members as they arrived and a reminder to me to help myself to the licorice drops he always kept on one side of the console, below the array of knobs and switches that activated the different combinations of pipes.

I did not understand this then, but my father was teaching me something I only began to grasp when I was much older. The lessons were ongoing, continuing at the Sunday afternoon concerts of the orchestra, on whose board my father remained, and whose music director was the Austrian conductor Josef Krips.

My trumpet teacher, Gene Bishop, the orchestra's personnel manager, once played in John Philip Sousa's band. The man who had to impose discipline backstage, making certain all the players were on time, he must have been the gentlest person who ever guarded the door of a conductor's dressing room. Balding, he had a thick, wide moustache and enormous brown eyes, which looked even larger behind his silver, wire-rimmed glasses, and his eyebrows, which were the same gray color as his moustache, were as expressive as the multiple furrows of his forehead whenever he smiled, which was often, or placed an index finger to his lips to signal quiet.

"Shush," he would whisper, as I entered Josef's dressing room during a concert intermission, "the maestro's changing his shirt."

Mr. Bishop smoked Camels, and a tiny piece of tobacco or cigarette paper was often visible on his moist, upper lip. That was his "money" lip, the one that had enabled him to have a long trumpet career, and that must have impressed the man whom an entire country used to refer to as the March King. He didn't play often by the time I was studying with him—only during an occasional Wagner prelude or one of the Mahler symphonies or during the last movement of the Sibelius Second Symphony.

I remember exactly where I was sitting the day I heard that piece for the first time. I had moved from our customary place deep in the center rear of the hall to a spot midway toward the front, on the right side, in an empty seat next to that of a friend from school whom I had arranged to meet. Looking straight ahead, I was in line with the trumpets, who sat in the rear of the orchestra, stage left. On a recent trip to New York City, I had bought an LP recording by Eugene Ormandy and the Philadelphia Orchestra of Respighi's *Pines of Rome*, which my father thought might "broaden my outlook." But it was during that Sunday afternoon concert concluding with Sibelius's Second Symphony that I first heard something that stayed with me long afterward. Josef was conducting, and I went backstage to see him during intermission. Mr. Bishop never questioned my visits to the conductor's dressing room, visits which began when I was too young to remember, and continued until I was old enough not only to remember but also to have known, had he ever given me such a sign, that I was becoming a pest. The indication never came, though I must have tried his patience. I have his autographs now, dozens of them, and a baton he gave me, with a cork handle, which had broken in half during a concert.

When Josef had first arrived from Vienna in 1954 to be the music director of the Buffalo Philharmonic, my father and he struck up a friendship, both personal and musical, which eventually led to annual Good Friday performances of Haydn's *Seven Last Words* at my father's church. I spoke to Josef after one of those services, too, as though it were another concert; what a forbidding look he'd given me when he sensed I hadn't been properly moved by the religious aspect of the occasion.

It was the closeness of my father's relationship with Josef that led to the christening one cold Thanksgiving morning of my brother, my sister, and me with Josef and his second wife, Mitzi, as our godparents. Thereafter, every Thanksgiving, we each received a check, deposited into our savings account. My first such check came with a handwritten note:

Love your parents.
Love music.
Love your country.

Josef looked upon almost any twentieth century composer as being modern, and his tastes were decidedly traditional, with a particular love for Mozart and Beethoven. Mozart was a god, the closest friend a musician could have, a guide to all that was beautiful in life. One of Josef's last recording projects was the late Mozart symphonies with the Concertgebouw Orchestra.

After Josef recorded the five Beethoven piano concertos with Artur Rubinstein as soloist, my father arranged for Josef and Rubenstein to listen to tapes of those recording sessions in the parish hall of our church while Rubenstein was in Buffalo for an appearance with the Philharmonic. The two men sat for an entire Saturday afternoon, listening to their recorded performances, nodding to one another over especially fine moments while smoking enormous cigars.

Occasionally, I would tag along with my father to a rehearsal. I loved being with him behind the scenes, parading through the hall after the lights had dimmed and everyone in the audience had taken their seats. When I became old enough to do this myself, it felt natural to me at intermission to go backstage and knock on the door of Josef's dressing room. Mr. Bishop would peer out over his glasses and a Camel and let me in.

"Ah, my Carl," was Josef's greeting as he studied the score for the next piece he was conducting while fastening the cuff links of another shirt. Repeatedly asking him for an autograph was an absurd request, but I thought it was a sophisticated thing to do. He always granted my wish, sometimes signing that afternoon's program, occasionally giving me a copy of a new recording, the jacket inscribed with my name and a greeting of affection.

I last saw Josef in 1969, when he conducted the Boston Symphony Orchestra at Tanglewood. As a young man, my father had been a member in 1940 of Tanglewood's first summer conducting class, whose most illustrious graduate was Leonard Bernstein. We came regularly for concerts when I was a boy, sometimes renting a cottage in the Berkshires, and we were always present when Josef appeared as a guest conductor. When Josef's Tanglewood appearance was announced, I was living in Providence, Rhode Island, just a few hours away, and had only recently been married.

For what turned out to be his final Tanglewood performance Josef had chosen to close with Schubert's "Great" Symphony. As his guests, my wife and I were seated in a box with his third wife Harrietta. Now, almost half my lifetime later, I remember few details of the performance, but I distinctly recall that upon its conclusion I walked backstage with my wife to greet my godfather, just as I had during those countless Sunday afternoons as a boy.

I had not seen him since he left Buffalo. He looked older, even a little frail, but my sense of being with him was otherwise unchanged. He embraced me and made a big fuss about meeting my wife. In response to questions, I spoke briefly about my early writing efforts and mentioned that we had seen his Buffalo predecessor, William Steinberg, conduct the BSO in Providence.

I knew better than to stay long in Josef's dressing room that summer Sunday afternoon. There was nothing I could say about the Schubert performance that Josef did not already know. I asked about Mitzi, who had died a few years earlier. She remained in my memory a mysterious presence, a petite blond woman who always produced chocolates for me during visits to their Buffalo hotel suite. Then she would disappear, leaving only my father and me and Josef, and I would watch in awe while he drew off almost an entire filtered cigarette with one enormous inhale and drank a whole glass of beer in one huge swallow.

During one of the earliest meetings between Josef and my father that I can remember, the soloist for that week's concerts was also present. Something had not gone right in that morning's re-hearsal, and so the soloist had been summoned to meet with the maestro. I believe the piece was the first piano concerto of Brahms, and if I can trust my repeated response hearing it years later, it was a passage near the end of the second movement when a ground bass adds tremendous tension to a sequence of descending chords the pianist plays. What I recall with great certainty is the image of my godfather sitting next to the soloist at the piano in the living room of his suite. Soon the two men, side by side at the piano in the living room of Josef's suite, were lost deeply in the score, which lay before them above the keyboard because it was too large to rest, upright, on the piano's built-in music stand. Rapidly turning the pages, Josef would suddenly stop at a place he had apparently marked and ask the soloist to play his part.

"Yes!" Josef would interrupt in a voice that was by turns impa-tient or passionate. And then, as if words could not fully explain what he was after, Josef would sing the phrase in question, all the while gracefully moving his arms, as if he were on the podium conducting. Music, I was never to forget, was a human activity of the gravest conceivable import; truly, from Josef, it came across as a matter of life and death.

As a child, I knew very little about Josef's own earlier life. My father, who to the day he died carried in his wallet a black and white photograph of a prisoner in a German concentration camp his bat-talion had liberated, told me that because one of his parents was Jewish Josef had spent the war working in a pickle factory. Though this fact may have made little impression on me then, as I now re-member the scene with the soloist in the hotel suite I am stunned to imagine the link in Josef's own life between the tragic event of the war and the inspired occasion of a musical performance.

What must have been going through his mind that afternoon in his hotel suite as he led the humbled soloist through what I am sure must have been a trying experience for them both? What did Josef *hear*? From what events and encounters and experience did his sense of the sound he was looking for originate? What was it that he *felt*, that he understood the composer felt and somehow, through the performance, would, if things worked out as they should, be felt by the people in the audience at the next performance? The concerto came into its final form, I learned much later, after the death of Robert Schumann, and Brahms may have composed the second movement out of both his grief over that loss and his love for Schumann's widow, Clara, a pianist. What encapsulation of the world as, in this case, Brahms had lived it, could yet be found again in the music these two men were making there in that dimly lit room in a brick building at the corner of Delaware and North in the city of Buffalo, New York, what sleight of musical hand, what transforming miracle of art, what willed, brave, human achievement?

Our house in Buffalo was set back from the street by a squared section of lawn, bounded on the sides by our neighbor's driveway and our own. Where his driveway bordered our lawn, our neighbor had built a concrete curb, and the man who mowed his lawn mowed also a strip about a yard wide of ours. Our neighbor insisted that the property line was "there, not here"—I can hear him emphasizing "there," unsmiling, as though he might have me arrested for trespassing if I ever forgot, but when I asked my father about it he just shrugged his shoulders. I seemed the only one in our family concerned over the incongruity of our space of crabgrass and dandelions, poorly cut by a heavy, hand-pushed mower, contiguous with the power cut, weedless object of our neighbor's pettiness.

Our reclusive neighbor, a retired businessman whose first name was Frank, lived with his sister. Neither had ever married, and their trips out consisted exclusively of short drives together in their black Cadillac; I never saw either of them so much as walk to the corner drugstore, four houses down the street. Their backyard, separated from ours by a high chain-link fence, was filled with flower beds and rose trellises, which they could see from their dining room window. My brother and I, who had turned our own small yard into a wiffleball diamond, were often in Frank's yard, retrieving a foul ball, that, because of the risk the retriever ran of angering Frank (he would rap his knuckles on the window and scowl if he caught us) counted as an automatic side out. Sometimes we played pepper with a real baseball, but that practice ended when a ball broke a window in Frank's garage and Frank called our mother on the phone and accused us of having no respect for other people's property.

The window of our second-floor, back bathroom faced the roof of Frank's garage, and one day I made the discovery that, by standing on the tile-capped side of the garage roof (reachable from the top of the chain-link fence), I could touch the window sill. Supporting my weight with one hand on the side of the house, as I leaned across the space between the house and the garage, I managed with my other hand to prop open the window, grab inside, and then pull myself into the bathroom. Beyond the daring of it, this was a momentous event: my brother and I could get into the house without a key. As we grew older, this became a favorite, if somewhat inconvenient entrance, particularly at night, since coming in through the front door meant encountering a dozing parent waiting in the living room or waking one of them inadvertently while walking on floors that creaked especially loudly at late hours.

Several black and white photographs taken by my father in 1949, when he had traveled alone to Buffalo on a house-hunting trip before we left New Jersey, were tucked into an envelope I found after his death. Missing are any shots of the backyard or the window above our future neighbor's garage, but there are two well-preserved prints of the front exterior of our house from different angles, and in one of these, taken from the street, the lawn is dappled, with sunlight coming through the leaves of one of the many elms that used to grow along all the avenues of the city. Not yet is there a curb where the lawn ends, but, instead, the ground slopes gently to Frank's driveway, and the curve of the slope contrasts with the sharp angle of the house's steep roof. The sunlight on the roof is so bright that the entire top of the photograph seems almost to glow, as though in anticipation of the aura of happiness that would surround that house for many years when we first lived there.

"Here you see the driveway," my father had written in black ink on the back of another of the photographs. "Note upper porch is smaller than below, since bathroom takes up part of space. There is the bay window." That is all. There are no people in the photograph, and nothing is said about the interior; perhaps he described that in a letter to my mother that was sent with the photographs. Though this is a point on which the first-time reader might disagree, I detect in the tone of my father's shorthand description more than a hint of the pride I believe acquiring the house gave him. There is also, even in these few words, a style that I recognize immediately as his—direct, personal, and without affectation. We would all, later, learn to distinguish between the positive expression of that personality and the manic joy that was often a mask for the sadness from which he suffered during the last decade of his life; but here, in this glimpse of what I now see as the end of his early adulthood (he had just turned 31), the contentment created by the prospect of a new job in a large, prosperous church, a home on a residential street far from the crowded Manhattan of his childhood, and a growing family—my mother was already pregnant with my brother—that happiness is evoked for me in those five final words: *There is the bay window.*

I did not go back to the house for many years after the hospital across the street bought it, but I understood it had been painted, the backyard paved over into a parking lot, and the rooms turned into neurologists' offices. The thought of an outpatient being examined in our former dining room was so far removed from my recollection of dinners there that my memory remained undisturbed, and I was able at will to return to our house, to climb quietly the fence by Frank's garage, cross the garage roof, and enter through the bathroom window to look around, pausing at each bedroom to gaze in their sleep at those whose daily lives I once shared...

...The back hallway lamp never works, but I can see my way from the lights through the window coming from the outside lamp over Frank's garage door. I leave my shoes in my bedroom, which is next to the back bathroom, and look down the hallway. It is dark, and the only

sound is of my own breathing and, from the opposite end of the hall-
way, my father's snoring. Never, as a child, did I hear my father describe
a dream, and I have difficulty imagining his midnight meditations.
There is, of course, the nagging problem of the water pressure; the pipes
are too small or too corroded, and whenever someone is using the water
in the kitchen a person who has just lathered his hair with shampoo in
an upstairs shower suddenly has no hot water to rinse. And the weather
forecast is for snow. Half the congregation will probably go skiing and
the other half will be unable to get out of their driveways. There may
not be enough tenors to do the offertory anthem...

... Standing in my parents' bedroom, at the foot of their bed,
my thoughts, too, turned to Sunday morning. My father always
left for church very early. In the spring and fall, when the weather
was good, he usually walked, and I often walked with him. Our
route took us along a street where many of the pillars of the church
lived. All the pillars were old and owned large houses. Rarely did
we make that walk without my being told that the woman whose
new Cadillac was being washed in the driveway by her chauffeur
had just learned that she had cancer, or that so-and-so's daughter
or son was flunking out of college or the parents were divorcing.

Some mornings the grass on the large lawns would be wet
with dew, and the air cool because Buffalo was located by Lake
Erie. There might be a heavy mist, too. All the homes on the street
had tall windows and solid-looking doors...

...I would be wearing my fire-engine-red sports jacket, charcoal
woolen pants, white tab shirt, and crimson tie, and my hair would be
slicked back with some of my father's Vaseline hair tonic. There are
puddles along the curb with rotten, water-logged leaves that the high-
way department missed in the fall, and the odor of the leaves mixes
with the fragrance of tulips and juniper on the lawn of the bishop's resi-
dence, which we have just passed.

We enter the church through the back door, where the kitchen for
church suppers is located, pausing for a drink of bottled spring water
dispensed in small paper cups. Then we walk across the carpeted floors
of the parish house, which is attached to the sanctuary, and we stop in
the church office, where my father shouts, "Good morning, boss," up the

stairs to the minister's second-floor study. Sometimes we climb those stairs to the large, book-lined room, the air smoky from the minister's Chesterfields, and he and my father discuss a hymn or a quotation the minister is planning to use in his sermon. Then we retrace our way, picking up several copies of the church bulletin, which my father encloses whenever he writes letters to friends, and we turn at the corner of a hallway and take a few more steps before opening the door to the darkened sanctuary, with sunlight filtered through the huge, stained glass windows that rise almost to the ceiling in a series on either side of the pews. The first thing my father says is, "Baa!," to test the acoustics, as though they might somehow have changed since the day before, which he spent practicing.

Soon, my father is sitting at the organ bench, playing one of the hymns that will be sung during the service. He has already set the register for this and the other music for the morning, and he runs through each verse of each hymn, since the registration varies by verse. At the end of the hymns he plays an amen. He has taken off his suit coat and is practicing in his shirt-sleeves. When he comes to the prelude and the postlude, he asks me to turn the pages for him. He has written notes in the margins of the music and over staves, and sometimes I am reading a marking for a fingering when he nods his head, indicating that I've missed my page turn.

Between pieces, he opens a box of licorice drops and offers me one. Then he begins to play again, the walls of the sanctuary shaking at a crescendo, and this time he whispers, "Now," or "Okay," when I am supposed to turn. Later, after the choir has come, I sit downstairs, below the choir loft, where a deacon is checking the bulletins on the table next to the center door.

At Christmas the church is always decorated with balsam trees that are brought in a large truck on the Saturday before the Sunday nearest Christmas. The church chancel is filled with the balsam trees and the entire sanctuary smells of the sap and the needles. Red ribbons grace the green trees and it is necessary, as at Easter, to hold two services on Christmas Sunday. The first is a shorter version of the second, which is still attended by so many that extra chairs have to be set up behind the last pews and the two doors on either side of the chancel opened so that people sitting in the chapel can hear the service.

When the service begins, I will sit again with my father on the organ bench, where I will see all the heads bow during the prayers. My father's head will not go down; he will be waiting for his cue for the choral amen, his arms raised, eyebrows arched, poised for what seems an eternity. I can hear people in the congregation coughing, I hear the minister say, "In the name of the Father, the Son, and the Holy Ghost," and next to me my father's robes rustle as at last he gives the choir its signal.

Later, I am kneeling at my bedroom window, which I have opened about six inches and through which I can feel the cold air on my face...

...There is snow, too, in the only photograph I have of the house today. Snow covers the front lawn and the roof of the porch, and there are tufts of snow in the shrubbery, now kept neatly trimmed. Whenever I tell people I grew up in Buffalo, they ask about the snow, but they are thinking of quantity and frequency, so I answer only in reference to the sledding in Delaware Park or skating on homemade, backyard rinks (we'd lug the hose out from the basement and water our rink each night).

I say nothing about the penetration of the cold when you walked outside late at night, and the welcome warmth of coming back into the house, the lamp on my father's desk left on, the smell in the room of the cigar stub in the ashtray. I say nothing about the winter Sundays when my father cannot find his car keys and we decide again to walk to church despite the temperature, and how deserted the streets are and how quiet, when we enter the church, the old building is.

Nor do I speak about the distant, warm land where my father lived the last years of his life, almost, I think, as if he sensed that by removing himself from our lives—removing his physical presence, that is—he might give us back some of the space his illness had occupied, a space so dense and deep it had by then obliterated first his work, then his home, and finally his family.

What man was this who taught a boy that the robin we've passed—there, on the lawn, waiting, looking around—sticks its short, sharp beak into the moist ground and plucks out gold? It is a spring morning, and I have to hurry to keep pace with my father. I am seven years old.

"I am the robin," my father says, "And you are my gold."

Years later, driving back from Boston, where my father had flown from North Carolina for a surgery on a hip he'd injured badly in an automobile accident when he still lived with my mother, we stopped for food at a Friendly's in a shopping plaza just off the highway. Soon after losing his Buffalo church position, he had received an offer from the American Church in Paris, but my mother did not want to go, correctly insisting that they could not afford to live there. An old friend found him a teaching job back in the Berkshires, where he also began playing the organ at the same church in Great Barrington he'd served as choirmaster before the Second World War. Except for brief visits he had not spent time there since the summer when an old girlfriend of his gave us the house where she and her dentist husband lived. We had stayed all that summer, swimming in the Green River and picnicking on Mount Everett, my father with a baseball cap on his head and a corncob pipe in his mouth, grilling steaks in a stone fireplace by a pond off the dirt road that led to the peak. He was terribly unhappy after his return, and when another friend persuaded him to consider moving to Tryon, North Carolina, he had leapt at the prospect.

I pulled the car up to the restaurant and opened the door for him. Handing him his crutch, I held his free arm as he got out, slowly stood, and then gingerly made his way into the lighted building, where we found a booth near the soda fountain. I helped him off with his coat, then returned outside to park. He hadn't opened his menu when I came back in, and I was frightened by his look, which combined deep hurt with anger at the loss of a world he had loved. His first words were a fleeting reassurance.

"What'll it be, old boy?" he said.

We both ordered sundaes.

"Got a light?" I asked, reaching for the cigarettes I'd bought in anxious anticipation of this visit.

"Always have matches," he said. "That was one thing about being in the hospital. I had almost no desire to smoke."

Our waitress brought us glasses of water.

"Sure you don't want a hamburger or something?" my father asked.

I shook my head. His hair was turning gray. His hand shook slightly as he took a drink of his water, and when he put his glass back on the paper mat he spilled a little. In great detail, he described how a piece of plastic was attached to his femur, which had been inserted into a plastic hip socket.

"You wouldn't believe how much it hurt before," he said. The pain was gone now. Eventually, if his recuperation went well, he'd be walking without a limp.

"My doctor says I'll play the organ again," he said. "Even be able to use the pedal. We'll see."

I asked the waitress for some coffee.

"Decaf," my father said, adding to me in a whisper, "Caffeine's no good. Can't sleep."

"How are you, Pop?" I asked, as I reached with my hand for his.

"Sometimes I think I can't stand it anymore," he sighed. "They tell me to take it one day at a time, but that's easy for someone else to say. I don't know what I'm going to do, but I'll manage."

"Of course you will," I said, withdrawing my hand. "You're going to be fine. You'll probably outlive us all, Pop." He was staring toward the large, plate-glass window by the restaurant door.

"I think it's starting to snow," he said. "The driving could be bad."

I excused myself to call my wife. Looking at my father's back, I saw him reach into his pocket and pull out his pipe. He used the end of a spoon to clean the bowl, then tapped it upside down against the ashtray. Again reaching into his pocket, he brought out his tobacco and began to fill the bowl. He needed two matches to get it lit. The smoke from his pipe drifted toward the ceiling.

He was wearing his navy blue sports jacket, which my mother had bought him one Christmas during a family campaign to spruce up his wardrobe. Unlike his impeccably dressed brother, my father had often favored checkered jackets with striped shirts and ties with wild prints. He'd gone along with our attempts to change the way he looked, but the result was somehow the same; he'd sneak in a bright yellow tie or green pants. For a while, his one other concession to vanity in his appearance was his hair, which he let grow longer, before it was the fashion for a man his age. Then he added a goatee. His hair was still on the long side, but his face was clean shaven now; none of his clothes fit well because he'd lost weight in the hospital.

It was snowing hard when my father and I left the restaurant, and the driving was slow. The weather became the focus of our conversation.

"Are you happy?" I asked my father finally. Using his hands, which he placed under his thighs, he shifted his position in the seat.

"I'm happy to be with you."

"That's not what I meant."

"What do you mean?"

He had been alone, late at night, when he'd driven off the road into a telephone pole that had broken in two. After visiting my father at the hospital the next day, I had gone to the auto wrecker's yard to claim my father's belongings, which were still in the car. The windshield was shattered and the steering wheel had been pushed into the crevice of the car seat. Broken glass covered the seat and the floor, and dried blood was splattered on the steering wheel. The glove compartment was open, but nothing had been taken from it. I sorted through gasoline credit cards, the registration, an envelope with the insurance policy in it, some church bulletins, an empty brown bag, a small metal container of aspirin, and a few maps. Under the seat I found a pipe, and on the floor behind the front seat there was a small bag of groceries and my father's briefcase.

"You were lucky not to have been killed," I said to him as we neared our Conway farmhouse.

"Maybe," he replied. "I'd rather not talk about it."

The snow had stopped and stars were shining as we entered the driveway, and I saw my son's face staring out through a kitchen window. He was waving.

"There's your grandson," I said.

"I see him," my father replied. "I've been looking forward to this so much."

I brought the car as close as I could to the back door.

"Well, it's been a long trip," I said, turning to my father. "I hope you're not too tired."

"I'm glad we had this chance to be together," he said. "You were kind to come and get me."

Though he lived another year and a half, I saw my father only once more, in New York. He had composed an anthem for a choir my brother directed, and my father conducted the premiere. Afterwards, we had brunch in my brother's apartment where I gave my father a box of cigars as an early birthday gift. We wrote each other often; he was so upset with one of my letters that he sent it back to me, with marginal numbers added to correspond to his responses, which filled a separate page. After I received his answer, I wrote him another, longer letter, but I was talking to myself. On the phone, he spoke of moving again, when his hip healed—or when my mother joined him, as if the decision she had made not to follow him to North Carolina were somehow going to be changed.

"I'll take a job somewhere, selling tickets at a train station," he said.

"What about your music?" I asked.

"That's over," he replied.

The final time we spoke, his voice on the telephone was faint, almost a child's voice in pitch, insistent and plaintive in tone. It was an evening in early August, and we had just finished supper. After years of emergencies during which I had dropped whatever I was doing, I was nervous when I heard the phone ring. Though it was a relief to know it was him, not someone else calling to say he was in the hospital again, I had difficulty assuming my natural speaking voice when I heard his.

"I need to visit," he said.

"When, Pop?" I replied, scribbling a note to my wife who was standing next to me. "When did you want to come?" My wife jotted down the dates of open weekends.

"What's good for you guys?"

"Labor Day weekend. I have a day off and could probably take another."

"That's too far away. I want to come sooner."

I tried to keep my voice calm. Though I knew something was wrong, I did not tell him to come the next day.

"How about two weeks from now?" I asked.

A few days later I was at my desk at the college where I worked, when someone identifying himself as a coroner called and, after the briefest of introductions, told me my father had died of a heart attack. My hand shook as I held the receiver, but I was able to reach for a pencil and piece of paper and write down a phone number and the coroner's name. Then, in a gesture I could only have learned from my father, I thanked the coroner for calling. It was a brilliant afternoon, the sky the color of my father's blue eyes and only a whisper of wind in the air.

My brother and I flew south to arrange his cremation and collect his belongings. He had lived in North Carolina about three years, and, though in addition to his visits he had sent us photographs and letters, I had never seen his last church in Tryon or any of the apartments where he had stayed. What we found when we opened the door to his place forced upon me a painful image of how his life had ended.

The day was hot, and the sounds of the sleepy town outside were barely audible inside those walls. A window by the kitchen table was open, and through the screen came the occasional thump of a car going over a bad spot in the nearby street and the persistent shrilling of cicadas in the yard. An unmade bed stood by an open, curtained window, and boxes of my father's belongings rested in each of the corners of the room, along one wall, and on either side of a desk weighted with papers and photographs and a piano piled with music. The bathroom sink had been knocked to the floor in a fall, and I tried to right it. We cleaned the toilet and the kitchen sink and counters and closed the cupboard doors, leaving condiments and other cooking materials for the next tenant. The food in the refrigerator we threw away. Most of his clothes, which had been stored in a damp basement before he had moved into this apartment, were mildewed, and we discarded them. We left the rest in a closet for the landlord, who said he would find someone who could use them.

In the drawers of his desk were old newspaper clippings, many of them reviews of concerts he had given years ago; letters, recent and old, were mixed with bills and bank statements and prescriptions. A letter to a friend, written in a scrawl and dated the day of his death, lay on the felt top of the desk, and near it I found an envelope, unsealed, in which was a letter to me, written several months before and never mailed.

Hesitantly, I opened it and started reading. Despite all the difficulties that defined the final years of my father's life, I was unprepared for this last message he left me.

To paraphrase, it began, *"please let aching dogs lie." At this point, I don't need any preaching. It is a major accomplishment if I can 'crutch' it from one end of the room to the other. I now have my 3d cast—& will have one for at least another 6 weeks. I am in constant pain— have had ulcerations under the cast—& every time I move, it is sandpaper on raw flesh. I spend practically the whole day with the leg elevated—otherwise it swells up (the foot) like a football. I am not seeking sympathy. I could be much worse off. But as the time goes on—it is not better—but worse. There is not an awful lot one can do, lying in bed with your foot elevated. The first thing I think I'll give up is writing—it is hard in bed—and I get little reward.*

This may sound like a negative note—& in a way, it is. Why try to disguise? I am jobless (thank God on that one), have no future—at the age where no opportunities are readily available—don't really care.

Heaven only knows when I'll see you guys again. But I plead with you, at the present time, hold off for a little while. I'm in need of the slightest ounce of encouragement to keep going to get thru a day. I'm grateful to have Winky as a companion—while my landlady is in Florida. She is comforting & affectionate (even tho it is a big effort to attend to her needs).

I spend the better time of the days thinking about all of you. Just the thinking is about all I have left. All I'm really trying to get across is that I'm terribly lonely.

A friend gave me a black and white television (and I've learned to live with 1 plate, 1 knife & fork—possessions no longer mean anything to me—even a car—which, at the present time I'm forbidden to drive by my doctor—but which I probably can't afford—so if, & when I can walk again—I think I'll do without a car) (could probably do with a 2nd hand—but that is always risky). I think I'll just resign myself to sitting in my landlady's lovely garden—and keep the waiting game— hoping my turn comes up fast. I've had a rich life—in many ways—the greatest gift is you 'kids.'

I had no idea I could rant on like this. But you may as well know how I feel. I am pretty much alone—not that that is bad—one's own company is not the worst.

You can send this letter on to your brother—for I'm not up to writing two.

I have bared my soul. I hope I haven't depressed you. I am just being honest. I am so lonely it hurts—coupled with that, I also hurt physically.

You have always been a sympathetic person—and therefore I feel I can write you from the heart.

Love, Pop.

I put the letter back in its envelope and wept.

We scattered his ashes near a mountaintop in his beloved Berkshires a few miles from Tanglewood. It was a place where my father and mother used to go blueberry picking when they were younger and where, as a family, we used to picnic. My father had always loved views, and there was a magnificent one from that spot. His favorite flower, mountain laurel, framed the trail leading to the place where we gathered. Before I opened the plastic bag of white ashes I had carried in a plastic container from North Caro-

lina, we each said a few words and my mother read Psalm 139.
Then we held hands and sang a hymn, the music to which an old
friend had xeroxed, someone who had once been a member of the
junior choir my father had directed when he first came to the
Berkshires before the Second World War.

I was surprised that the ashes weighed as much as they did,
surprised too, at the faintly sweet scent they gave off. The day before, in my kitchen at home, I had practiced opening the bag, to be
certain I would know how to do it on the mountain. And how
could I be sure, I wondered, that these were my father's ashes?
Then I had noticed, near the top of the bag, a piece of metal that
had not been melted during the cremation. I picked this fragment
from the ashes and held in my hand a screw which I slowly realized was a surviving symbol of the hip operation my father had
undergone two years before.

4

"Hola papá, ¿cómo estás? Right now you are going to the bathroom on the plane. I'm thinking and wondering if you were working on your book a minute ago or if you were just staring at the
screen. If you were writing, what could you write about, we haven't
even arrived yet. I wonder what it will be like, probably fun, how
could it not be.

"I'm reading *In Cuba I was a German Shepherd*. It's really good,
I recommend it to you. It's a little like *Drown*, that other book I
liked so much. I was wondering about the author...I think if you're
a really good writer, the reader knows you before you meet. That's
why I liked *Drown*. I felt like I spent years with the main character.

"Blah blah blah, I'm just writing this so you have something to
read in five minutes when I take a nap or chew some more gun.
Gotta go, I'm gonna write some Spanish stuff for you to practice. I
have to remember to practice Spanish on the trip. By the way, I am
dying to have Mexican food, just thought I'd let you know. Well
that's all for now folks. Until next plane ride, Maren."

We are flying west to join Wynton and his band for a week, starting in San Diego. The date is June 18, a Friday, and Maren has just finished ninth grade—the day before, night before really, because she was up until about 3:30 writing the last of the papers that, cumulatively, helped her make up for some school time she had missed. Surprisingly, she does not seem tired, though I had to wake her twice for the early morning, one-hour drive to the Connecticut airport, where we caught a short flight to our connection in Newark.

Having come out by tour bus on a two-and-one-half day, non-stop drive from New York, the band (this is Wynton's quartet, with the addition of a fifth player, saxophonist Walter Blanding Jr.) has been in California since last Sunday—in Santa Barbara yesterday, Santa Cruz the day before. Wynton has invited Maren to come along on this trip. We were talking in Boston, where the new group was playing in Symphony Hall just four months after the *All Rise* performances, when he mentioned the idea, which Boss Murphy enthusiastically seconded.

"Let her be around some men who are doing something in their lives," Raymond had said.

Raymond, a/k/a Boss Murphy, joined Wynton's entourage almost by accident in 2000 when he got a call at his home in Washington, D.C., from his high school classmate, Wynton's longtime technical assistant and sometime roadie, Dennis Jeter (whose musical career as a trumpet player received a huge boost when he was a teenager and Wynton offered to pay his tuition at a summer music camp). A mortician by profession, as well as an active member of the Navy reserves, Raymond also has a license to operate a bus. When Wynton needed someone on short notice to drive him in the Winnebago he prefers to planes for long trips, Dennis suggested Raymond. Rock solid, a man you trust immediately based on his steady demeanor and unwavering certainty answering questions about the people and situations you encounter on the road, Boss Murphy is always on time, never complains, has a great sense of humor, and intuitively understands his place in the band.

Though he knew little about jazz when he first came out on the road, he is now an expert. And Raymond *cares*; every so often, he'll send me an email or leave me a message on my mobile phone, asking how my family is doing.

When I saw him and Wynton in Boston, just a week had passed since we'd been together briefly at a runout in Tarrytown, north of New York City. It was an early spring night, with a chill in the air, and you could feel the presence of the Hudson River a few blocks down the historic town's Main Street from the old theater with the lights in the marquee shining brightly and the steam in the heating pipes backstage making funny noises while the band members munched on some homemade barbecue before the first set. Wynton visited with an old friend from Juilliard and then a group of school kids came in, wanting their picture taken with him, and after Wynton had obliged he let another kid hold his trumpet and told him to practice. Soon Raymond poked his head into the tiny dressing room to say, "house is ready," and Wynton asked for his horn back and very slowly walked toward the curtained stage where he lit up the full house with a fiery tune, "Free to Be," from a new CD, combining a syncopated, partly staccato, blues-based melody inflected with lots of half valve smudges and bolts of very high slurred intervals and all propelled by a swing that jumped off the stage, made you want to stand up and dance or run out into the street and shout. The name of the new CD was *Magic Hour* (of which, Wynton said when he announced the title tune on stage, there are actually two—for children, the hour before they are put to bed, and for adults, the hour afterwards).

Magic Hour is also the name of this tour that Maren and I have joined here in San Diego, where the weather is cloudy and cool as we step outside the door at the baggage claim, waiting for our luggage. From the airport, we call our hotel for a ride. A perky guy who says he's lived in the area all his life transports us in a van, talking about the city as he drives to a peninsula that juts out north of the harbor, which we can see as we look across the water. I remember that view from a trip here more than a decade before,

when the septet played a gig downtown, near the marina where
the sailboats for an America's Cup race were moored, on the same
evening that Wynton's father Ellis was performing with former
septet pianist Marcus Roberts, who is blind, at a convention for
optometrists.

Almost at the tip of the peninsula, we pull over to a low-slung
series of attached, wooden buildings that comprise our hotel,
Humphrey's Half Moon Inn & Suites, which from early spring
until late fall presents a series of concerts, most of them with pop
stars.

"Hey, man," a fellow in a nice shirt and blue blazer greets me,
offering his right hand, "you must be the manager."

Maren pokes me.

"Do you believe that?" Maren says, remembering my stories
about the frequency of such greetings. "Tell him you play second
trumpet," she continues, but I let it go. I'm tired, Maren is hungry,
and judging by the time (just after three o'clock) the band should
be getting ready for soundcheck soon.

Our third-floor room looks out on a courtyard that has been
set up with rows of chairs facing a stage where the musicians will
play; from our vantage point, to the left of the stage you can see
more water and the masts of several sailboats bobbing up and
down. Maren wants to unpack before we eat, so I walk back to
ground level and then along the edge of the courtyard toward the
stage, veering left where I see an opening in the courtyard wall and
the water beyond. With a much better view of what I now realize
is a marina, I am stunned by the sheer number and size of the
boats, not just sailboats but ocean-going yachts. Who owns all
these boats? Where do they live? And what does a person do to
earn the kind of money a toy like this can cost? I don't feel judg-
mental, just curious, but it's a form of curiosity that over the years I
have kept to myself, or the source of it, a questioning that goes
back as long as I can remember, defining who I am to myself, as
opposed to the personality I present to the world.

Do other people have these secret selves, I used to wonder, and if they did, if we all did, what prompted the secrecy? During those hikes I used to take to that hilltop in Vermont and the childhood walks to church with my father, there was always a voice within me, talking "to" me, asking question after question.

Who cleared this pasture? What happened to him?

What did the people on this street *do* behind the enormous doors of their enormous homes? Were they watching me and my father as we walked?

And what were the secret sources of my reticence to speak these questions? Was it something in my nature, some intrinsic part of whatever was just me?

The sun tries to burn off the fog as I watch the wind make little waves in the water of the marina and I decide if Maren and I are going to eat we'd better do so while we have the chance, before soundcheck. I return to our room where Maren has unpacked all her stuff and put it neatly in drawers, and we wander to the grille that also looks out on the marina and order drinks, a Coke for her and a Chardonnay for me. The waitress says if we wait a few more minutes the happy hour appetizers will be out and they are a meal in themselves. Maren asks if she can order a taco, but I wait for the appetizers, not really talking with her about anything in particular, and then two men in white coats appear pushing an enormous tray of shrimp and beef.

Turns out we could both have waited a little longer and eaten with the band, which will be served dinner in a room behind the stage after a very informal soundcheck that is already underway when we return to the courtyard performance space.

"Where's Wynton?" Maren asks Carlos Henriquez, the young bass player who like Walter Blanding and pianist Eric Lewis is also a member of the Lincoln Center Jazz Orchestra. Eric is missing, too; besides Carlos and Walter, only drummer Ali Jackson is here right now.

"They're coming back from LA," Carlos says, meaning Wynton and Eric. "They were playing today at Ray Charles's funeral."

And he explains that they left for Los Angeles (where we are traveling tomorrow) early this morning, to participate in what for Wynton was something he has been doing since he was a boy, marching in funeral parades in New Orleans—a ritual commemorated subsequently in his own music in the funeral marches he has composed for such works as *Six Syncopated Movements* and *All Rise.* These days, he often performs at such occasions alone, or with just his band, but this time he played with Stevie Wonder, B.B. King, Glen Campbell, and Willie Nelson in a long service held at a church with a very long name, the First African Methodist Episcopal Church.

Maren has met Walter before, in New York, when he brought his twin daughters along on a July Fourth celebration several years ago in which the band took a ferry from Manhattan to a spot across the Hudson River in New Jersey not far from Ellis Island. There, against a backdrop of the twin towers of the World Trade Center, the musicians performed in a striking silhouette that took on an entirely different feeling when I remembered it after 9/11. That cataclysmic event was publicly observed by Wynton at a gig two days afterwards at the Hollywood Bowl, when he played a stirring solo national anthem before the Lincoln Center Jazz Orchestra joined the Los Angeles Philharmonic in a resonant performance of *All Rise.* The musicians then went into a Los Angeles studio to record the work, and immediately afterwards Wynton and the band left on an all-night and all-next-day bus ride to Seattle to keep a performance date that had been scheduled months before.

Like Walter, although younger, Carlos has known Wynton since he was in high school. His LaGuardia School for the Performing Arts winning participation in Jazz at Lincoln Center's annual Essentially Ellington high school band competition led him to his position today, after bassist Rodney Whitaker decided to accept a fulltime teaching position at Wayne State University in De-troit, partly in order to be at home with his large family. The shift in personnel, typical of many changes in Wynton's bands, made Rodney another member of the fraternity of former Marsalis sidemen, some of whom such as pianist Marcus Roberts and trombonist Wycliffe Gordon have gone on to solo careers and almost all of whom stay in touch with Wynton, sometimes returning on special occasions to perform again with him.

"I *live* in Detroit," Rodney said to me before leaving the band. We were enjoying cognac in the bar of a hotel in downtown Buffalo, where the Lincoln Center Jazz Orchestra had just performed on a chilly April night in the same hall where the orchestra played back when my father was its manager for a short time. Wynton had accepted my offer to drive him from the hotel to the gig in my rental car, "if I knew the way," and we'd gone right up Niagara Street, passing Johnny's Rendezvous, a speakeasy-like place where the owner used to let you in after you knocked (this was in high school) and make drinks that were so large and so strong that one lasted much of an evening. In the car I talked a little about my godfather, but Wynton seemed not to be listening, and I said nothing further to him about Buffalo while he was warming up in the same conductor's room where I used to visit Josef so many years before during those concert intermissions. The last time I'd been in this spot, I realized, was as a college student when I'd flown home for my dad's appearance as soloist with the orchestra in the Poulenc concerto, and I tried in my memory to hear the gorgeous quiet melody that comes right before that piece's climactic chords, but I could not summon that sorrowful music just then.

"I'm listening to the radio the other day," Rodney continued in Buffalo after the gig, "and this cat comes on and says whatever about business this and development that in Detroit, and then he says the city will turn around and then, '*people* will live there again.' So what does that make me and family?"

Rodney shook his head, took another sip of his drink, laughed loudly, then sighed, repeating the word again, "people!" and I told him about the time I interviewed Freddie Scott, a former wideout with the Detroit Lions, only time I was ever in Detroit other than changing planes at the airport, and did he remember Bob Lanier, I asked Rodney, played for the Pistons, All Star, biggest shoes in the NBA, size 22 I think, used to be on display in the lobby of the Basketball Hall of Fame, and Bob went to my high school I added, and check this out Rodney, *"check this out,"* yo *Swigeland!* I can hear Ronnie Carbo saying to me in my head, Bob Lanier didn't make our high school team the first year he tried out.

Damn.

I don't know how many children Rodney has, I mean the exact number, not because he wouldn't tell me—he loves to talk about his kids, one tour I remember he brought one of them along for a week, like Maren is here now—but it never came up. We never engaged in one of those "interviews" like I had with Freddie Scott in which I asked what books did you read in school and who was your biggest influence and how old were you when you learned to read music and then wrote something like: *It was a fall day in Detroit and wide receiver Freddie Scott felt his sore ribs and wondered if he'd be starting against the Jets this Sunday.*

Rodney and I did actually talk about books a lot, because he was always reading something on the bus and I'd be curious, what was it that he liked so much about *Tuesdays With Morrie* I might ask, and we'd be off, like when David Robinson would be on his Thomas Mann kick, or Malraux, David who collected first editions of the books he loved but read them in soft cover so the first editions would remain in excellent shape, kept them with his huge recording collection at his house in Texas, his crib but I didn't use that word; it was what had caught Wynton's attention when they first met in the late '80s, David an accountant then, coming to gigs when Wynton was in town, inviting Wynton one night after a gig to his *crib*, and Wynton thinking after he saw the collection, he told me later, "if this man who is an accountant can love these books and this music and know what he knows, he can learn how to run the sound and lights at a gig," and that is how David joined the band (and now sound technicians at some of the greatest halls in the world where the band has played ask *him* for advice). But I bet that first night when they talked Wynton never asked Rob where he went to high school, or how old his car was, or did he enjoy beer (he does). And I am sure Rob since has never said the same to Wynton, though they might *talk* about anything—women, old age, Yeats, shoes, hats, Picasso, baseball (but not Rob's favorite player, Barry Bonds, about whom no one, not even Wynton, has ever won a debate on any point with Rob).

At the San Diego gig an even older woman dressed in a sweater and long skirt with a floral print takes a seat near the stage just before the musicians themselves come out to enthusiastic applause, and throughout the first set this woman moves her entire body to the music, her face when I catch it from the side anticipating chord changes as she raises an eyebrow, breaks into a smile, then closes her eyes. It's chilly here, with the temperature hovering around sixty and a sea breeze blowing in from the marina. I switch locations between tunes, looking up toward the balcony where Maren has said she wants to listen from our room. Mostly, I think, she's sleepy, but she also seems intent on defining a space between the two of us, I suppose so she isn't suffocated by my enthusiasms or advice.

Where's she gone? It's between sets and I've walked up to our room to check in on her, see if she's awake, ask her if she wants to come backstage to say hi to Wynton, who got back from Los Angeles with barely enough time to change his clothes before the start of the gig. But she's not in our room. I walk over to the window and look out but certainly can't spot her in the midst of all these people sipping wine and talking below me. On the way back down, near where the stairs intersect with the entrance for concert-goers who aren't also staying at the hotel, I run into Dennis Jeter, who's along on this tour to sell some simple choices of merchandise, mostly tee shirts, and copies of the *Magic Hour* CD. Doing this represents something of a coup for Dennis because Wynton has had a longstanding policy of not promoting himself commercially at gigs; in all the years I've heard him play, not once has he ever so much as said, "And now we'd like to perform a tune from our new recording…"

Dennis—or Petey Jetey as Wynton sometimes addresses him to his great annoyance—says he thought he saw Maren a minute ago, but he's a little distracted as he discusses a sale with someone who doesn't have the exact change (everything is an even $20). Short, with a perpetual smile on his face and a voice so high it sometimes cracks, Dennis is constantly moving, as if there were no way to contain the energy in his squat body. An aspiring singer as well as accomplished trumpet player, graduate of the Manhattan School of Music and impresario of his own web-design company, Dennis two years before left New York City with his Dominican wife Betty and their two cherubic daughters for a distant suburban domain in Stroudsburg, Pennsylvania. When he's home he often works around the clock on multiple projects in a studio/office out-fitted with so much high-tech gear it has the look and feel of an electronics store. He'll take a very occasional break to hit golf balls at the local driving range and he used to enjoy skiing in the winter, but with the added commute to New York and the time he spends on the road with Wynton or for his singing career he says he really has few free moments.

"Did you meet Kevin?" Dennis asks me.

"Kevin?" I reply, drawing a blank, and then I remember Raymond's phone call the day before, mentioning the number of people who would be on the tour bus and how maybe somebody might need to be in a rental car for the short San Diego-LA drive. "We've got a magician with us," Raymond told me (along with Wynton's teenage son Simeon, a friend of Simeon's, and Wynton's sort-of cousin Maurice, chef extraordinaire, formerly of New Orleans and now living in Arizona).

"Kevin's the magician?" I say to Dennis rhetorically.

"Right!" replies Dennis, who favors exclamation points in his speech.

"No, I haven't met Kevin yet, but let me find Maren first. Which way did you think she went?"

And just then, as I am beginning to fight a slight sense of anxiety, I feel a tap on my shoulder.

"Dad, there's an usher who says nobody can go backstage without a pass."

"Girl,"—how she dislikes it when I call her that—"where have you been?"

"Nowhere. Jeez."

"Well I was looking for you. Please stick around."

"Where am I going to go?"

"All right."

"Whatever."

"What did you say?"

"Nothing. I'm sorry. Dad, can we go see Wynton?"

Which we do, and will again after the second set, though we don't linger, it is late, we have been up a long time, and his suite is crowded with some people Maurice wants to introduce him to. A huge man with an even larger personality, Maurice has been showing up in Wynton's life on and off for as long as I can remember, sometimes to cook his famous gumbo, sometimes just to hang, which seems to be the case here in San Diego. We haven't been in the room together more than a few minutes before Maurice is asking me again when we're going to write that best-selling cookbook he always brings up.

"Oh, man, it will be some kind of great cookbook!" Maurice says, squeezing my hand so hard it hurts. "Who's this beautiful woman you got with you?"

And I start to introduce him but he interrupts.

"I know this is your daughter, man. Met her that time at Wynton's."

I'm not sure which time that was. When Whitney was singing the blues after a gig? Place was crowded, Wynton had his horn out, think Wess did too, and Whitney told people her last name was Marsalis but Wynton seemed not to be bothered, nobody got hurt, nobody died, just a crazy happy moment in a lifetime of fantastic moments.

*

Before leaving San Diego on Saturday morning, Maren and I, still on East coast time, have an okay breakfast in the same place as we ate last night, check out, and leave our bags by the silver tour bus parked in the lot with the harbor view. It looks like no one is in a particular hurry to get going, though the band is scheduled to play tonight in the Hollywood Bowl as part of the *Playboy* Jazz Festival. According to my son, who lives in Hollywood, the hotel we're staying in is "tragically hip."

"Everything's painted white," he wrote in an email, "the furniture in your room is for sale, I mean they tell you how much you can buy it for." The bar downstairs is supposed to be a scene, too, he says, especially on Saturday night.

I've been visiting LA for half my life, since my college friend Stuart, the same person who met Wynton that time at the workshop in Oakland, was living in Venice Beach and making a living as a screenwriter. I vividly remember flying into LAX at night, the lights of the vast metropolis shimmering in every direction as we prepared to land, and Stuart picking me up at the airport in his black Mazda sports car convertible with Bruce Springsteen blaring on the tape deck. Years later, after Stuart had married and moved to Israel but before my son had come out here, I arrived via tour bus with Wynton's septet, with Harold Russell at the wheel, all the way from Las Vegas, where the septet had played a one-night gig after a much longer, all-night drive from Boulder, Colorado.

We stayed that time at an expensive hotel called the Westwood Marquis, a few blocks from an old theater, the Westwood Playhouse, where the septet was joined during one set by pianist Eric Reed, who'd played briefly with the septet after Marcus Roberts left the band. Like many band members before and after him, Eric was sent "to the woodshed," which meant home to work on his instrument. When he showed up that night in Westwood Wynton was still trying out other, new pianists, and Eric came in and played just one tune, and everyone there knew the gig was his again. It was Eric who would play the hypnotic, foot-stomping preacher's sermon near the end of *In This House*, which brought Bobby Short backstage to congratulate him after an especially exciting performance at a summer festival in Nice, France. Eventually he became restless, making remarks like renaming *Big Train*, a big-band piece of Wynton's from the mid-'90s, "Long Train."

Arriving in Los Angeles today from San Diego, Kim the driver gets off the freeway somewhere south of Anaheim and we lose some time creeping through city traffic. Kim stops for gas at a place with a paved, vacant lot adjacent to the fuel pumps, and David Robinson finds a football in the back lounge of the bus to throw around while we're waiting for the large tank to be filled. Maren, whose hand hasn't quite grown enough to grip the ball at its seams, holds it near one end but manages to make a pretty good pass to Wynton, who fires it to Rob, who tosses it back to Maren.

"Okay, girl, I'm open," Carlos hollers, running as if he were a receiver.

Maren throws a little behind him but it's still good for a completion.

"Touchdown!" someone says, but I'm only half listening, trying to reach my mother on my cell phone.

Since an emergency at Christmas, when I had to fax her doctor a copy of her living will, my mother has been in and out of the hospital a few more times but is now, miraculously, living at home—frail and not yet able to walk—with my sister in a small coastal town north of Portland, Maine. At Easter I visited with Maren and my wife and we all went out to dinner at a seafood place; just before this trip I went up again with my older daughter Anna, home for the summer from circus school in Montreal, and we pushed my mother in her wheelchair on a long walk down to the tidal river a half mile or so from my sister's. It was a sunny afternoon, a little chilly for June, and with the talk in the news about the anniversary of D-Day I found myself asking my mother again about the time she met my uncle at the train station in New York after he was released from Walter Reed Hospital.

"We went out for dinner then," she said, a fact she had not before shared with me. "And then we went dancing at the New Yorker. There were lots of places in those days, where you could dance."

"But I thought he was still so weak," I said, meaning my uncle, a prisoner of war in World War II.

"He was," my mother replied, and then stopped speaking for a few minutes, lost in her recollection. We had reached a spot on the path by the river that overlooked some falls, and we watched the water running over the rocks. On the return we stopped for ice cream cones at the corner store on the town's Main Street.

"We're supposed to be there already but I think we may be lost," I'm saying to my mother now, as I watch Maren run across the pavement for a pass from Rob.

"Yeah, she's fine, we're both still a little tired but we got lots of sleep. Christian's meeting us when we get to the hotel. He's coming to the concert tonight, then tomorrow's an off day, no travel either, we don't leave for Albuquerque until two a.m. Monday. Yeah, that'll be a long ride, twelve hours I think and we're only there overnight and then it's on to Santa Fe. I love you, too. Let me put Maren on."

Back on the bus it soon becomes clear that we are not only lost but we're going to be late. Oblivious to "where" we are—*fact is: we are on a bus*—Wynton has been arguing with Eric Lewis about the availability of images on the internet of Iraqi hostages and, more specifically, of the beheading of an American hostage. Only half tuned into the debate, which if I'm following it correctly focuses in part on Eric's insistence that the power of such an image to repulse resides only within the viewer, I have been keeping an eye out for familiar landmarks while trying also to keep a little distance from my daughter, who is more than holding her own as the only female among fourteen passengers and Kim the driver (earlier plans to lighten the load by adding that rental car were dropped, no reason given; no questions, as I learned long ago on the road, asked). When I am sure the direction we're going is west, not east, I break another rule of the road and, indirectly, comment on someone else's job by mentioning to Boss Murphy that I think we're heading toward Santa Monica and the Pacific Ocean, not Beverly Hills and Hollywood.

"Let me check with Kim," Raymond says, and in a few minutes we've reversed our course. I call my son to confirm our route, but not our arrival time, having quickly sensed I've already strayed as far as I should: we'll get there when we get there.

By now Wynton and Eric have transposed their conversation to music, and Wynton is recalling when he started to *hear* saxophonist Sonny Rollins. The key word, Wynton is saying, is *intent*, as in what was Sonny's intent?

"And when you've peeped something like that out," Wynton says, citing his discovery of Sonny's intent in the soundtrack he composed for the Michael Caine film *Alfie*, "when that happened for me with Sonny, I couldn't wait to get back to my hotel room after a gig to listen. It was the same when I first heard *Giant Steps* and started to peep out Trane. I wanted to rush home from school and listen to it again. And it's so rare now, to have three or four musicians of the caliber of that band in the same room together at the same time."

The discussion morphs to Wynton's own work, including *All Rise*, which Eric has been learning for a repeat performance next month with the Boston Symphony Orchestra, this time at Tanglewood (in what, so far as I can tell, will be the first-ever presentation there of a single work written by a living composer and comprising an entire program). There is a direct relationship, Wynton is saying, between the chord progressions of his much earlier *In This House, On This Morning* and *All Rise*, one of many aspects of his work, he laments in a later conversation, "that no one has bothered to explain. No one listens to *In This House*," he continues. "But it will come around."

Eric, whose place in the Boston performances of *All Rise* was taken by seventeen-year-old Juilliard student Aaron Diehl, has apparently put aside whatever objections he had to the work's text, which Wynton also wrote. His focus seems to have shifted to the meaning of the music.

"I really put something in that first movement," Wynton says in a rare boast, but his explication of the score is cut short because we have finally arrived at the Mondrian Hotel in West Hollywood, after a four-hour drive that should only have taken two. No one complains, in fact no one else seems to have noticed. *Fact is: we are here.*

Well, almost. Perhaps because of the high cost of real estate at this end of Sunset Boulevard, the Mondrian has been constructed with a minimum of space between the front exterior of the building and the curb. So, to stop the bus where bellhops can unload the luggage while other guests are pulling in and out of the valet parking area is difficult. Kim decides to deal with this after we all get off, because Raymond has already returned from the lobby with room keys for everyone; he even has mine and Maren's, with the understanding that when we check out we'll explain to the front desk that the charges go on my card, not the band's.

"Nice!" exclaims Maren, when we get to our room. "Very cool."

The walls and all the furniture are indeed white, with white curtains framing two large windows that look out in the direction of the city's vast, distant downtown. Maren immediately begins to unpack and she's still carefully laying out her various creams and sprays in the bathroom when there's a knock on the door signaling the arrival of her brother.

 Ten years older than Maren, Christian left home when she was still in elementary school—he came out here two days after his college graduation. The two of them talk on the phone occasionally and they used to email one another, before Maren broke not only her addiction to instant messenger but her interest in written correspondence. Until recently a production assistant at *South Park*, Christian's been working the past few months at a small talent agency nearby, while continuing to write a screenplay at night and during whatever weekend time he isn't either biking or working at a bike shop by the water. He was at the bike shop today, but took off early to meet us when we called to say we were getting close.

"You guys eaten yet?" Christian asks.

Even if we had, I know Maren's response would have been the same enthusiastic, "Where shall we go?"

Christian says there's a place, Saddle Ranch, practically across the street.

"We can sit outside," he adds—which is what we do, at a table perched on a sidewalk in a space so close to the street you feel you could reach out and touch a passing car.

"I don't know what the deal will be tonight," I say. "The last time I was there it was so crowded backstage no one really got any food." I don't need to repeat another road rule: *Eat when you can.* We each order an early dinner.

"Something to drink?" I ask my son, expecting him to ask for beer.

"Water's fine," he says.

"California," I think, remembering but not mentioning my surprise when I arrived at Stuart's that time in Venice Beach and he had installed in his apartment an electronic device he called an air ionizer.

Two hours later we're waiting in the lobby of the Mondrian for Boss Murphy to give the signal that the vans to take everyone to the Hollywood Bowl are ready. One by one the band members saunter down, and we have more company, too.

"Miller!" I shout, addressing Wynton's Tennessee friend, John Miller, a sometime filmmaker, writer, and all around go-to guy who just shows up wherever—often New York, and usually having just had a drink, or two, or on his way to get one. In New York a few years ago, on a winter's night, I had stopped at Wynton's after a rehearsal and Miller was visiting, and there was nothing to drink. It was late, too.

"I know a place that will be open," Miller said, so I followed him up Amsterdam Avenue, past a closed liquor store, and we continued in the bitter cold, the wind blowing, for several more blocks beyond where Amsterdam crisscrosses with Broadway, until finally we were in luck.

"Let's get some Sherry," Miller intoned. "Skain's been liking Sherry."

So I bought a bottle of something, can't recall what but it was expensive, and we brought it back with us, and then I was afraid I was going to miss my train at that point—I was staying at my brother's, just outside the city—so I left. When I came by the next night the bottle was empty.

In the Mondrian this night Miller is talking with Wynton's dapper doctor friend from New Orleans, Ken Mast, whom everyone addresses simply as K., and who has just self-published his first book, a mystery, and who is also Miller's occasional film collaborator, in fact they've recently completed a project with another friend of Wynton's named Todd Williams, not the Todd Williams who used to play tenor sax in the septet but someone who lives out here and works in the movie industry.

"Have you seen our movie?" K. asks me.

"Which movie is that?" I reply.

"The N-word documentary," John interjects. "Damn, Veeglan, you got to see this one, this is a bad-ass film." And then he lowers his voice a little, as if to share a confidence, and puts a hand on one of my shoulders. "You know the N-word, Veeglan? You know what that is?" And he sort of howls and smiles and slaps me on the back. "Damn, you got to see this one!"

Except for Wynton the band is assembled now in the lobby and Raymond tells them to take the first van and we'll see them there.

"What's Wynton's room number?" I ask and then head upstairs in the elevator with Christian and Maren. K. Mast comes along, too, but Miller remains in the lobby. He's started a conversation with a couple of young women who wonder who these musicians are and is this the gig they have tickets for they ask though it is pretty clear they don't have tickets to anything nor the slightest inclination to purchase them.

"Great One," K. mockingly greets Wynton, who is still ironing his shirt while Simeon and his younger brother, Wynton's third son Jasper, who lives out here with his mother, finish room-service burgers in the adjoining room while watching a baseball game on television without the sound. In less than half an hour Wynton is supposed to be performing before more than 20,000 people at the Hollywood Bowl, but from his demeanor you would think he is getting reading to attend a meeting of the PTA at Jasper's school.

"Hey, little Swig," Wynton addresses Christian. "What's happening?"

Then the phone rings.

"Yass, yass, thank you, we're on our way right now," Wynton fibs to Boss Murphy. It's another five minutes before we are out the door and soon stuck in stop-and-go traffic on Hollywood Boulevard.

In the front seat, with Jasper sitting on his lap, Wynton takes his mouthpiece out and starts playing a few drills on it to warm up.

"Sorry, boss," he says to the driver. "How long a drive we got?"

"Can't tell, this traffic."

"Anyone know what time we go on?" Wynton asks. Not waiting for an answer, he continues playing a tune on his mouthpiece while the van creeps uphill toward the venue. Jasper tickles one of his father's armpits and Wynton feigns a blank expression, as if he were a wax figure, and then breaks into laughter. When we finally turn at the entrance we bypass hundreds of cars double and triple parked and pull up to a gate backstage, where we follow Boss Murphy to a lady at a table who is dispensing passes. With Jasper in tow, Wynton has disappeared through a stage door, and before we have found our way into the amphitheater we can hear master of ceremonies Bill Cosby introducing him as the floor of a revolving stage makes a semi-circle, so rather than walking out the band simply appears suddenly, having been seated on the hidden side of the stage as Cosby spoke and then emerging while they begin playing.

The mixed, boisterous crowd, which has been here for several hours eating and drinking and listening to other acts, erupts in a prolonged ovation. Folks in the lower portion of the bowl are seated at tables that are roped off from the upper seats and watched over by zealous ushers.

"Follow me," K. says, and when an usher asks to see our tickets he tells her he's a doctor and we continue to the front section, a little to one side, where an older guy eyes us suspiciously as we find an empty table.

I don't like it down here, so close to the giant speakers on either side of the recently renovated stage, the speakers necessary I gather because the amphitheater space is so large. The amplification seems designed more for a rock band, so there is a tinny, hollow sound to acoustic instruments; even the piano sounds canned.

"Let's move," I say to my kids, and we are soon standing in the cross aisle that separates the upper and lower sections of the bowl, which is literally carved out of a hill and, were we to climb to its top, would I imagine present a view of the vast city, like it looked that time I flew into LAX at night. An usher asks us to move, and we walk now to the side, where the smell of marijuana mixes with the fragrances of many perfumes and the aroma of food.

On the clock, with a directive not to go over because another act is waiting to follow, the band plays a short set, and Wynton keeps his stage chatter brief. He's played here many times over the years and it's always a challenge to know what will work. When he played *Big Train* at the 2000 festival many in the audience tuned out; it was the wrong piece for this venue.

"We'd like to conclude with two songs for the memory of two musicians," he says now, and he announces their names—Ray Charles and the jazz drummer Elvin Jones, with whose band Wynton had once toured Japan (and with whom he recorded some of the music on his 1991 three-CD blues cycle, *Soul Gestures in Southern Blue*). The two tunes are a stirring version of "Rugged Cross" and a New Orleans-style arrangement of "Down by the Riverside," during which many people in the crowd wave handkerchiefs in the air, as if they were second-lining in the Crescent City.

An old man with his handkerchief leads several other men and women in a spontaneous parade toward the front of the bowl, and some of the women raise parasols up and down as they move to the rhythm of the music. The cheering that comes at the end sounds more like what you would hear at a sporting event, loud yells and cries for more.

Afterwards, Wynton deals with the usual backstage LA throng, which also includes Jasper's mom, to whose home Wynton is going later. I am about to tell him what a sad display the set was when I sense he is already someplace else, some brief braggadocio an uncharacteristic cover for the complex of emotions he must be dealing with at this moment, with the mother of one of his children nearby, a gaggle of wannabees competing for his patient attention, the usual myriad of problems elsewhere to deal with (focused this time on raising the remaining capital for the new hall in New York; completing the program plans for the first season), and the long part of this tour still ahead, with gigs in St. Louis, Cleveland, and Montreal after Colorado, which is as far as Maren and I are going. None of this is ever mentioned in conversation, nor the painful cyst on his upper lip (that will eventually force him to cancel the Montreal gig, a distressing first in his career).

Another backstage visitor, seated in his wheelchair and greeting friends as if he, too, had been performing, is D.J. Riley. He has just moved back to Los Angeles after spending the past year or so in New Jersey, near his parents, following the death of his sister from Morquois syndrome, the same disease that has incapacitated D.J.'s body (another sibling, a brother, is healthy). His sister's last wish, D.J. said, was to attend a Jazz at Lincoln Center concert and meet Wynton, which she was able to do shortly before she died after D.J. got in touch with Billy Banks, Wynton's first road manager, who in the old days did everything from making hotel reservations to driving the band's van.

"That meant so much to her," D.J. told me, when I had visited him two years ago in his home here in LA before he left again for New Jersey. Driving over from my son's on a sunny afternoon to a neighborhood near but not in the city's South Central section, I had turned onto a tidy street of nearly identical bungalow-design houses, each with its own driveway and unattached garage. Separated from the street by a weedless lawn, D.J.'s one-story, brick house looked unoccupied from the front, with the windows curtained and the door locked, but around back a nurse on her way to do errands greeted me cheerfully and told me to let myself in, I'd find D.J. in his room in the rear.

With only his head visible above a shroud of sheets and blankets, he was seated near the end of his bed in a wheelchair that had been retrofitted with various devices to help him answer and talk on his phone and to manipulate his nearby television and computer with voice-recognition commands and signals that he made by blowing into various tubes. The walls of the bright, sunlit room were lined with shelves piled high with medical supplies. Throughout our hour-long conversation, there was a constant stream of calls from people in Los Angeles and elsewhere in the country. And at one point D.J. made a call himself to a radio station where he said he was going to be hosting some kind of talk show, if I got the story right. With clarity and passion, he moved quickly from one topic to the next, interweaving his observations with frequent quotes and illustrating his points with regular references to musicians and their music, including the young musicians with whom Wynton was always working:

"Art is something that is not only beautiful in itself but is something that connects with the needs and desires and hopes of the people that need it. It molds itself to provide a tool, a mechanism for us to uplift ourselves and strengthen ourselves and the people we care about.

"I'm optimistic. Still. After forty-two years.

"Do you concentrate on what isn't in your life and blame your shortcomings and your troubles on what isn't?

"Or do you find a way to take the pieces of life that God has given you and maximize them to some kind of joy, maximize them to show how more can be made out of little—if one's desires and motivations are to add?"

D.J.

Sunday morning, early, quiet streets, cloudy sky. Maren's still asleep back in our room on the foldout couch, that breakfast place Frank Stewart and I went to one time, Duke's, is too far to walk, and I will have to settle again for Starbucks, with a stop at my favorite

Sunset Boulevard bookstore for newspapers. It's pleasantly cool at this hour, but maybe not comfortable enough to sit outside. I must remember to get something to take back for Maren and to call Christian, see if he's up yet, ask him where can we all have brunch?

Last night, coming back to the Mondrian, most of us were packed into one van, with Jasper and his dad again sitting in the front seat. The two women Miller had met earlier, who had managed to hustle a ride to the venue in one of the vans, had disappeared after they had been given tickets that, someone said, "they probably scalped." This certainly hadn't fazed Miller, who was in rare form in the back of the van talking so loudly that Wynton finally asked him to quiet down, which he did not do.

"John, I'm gonna *dis* you if you won't stop," piped up Jasper.

Then they went back and forth, Jasper continuing to repeat his "dis" threat, all the way to the Mondrian, where Miller headed straight for the outdoor pool and terrace, which had been turned into a giant bar. The bouncer wouldn't let Maren in.

"That's okay, Dad, I'm tired," Maren said. "I just want to watch a little TV and go to sleep."

So, my son and I joined Miller for a drink, and he proceeded to introduce us both to some women he didn't know. We were standing near a railing at a corner of the terrace, the three of us, and Miller turned to the strangers next to us, offered to buy them a drink, and then said, "Please say hello to my friends here," and then disappeared. We left, too, a little while after that.

"What time is that Dodgers-Yankees game?" I'm asking my son now, on Sunday, late morning, at this Mexican place we've come to for brunch.

"It's a sellout," Christian replies, but I'm undaunted. The Yankees are Maren's team, and I have a vivid memory of taking Christian to Chavez Ravine, the Dodgers' ballpark, when he was an infant and we were visiting Stuart.

"I think it's a late start," I say, "for television back east." I can't understand why I didn't check in the newspaper earlier, but in Christian's car I call the box office.

"Five o'clock!" I announce. "Do you want to go? Someone will be selling tickets."

With very little further discussion we decide to give it a shot. It's a fairly short drive from where Christian lives, and he says he knows how to avoid the freeway. We leave his apartment for the ballpark at three and can see its light towers ahead in less than half an hour. What if we can't get in? Or what if the only tickets being scalped are hundreds of dollars a piece?

Somehow certain this baseball game idea is going to work, I scan the neighborhood for signs of scalpers, and then I remember that in Los Angeles everyone drives everywhere and that here in Chavez Ravine you park your car in a lot located near an entrance on the same level as your seats. There are no scalpers until we begin inching forward in the traffic lanes that lead toward the lots, which surround the park and are fenced in. All scalping transactions, I finally grasp, must be conducted from your moving car, before you reach the gate.

"Watch your wallet, Carl," Christian says. It's what he's always called me—my name.

I'm sitting in the seat next to him and I can see several men holding tickets in the air. As soon as I put the window down they start elbowing one another for the chance to make a sale. Afraid we may miss out, I buy the first trio of tickets that someone offers, at a relatively small markup, and not until we've moved forward and I've looked at them do I realize they are not together. I jump out of the car and run back to the scalper who sold them to me.

"Nothing I can do about it, man" he says. "Just hold them like this"—and he shows me how to hide the seat section identification on the odd ticket—"and he'll let you in the same entrance." Then he turns away to make another transaction and I have to sprint to catch up with Christian's car.

The little scam about the entrance works, despite the fact that the ticket whose section identification I am disguising is for an entirely different level, and we walk around the beautiful park along the right field foul line to the place where two of our seats are located and where, 25 years earlier, Christian had attended his first baseball game perched on my chest in a Snugly. For the first inning, no one is sitting in the adjacent row, and I'm able to enjoy the game with Christian and Maren while remaining wary that I may have to move. In the top half of the second a group of people begin to file into the empty row, and as I stand up I explain my predicament.

"That's cool," the young man next to us says. "My buddy's not here yet. Me and my girl will move over one."

"Let me buy you a beer," I say.

"You don't have to do that. But thanks."

The rest of the game passes in a kaleidoscopic blur. Maren's favorite player, Derek Jeter, hits a home run, but the Dodgers win. On the way out she and I apply for Dodgers Visa cards in order to receive free Dodgers tee shirts.

"What should I put down for assets?" she asks me as she fills out the required application.

"Make it up," Christian says.

I'm feeling wistful about our imminent departure, though it's several hours away. I remember the first time I visited after Christian moved out here, when he was renting a one-bedroom apartment he could not really afford. We drove to Palm Springs, where I had a magazine assignment, and he got sick, couldn't swallow food his throat was so sore. We drove back without conversation and I was tempted to change my departure flight because of his health.

"I'll be okay," he insisted, in a whispered tone that I interpreted as, "I'm on my own now, really, you can head home."

And so I did, leaving very early the next morning, still dark when I started for the airport and, following his directions, drove much of the way on city streets instead of the freeway, parts of sleeping Los Angeles a ghost town that mingled with my mood,

the ghosts of my first-born's receding childhood chasing one another in my memory, summer nights when we played baseball after
dinner in the field behind our Conway barn and I could still remember the first time he hit one on the fly into the neighbor's
lawn, and the winter when he wanted to learn to skate and a friend
at the prep school in the next town said he could skate on Saturday
mornings with the faculty kids, said we could both come actually if
I'd help out, so I became a hockey coach and he got so hooked on
hockey we started going to the games at the school, we'd drive
down late on a weekday afternoon, they usually began at four, and
between periods we'd run across the street to the local market that
sold coffee and hot chocolate and usually still had some doughnuts
left, and when I got the golf bug he did, too, joining me at the
Greenfield Country Club if I promised to rent a cart, which he
would drive; sometimes we'd take a picnic along with us and park
the cart in the rough near the woods by the covered bridge over
the brook between the seventh green and eighth tee; he'd go to
concerts with me, too—when I was working on a book set in Boston he came along sometimes, once I remember on the return
home complaining about the cigarettes I still smoked then and
soon after that, on a solo trip, I stopped at a Burger King on the
Massachusetts Turnpike for a very lousy late-night snack and
when I reached into my pocket afterwards there was just one cigarette in the pack, crumpled, and I looked at it, fingered it, smelled
it…and threw it away with the remains of my meal, and have
never smoked another one since.

Leaving Chavez Ravine, traffic so bad we don't move in the
parking lot for more than half an hour, Maren says, "I'm hungry,"
and Christian says, "I know a good place for Mexican takeout,"
and so we drive there in the June dusk, it's nearly nine o'clock by
the time we find it, and we each order burritos, which we bring
back to Christian's apartment, stopping en-route for a bottle of
wine and I treat my son (and myself) to something good, which
we open to have with the burritos.

Maren takes one bite of hers and looks at me as if to say, "Is
yours okay?"

The chicken is overly charred, the sour cream and salsa don't seem fresh, the taco itself is a little stale.

I take a sip of the wine and ask Maren if she'd like to try a little.

"Sure!"

Then we return, grim-faced, to our burritos.

Finally Christian speaks up.

"I don't think these are happening," he admits.

Maybe we can get a snack at the hotel. Or, for Maren and me, there will be food on the bus, which is now not departing for New Mexico until three a.m. because everyone except Wynton is playing a gig that Ali Jackson arranged at a local club. Since he has to be at work the next morning, Christian says he won't be able to stay up that late with us, so after watching part of a lousy DVD from his roommate's vast collection, we start back for the Mondrian.

With our budget for the trip in mind, I checked out earlier and left our bags with the concierge. It's close to midnight now and the Mondrian's dining room is closed. Bribing him with a small tip, I persuade the bartender at the adjacent terrace to let us sit at a table in the empty, darkened dining room.

There isn't a lot to say. We're tired, and Maren and I have several more hours to stay awake. Christian tells me a little more about his latest screenplay, a thriller for a small production company where he started as an unpaid script reader, and we laugh about the treatment for a television series we wrote together the year before, which in the labyrinth of Hollywood politics basically never made it past my agent.

"We really needed a pilot," Christian says, and I nod. The idea for the show was a kind of golf Cheers, set at a fictitious resort on an island in the Caribbean. The main character was a man named Benny Motion, a teaching pro at the resort's golf course, divorced with two kids who live with his former wife back in Florida, where Benny had failed to earn a living as a competitor in mini-tour events. His sidekick was a guy named Peter Madison, which was the name I gave to my surrogate character in many of the unpublished short stories I wrote on those early mornings at the dining room table when we lived on the dairy farm when Bonnie was pregnant with Christian.

"I should really be going," Christian says.

"I know," I reply, staring at him, six feet tall, a very lean 190 pounds, his hair still blond, his eyes my father's blue.

We walk to his car, which the valet said as a favor he could park free by the curb, since it was quiet this Sunday night.

"You take care," I say, realizing with a sudden start that we probably won't see him again until Christmas; he's already told us he won't get a vacation this summer, having started his new job at the agency so recently.

"'Bye, Christian," Maren says, giving her brother a last hug. And he's gone.

"'If you can't play the blues,'" Wynton said the other night, quoting Lester Young, "'you can't play shit.'"

Or leave Los Angeles long after midnight, the streets of the city seeming to pass by us instead of our moving through them, traffic lights changing, an occasional car or truck ahead, not a person out walking so far as I notice. Inside the bus's crowded front lounge, the talk begins with baseball, with Rob expounding on Ken Griffey Jr., and then we shift briefly to golf, why didn't Tiger win the U.S. Open that just concluded, Wynton asks, not really caring, I think, from the sound of his voice but he knows I follow the sport. In between bursts of conversation I listen to the soothing sound of the wheels on the pavement, a kind of steady hum against the drone of the gears when they are shifting, peaceful somehow even though they are propelled by a machine; the sound and the sense of a lighted, closed place, a secure environment, creates and then reinforces the feeling that we are not simply moving on but like the music putting behind us whatever we just did, whatever we just experienced, good or bad, happy or sad, it's gone, over, and we are physically traveling toward tomorrow.

Carlos, who along with Ali thought about flying to Albuquerque because the bus is so full, is bummed about the gig at the Hollywood Bowl. Constantly questioning himself and the band like this, Carlos couldn't really hear on stage, he says, by which he means hear the other members of the band, but he also wonders what the audience heard. He couldn't pick up its vibe, all those people and the big stage.

"It is what it is," Wynton says, too tired for a prolonged conversation just now, and still it seems affected by whatever went on after the gig, though he won't say anything about it; if there is a response, it will come in the music at the next gig, or in what he is writing just now (a long delayed piece to be premiered this winter during Jazz at Lincoln Center's first season in its new hall). Dennis Jeter and Ali have already made their way to the triple-tiered bunks in the middle section of the bus, and Walter looks ready to follow them.

"How're you doing?" I ask Maren, who was drooping during the last hour at the hotel but has now revived.

"I'm fine, Dad. Go to sleep."

So I do, stretching out on one side of the rear lounge, my favored napping place ever since I got claustrophobic on a septet tour when, sleeping in a floor-level bunk on a night-time ride through the Rockies, I awoke to use the john and realized when I went forward to say hello to Harold Russell that we were in the midst of a snowstorm. All I could think about after that was being in that bottom bunk with the bus rolling over. Of course that never happened, not with the world's greatest bus driver at the wheel...but once the idea lodged itself in my mind I couldn't get rid of it, like a tune you start humming to yourself and can't stop.

Well into the morning, the sensation of slowing down triggers something in my unconscious. Blinking, I peer out through one of the blinds to a startling brightness, the air clear, some kind of conifer near the place we've parked, and from other trips and my own inner gyroscope I conclude we must be somewhere in the vicinity of Flagstaff, Arizona. Kim confirms this after I pass through the quiet darkness of the bunks, with no one including Maren stirring, to the front of the bus, where Rob has been watching a movie.

Outside at this truck stop the air is also quite cool and I wish I were wearing a sweater, but it feels good to be walking a few steps, moving my arms, taking deep breaths. I wonder what Christian is doing. Must be on his way to work. I'm about to call him but I then think no, let him be. I'm thirsty and a little hungry and could kill for some coffee though I don't imagine the stuff they sell here will be anything to rave about.

How true.

In less than two hours we are crossing the Arizona desert, and just about noon we enter New Mexico, where there's another truck stop at which Kim has to pay a special tax. Everyone's awake now, an old DeNiro flick is playing, even Wynton is watching it while he gives Simeon, sitting next to him, a backrub.

"Longest drive I ever remember was twenty-two hours," Dennis Jeter says. "Winnipeg, Canada to Interlaken, Michigan. We were in a Winnebago, I took turns driving and Wynton had us listening to a book on tape, it was either the *Odyssey* or the *Iliad*."

By mid-afternoon we're approaching downtown Albuquerque, and Rob starts talking about the promoter for tonight's gig here and tomorrow night's in Santa Fe.

"Bumble Bee Bob," Rob says, his lips puckering on the alliterated B's. And then he repeats the first two words, annunciating slowly: "Bum-ble-bee!"

The bus pulls to the curb, the door swings open, and waiting to greet us is the very person whose name Rob has been having fun saying, a bundle of energy in his late 60s with a yellow cap on his head, the cap decorated with the oversize likeness of a bee.

"Bumble Bee!" Wynton says with a smile, as if this word were part of a chorus. And right at that moment I realize I know this man, just not his nickname. He was a cattle rancher when I met him more than twenty years ago, interviewed him in Santa Fe for a magazine article, visited his enormous ranch with its house up on a hill outside town with views in every direction of the mountains, came home and told my wife if we ever decided to move I had found the place. Bob Weil is his real name, and he's a concert promoter now—and a restaurateur, I'll learn tomorrow when the food after soundcheck is catered from the "beestro," Bumble Bee's Baja Grill, that he and his second wife B.J. began two years ago.

"Howdy," he says to the new musicians he hasn't met before, while Wynton and Rob—and me—are greeted with bear hugs.

"Dad," Maren interrupts, "I seriously need a shower." And so we head up to our room, with its view of a downtown sculpture park that I explore after the desk clerk I call tells me no, this Hyatt doesn't have wireless internet yet but some people say you can pick up the city's free connection in the park.

No such luck, and once again I settle for Starbucks, where I can't decide whether or not to have an extremely late and not very nutritious breakfast or be patient and wait for an early, possibly more balanced supper. And then I realize we've lost an hour, we're on Central Time now, and will there even be time before the gig for food?

The recently renovated KiMo Theatre, a short walk from our hotel, is a curious blend of art deco and Native American iconography. Backstage, on a stairway landing, a kind of open closet serves as a shrine to someone named Bobby who, an inscription reads, "was killed in this building in 1951." No explanation, no other details. The band is playing two sets tonight, with our magician Kevin Lee opening the second with several sight gags. The house is packed for both sets and clamors for an encore at the end of the second. Wynton obliges with an extended solo blues, some of it played so quietly it's as if Wynton were whispering through his horn.

"I really got to something there," he says later, in response to a compliment, but this is as far as he ever goes in trumpet talk. Quickest way to end a musical conversation with him is to say something like, "That was cool, the way you turned that trill on the low C and B into a rhythmic figure for the following phrase."

"What trill? What phrase?"

To my disappointment, Maren misses the blues. She's been hanging out with Simeon and his friend, and all three of them are ravenously hungry as the gig concludes.

"I'll walk with them back to the hotel and we'll get some food there," I say to Boss Murphy.

"Okay," he responds in a clipped, almost staccato voice, as if he had for a second thought this was one of his Navy reserve weekends. He's helping Rob deal with the folders of music and the wiring onstage while keeping an eye out for Wynton, who is supposed to make an appearance in the lobby to meet some of the benefactors of an area jazz foundation that Bumble Bee helped found and to which he has donated generously.

When the four of us get back to the hotel the dining room is closed, but the bartender says the teenagers can order off the appetizer menu, so we take seats at a table large enough to accommodate the four of us and saxophonist Walter Blanding, who was asking at the theater where he could eat. Conversation until Walter's arrival consists of chitchat about sports and school; I remember from Christmas the year before, when Simeon was along when his father was a sideman at the Ali Jackson gig in Boston, that Simeon had more or less stopped doing his school work for a while, and I ask him now is he back to his books?

Smiling, he shrugs, passes as well on a question about the clarinet, and reports that his older brother Wynton Jr. is still playing soccer. There's a lot of pent-up energy in Simeon, always has been, and I ask him about his chess. Until recently he was beating his father regularly, but then Wynton started playing a lot, at home as well as on the road, and the matches have become closer.

"I let him win sometimes," Simeon says, and laughs. His eyes dart around the room. "Think that hamburger will be here soon?"

Before I can answer the waitress appears with the food, almost simultaneously with the arrival of Walter, who orders a plate of baby-back ribs. He sits at the opposite end of the table from me, with our young guests between, so it's a little difficult to make out every word as we catch up on bits of family news. The son of musicians, born in Cleveland but raised mostly on Staten Island, where his parents moved when he was ten, Walter's in his early 30s. He lived in Israel for several years with his first wife, the mother of his twin daughters, and he's married now to a woman from Italy. In addition to playing in two of Wynton's bands he's earning a degree at the New School in Manhattan, where he lives. It's a complicated life, but you always get a sense when you're talking with Walter that he sees the clear line, stays focused on what follows, whether it's to meet his daughters after school or visit his mother, who has remarried since the death of his father and to whom Walter bears such a striking resemblance that they could pass for brother and sister. Walter speaks in a clear, cadenced voice, filled with both empathy and joy, which are the qualities beyond the extraordinary technical skill that immediately strike you when he's playing the saxophone.

Pianist Eric Lewis must have had Walter in mind when he gave me his definition of jazz. "Jazz music," says Eric, "is the sound of someone's dance sensibility."

This is the same Eric who earlier this past spring, in a gig at the Troy Savings Bank Hall in Troy, New York, brought the audience to its feet in a standing ovation *during* a tune—it was after a long improvisation in which he more or less surveyed the entire history of jazz piano, going from stride to ragtime to swing to blues, all in one improvisation lasting perhaps twenty minutes, with gradations of volume and velocity, complicated chord changes with stretched fingerings that had to have challenged even his enormous hands, and all within a logic of rhythm and form that gave the improvisation not simply an aesthetic coherence but an artistic inevitability.

And so in Santa Fe, the night after Albuquerque, *I'll Remember April* is the tune in the first set when Eric takes off again, the whole band does, Walter and Carlos and Ali and Wynton, nothing like what they just played in San Diego or Los Angeles and yet the very same core, nothing's changed in that, the heart of Saturday's "Rugged Cross" is now the base of "Blues in Bogey," and how I wish Maren were sitting with me behind one side of the opened curtain, onstage, where I can see and hear the band but the audience cannot see me, my preferred place to sit, the spot I've always claimed going all the way back to that gig in Nebraska when Wynton invited that old woman to sit with the band on stage and when I commented on it afterwards invited me to do so, too, but I concluded that I liked it better in the secluded, darkened intimacy of the stage-wing, where once at a gig in Hartford, Connecticut,

Billy Banks who was road managing a runout and his wife Laurie stood, not sat, in the same place between tunes and as soon as the music began again they danced, just the two of them, there on the hidden side of the stage, and another time I remember was in South Carolina, Greenville was the name of the town, where we'd arrived after a long day's drive from Durham, where Wynton had played a long blues with a young boy at a school assembly, and then in Greenville backstage during soundcheck I'd started a conversation with a member of the theater's staff, think she may have gone to the university whose theater it was, Furman its name, anyway she had never before heard jazz and so I was telling her about that tour, remarking on the interplay between Wynton and Wycliffe Gordon, the extreme degree of their coordination and the intensity of hearing that it required of them, and not just hearing of course but also of responding, I meant how they heard and then responded to one another, funny word, respond, made it seem a little academic, but Tami I believe her name was responded to what I said and so we continued the conversation afterwards, my father was stationed near here when he was in training camp during the Second World War I said, right up the road more or less and she said where and I said Spartanburg and she said yes it's not that far and I asked did she know a town north of Spartanburg, it was actually just over the state line in North Carolina, town was called Tryon, and Tami said she'd heard of it but never been there and why did I ask, and I said, "That's the town where my father moved before he died."

Wynton, playing a solo at the end of a tune by Coleman Hawkins during the second set in Santa Fe, sounds a high wail and then cuts to a New Orleans march, moves momentarily into a melody before unfurling a blazing sequence of arpeggios, finally finishes with a kind of whistle, and all the while, sitting next to me now, having missed the first set because she volunteered to return to the hotel half a block away...to fold Wynton's laundry...Maren taps her feet while she listens, and then in *My Ideal* Maren moves her head and her shoulders.

"Let's walk the other way," I say after the gig, outside the theater, and I mean let's walk a few blocks in the other direction from
the hotel to the square, where some of the oldest buildings in
North America cast a mystical spell on this clear night: so many
stars visible here in these hills! More interested in the closed shops
we pass than the historic church at the center of the square, Maren
runs ahead on the return, reminding me again very briefly but very
sharply that she's fifteen, not fifty. Again on the next day's ride to
Denver I realize this when, driving by Colorado Springs with tow-
ering, snow-capped Pike's Peak looming over the high, western
horizon, I try to catch her attention.

"Look, Maren, the Rockies!"

"Yes, Dad?" she says, looking up from the CD she's selecting
for her Walkman.

At Loews Denver Hotel, located in the southern end of the
city, several miles from downtown, she comes to life when she no-
tices a strip mall within what she perceives as walking distance.
With a promise that she'll stay in touch with me on her cell phone,
she negotiates permission to visit the stores across the street.

"Remember we have to eat here at the hotel before the gig," I
tell her, because Boss Murphy has explained there will not be a catered meal at that evening's venue, the Denver Botanic Gardens.
There, the band will play two sets in an outdoor amphitheater,
while Maren helps Dennis Jeter sell out the last of his tee shirts,
and when I understand how content she seems, smiling at prospective customers between sets, correcting Dennis on the way to
fold a shirt, I leave the crowd and wander at sunset away from the
stage toward the nearby flowers and trees, water running in the
pool of the spacious Japanese Garden area, birdsong mingling
there with the music that I can still hear from afar. A plane flies
over. By another pond in an area called the Monet Garden, where,
appropriately, water lilies have opened, the rock I sit on is still
warm from the afternoon sun; two kids with bare feet test the water
and a bird swoops in for a drink; drinks; stands still; drinks again;
flies off.

With the first cool air of evening, the music becomes louder as I walk back closer to where I started. Eric is in the midst of another virtuoso improvisation, this one on "Cherokee," the speed breathtaking and somehow he has added a stride chorus that he will repeat in a different tune in a very different format several hours later. After midnight, in the midst of a long phone conversation from his hotel room regarding Jazz at Lincoln Center programming choices, Wynton receives a phone call from Eric, who with Walter and Carlos has traveled after the gig downtown to the oldest jazz club in the city, El Chapultepec.

"I'm coming," Wynton says to Eric, and then to me, "Swig, Maren can hang out here with the boys, they can watch a movie or play chess, Boss Murphy will check on them."

And we go, a taxi takes us, we get there the long way, driving by the new stadium where the Denver Broncos play and the old one where they used to play and finishing finally in a boisterous neighborhood right next to Coors Field, home of the Colorado Rockies, the construction of which has clearly triggered a commercial gentrification of the neighborhood with sports bars and grilles and discos all doing a booming business tonight even though the Rockies are out of town. But Chapultepec, at the corner of Market and 20th, looks like it hasn't changed in fifty years, the walls lined with photos of jazz artists and other musicians, the tables by the small bar packed with people of all ages, most of whom to judge from the air quality must be smokers, and a small band plays a blues by the doorway at the end of the bar, the door open, the lights low.

A slight stirring of recognition occurs amongst the intimate crowd as Wynton takes a seat at a table. Jerry the owner, with a cigarette dangling from his lips, asks Wynton what he'd like to drink.

"You have any cognac?" Wynton says. And Jerry brings him an enormous glass, from which Wynton takes just a sip before Jerry is at the front, saying there's a special guest in the house tonight and would you all please welcome...Wynton Marsalis! And Wynton begins playing with the combo that has been there all night, and then one by one his own musicians sit in, too, and it's a nice vibe here, nothing manic, no over-the-top would you believe b.s., and they keep playing until last call at 2:00 a.m., by which time two friends of Wynton's who happened to be there have offered us a ride back to the hotel, and we somehow all squeeze into a station wagon, one of the friends saying he'll sit on the floor of the rear luggage compartment. Our return route is through the city itself, along tree-lined streets and a neighborhood with large homes and then a few apartment buildings and then a business zone, this must be part of the area I watched from the window of Wynton's hotel suite before we left, a little sliver of an immense urban area, bounded by the mountains on its western side and the plains in every other direction, and the entire, invisible rest of the country beyond that jagged perimeter.

The next morning we put those plains behind us and begin to climb these mountains. We are on our way to Aspen, where the band will play a kind of runout gig, leaving soon afterwards on a long trip to St. Louis, but first letting off Maren and me. My daughter and I will stay over with Denver friends one more day before flying home. To expedite our drop-off, and make it possible to stick with the band to and from Aspen, I've rented a car in which I trail the bus as it leaves Loews Denver Hotel and, inadvertently, makes a loop around the hotel's vicinity until Kim figures out the location of the interstate's entrance. Then we go north, past downtown, before intersecting with I-70 west, before the turnoff for Boulder where the epic ride through that mountain snowstorm to Las Vegas with Harold Russell at the wheel began on what was a spring evening in Boulder, and we pass Golden where I was once startled to discover that rather than being nestled by the mountain stream pictured in television ads the imposing Coors brewery stands hard by a giant, paved parking lot, and we continue upward past Loveland Ski Area (closed for the season but still with lots of snow) to the Eisenhower Tunnel, where the road literally burrows through an otherwise impassable pathway to the other side of the Continental Divide.

Well before that landmark, I've left my rental car in the parking lot of a bank just off the highway in a small town in what are euphemistically called the foothills. Back on the bus, I interrupt a conversation Maren is having with Eric Lewis.

"Hey, beautiful," I say, "please help me remember this exit number when we came back tonight."

Absent-mindedly, I've been keeping an eye out the window while listening to the conversation around me. My cell phone rings, surprising me—I didn't think it would work up here.

"Where are you?" a friend from back east asks.

"Let me look," I reply, and instantly realize we've made another wrong turn. We're off the interstate, on the road south to Leadville, an old mining town, beyond which is a shortcut to Aspen—if you're in a car with good snow tires and maybe a set of chains just in case.

Four summers ago I was in a vehicle that took that shortcut, by mistake, and almost didn't make it. I was on my way to the same jazz festival we're heading to now, in a Winnebago with Wynton and Frank Stewart and a new driver named Keith. We'd just driven all the way from New York City in less than 48 hours, with a stop in Nebraska to watch a basketball playoff game on television, and we were meeting Wynton's big band at the Silvertree Hotel in Snowmass Village at Aspen, same destination as today, except that time we were going to be staying at Snowmass for a couple of days while Wynton rehearsed the band before it began a western tour. When Keith reached the point where the shortcut crossed Independence Pass the road was covered with snow—this was in June, too.

"Keep your eye on the yellow line," Wynton said that day to Keith.

"There is no yellow line," Keith had replied.

Now, outside Leadville, I say something to Boss Murphy, who immediately goes to Kim and whispers and Kim pulls over and calls the Silvertree on his cell phone. My interference isn't a matter of etiquette but, possibly, of life and death; were we to head up the narrow road to Independence Pass there would be no room to turn around and a reasonably good chance the bus would slip off the pavement, tip over, and fall several thousand feet down a mountain slope.

Kim isn't happy about having to turn around, and neither is anyone else on the bus because it means we have lost whatever opportunity there might be for a soundcheck or a hotel nap. We aren't back on I-70 for long before we have to pull off again, this time because the treads on one of the tires for the trailer the bus is pulling has burned off. It's late in the afternoon before we finally reach the Aspen/Snowmass fork in the road where we take the turn to the Silvertree, all the way at the end of the road, the hotel built right into the bottom of the Snowmass ski slopes, with an ersatz village surrounding it, and kids who are attending the resort's Suzuki music camp walk around carrying violins.

Maren and I have no hotel room for this brief visit, and so we leave our stuff on the bus. When I was here before, the festival took place in an open field just down the road from the hotel, but this year it has been moved to a tent in Aspen itself, several miles away. So we still have another ride ahead of us, after the band members have showered and changed. Rob is going ahead now, to check on the sound system, but I remember the shops in the village and am pretty sure they will still be open.

I follow Maren around the side of the hotel that faces a chairlift and ask her to stop by one of the lift towers.

"Why?"

"I want to take your picture."

"Oh, Dad, that's so corny." And she keeps walking downhill, toward the level where the shops are. So in the photograph I take you just see her from behind, wearing maroon pants and a white tee shirt over a long-sleeved tan turtleneck, her black purse dangling from her right shoulder, and swaying from her head long locks of her reddish-brown hair that she had cut and colored before we left on this trip, and she seems to be leaning with the angle of the hair, as if she were moving to some music she could hear in her head, and beyond her in the photograph are the slopes of other mountains forming a green valley, the early evening sky still blue with white wisps of clouds.

Maren quickly finds a boutique that sells jewelry and "stuff" and starts looking at earrings for her pierced ears. We are the only people in the store other than the shopkeeper, a blond-haired woman who introduces herself as Cyndi. She's deeply tanned and smiles constantly as she talks a little about herself, tells us she loves the snow but doesn't ski much anymore, says she used to date a comedian and travel a lot, is a Barbra Streisand fan and did we know Vince Gill, he stopped by the store just the other day.

"Why don't you pick out a bracelet," I say to Maren. "To remember our trip."

Cyndi helps her select something simple and gives us a deep discount on it. Maren leaves the store wearing the new bracelet, and we meet the band at the hotel lobby door and ride to the gig in a large van. It's almost dark by the time we get there, and while the band is being introduced we're invited to help ourselves to food in the commissary tent for festival employees. We listen to some of the music from behind the stage and then walk around its edge, near one side of the enormous tent, where an usher lets us through a temporary gate. Another, smaller tent stands adjacent to the main one, and I discover that our backstage passes permit us to enter this tent as well, where gourmet food and fine wines are being served to festival donors. I enjoy a glass of a California cab while Maren scarfs down some strawberry shortcake, and then I help myself to a second glass of wine and take it back with me as we find seats in the main tent.

"Can I have a sip?" Maren whispers.

"Sure," I say. "To a great week. I love you."

She squeezes my chilly hand; it's cold up here in the mountains at night.

"Love you, too."

Maren knows from much experience that one place not to get lost is backstage after a gig if you need a ride. And so she stays near me, while I keep Wynton in my line of vision. He seems in no particular hurry to be leaving, but I know from experience that when he's ready to go somewhere he goes, and if you don't follow along right away you'll be left behind. You could be one of his sons and he wouldn't wait for you (though he would, if you were one of those boys, be certain to ask someone to stick with you). Sure enough, just as he finishes a plate of food someone on the festival staff saved for him, he stands up, grabs his trumpet, and more or less bolts in the direction of the backstage exit. I run after him, and Maren runs after me.

By pure chance, no one else in the band leaves just then, and we end up together, the three of us, in the seat right behind the driver in an otherwise empty van. Maren sits between us, and we ride together back to the Silvertree. Wynton quickly starts a conversation with the driver, who tells us he lives in Las Vegas, where he works as a bartender, and is just helping out a buddy tonight by doing this driving while he visits for a few days.

"That was beautiful, what Eric did tonight on 'Magic Hour,'" I say. "I like how you've been letting him just end the piece himself, that lullaby."

Wynton sort of nods and mumbles some kind of "uh-huh" and asks Maren does she have enough room and, "I'm sorry we didn't get to spend more time together, you'll have to come to New York with your dad," and then, to me, "How did the band sound?" by which I assume he means in part how did it sound with Herlin Riley playing the drums tonight, Ali having left last night for a weekend gig at the Village Vanguard and Wynton's regular big band drummer and original septet member Herlin having flown in from New Orleans for this gig and the one to come in St. Louis.

"Nothing has meaning on its own," Wynton suddenly declaims. "You have to give it meaning, invest it with life. Another day in the world, we played a gig, and now we go home."

Or, in this case, back to the hotel, where the bus will be leaving in about an hour.

"You don't have a room?" Wynton says as we walk him to his. "Stay here."

Maren parks herself in front of a television and I follow Wynton into the next room, where the television was never turned off earlier. Wynton sits down and in silence we watch a few minutes of Sportscenter, then his cell phone rings and he disappears into the bathroom for a minute, comes out wearing jeans and a blue work shirt, and, still talking on his phone through a headpiece, sits down again, clicks the off button on the phone, sighs, looks past my shoulder into the room where Maren is now reading a magazine, shakes his head and smiles.

"This is what life will always be," he says, again without any prompting. "What it is. They eat great meals, they marry their old ladies, they make love, they blow into horns…but they have to blow beauty into them, into life. And then they die. We're just like the Romans hanging out two thousand years ago, Swig. Yass, yass."

Then he stands and without another word walks into the next room and starts to talk with Maren, says something to her about pimps and drug dealers but I can't really hear the conversation and don't try, try only to stay awake until we're on the bus again, where Kim thinks it will be about five a.m. or so when we reach the place where I left our rental car and so I wander to the back lounge, set the alarm on my phone for 4:30, and fall asleep before the bus begins to move.

The sound of that alarm a few hours later startles me. I collect my things and walk back through the darkened bunk area, poke Maren in hers, and find Wynton, Carlos, and Eric in the front of the bus, deep in a continuation of the conversation about staying together on the bandstand that began in Los Angeles. It's still dark out.

"Got a ways to go," Kim says, and I take a seat near him, drift in and out of the talk around me, watch the road, nod off, and then, "We're here," Kim is saying. I'd fallen asleep again and I stand now and walk back to Maren's bunk and wake her again, too, and by then Kim has the bus idling by our car, and he opens the luggage door underneath and I find our stuff and put it in the trunk of the car.

"Well, goodbye," Maren is saying inside. "Thank you so much."

"What, you don't have any hugs for us," Carlos deadpans.

Maren blushes, smiles, hugs Carlos, hugs Eric, and looks at Wynton, who pretends for a second like he's never met her. Then he does one of his whoops, laughs again, smiles, throws his arms around her and

says, "I love you, girl. You take good care of that old dad of yours." And we get off the bus.

Kim waits while I start the car, and not until I wave, signaling that we are fine, does he put the bus in motion. It's light enough to see now, the sun just coming up far off to our east, over the plains. The clock in the Camry flashes 5:15. Across the lot an old guy appears out of nowhere, must live down the street, he and his dog on their morning walk.

"Dad," Maren says. "Are we going?"

"In just a minute, Maren," I reply, not moving, and I wait while I watch Wynton's bus exit the lot, listening to its gears grinding, then the sound of its wheels as it disappears beyond some trees, and I think of the men on board, in motion like the music they make, and I think again of D.J., Sally, Wess and Monyure; Wynton's housekeeper Anna Castillo from Honduras, how she always finds some food for me if I drop in and he's not there, Anna who takes the train everyday from the Bronx with her young son, whom she drops off at school after the hour-and-a-half ride before she starts work.

"Dad, I'm so tired. Can we please just go? Please?"

And so we do, leaving the lot a few minutes after the bus, which when we get back onto the interstate has disappeared from view. Sitting in the seat beside me, Maren seems already to be asleep.

"Will the radio bother you?" I ask.

No response.

Hitting the scan button, I find a jazz station, and I turn the volume up a little. Maren doesn't stir.

I remember the day I almost missed my ride to the airport. I was using a van service that trip and when the driver rang the bell at the house we were renting after selling the farmhouse I was still asleep. It was 4:30 a.m. and he had other people in the van already he told me. "How many minutes do I have?" I asked. "Five," he replied and meant it.

Funny, I think that was the time we were all convening in Denver and then onto Fort Collins, and from there it was a short drive the next day to Wyoming, where I went on that walk in Laramie the following morning with Harold Russell and Darlene, before we left for Cheyenne.

There's a Charlie Parker tune playing on the car radio. Funny, the first time I was in New Orleans with Wynton, one night we went to get something to eat at a Chinese place near the tree-lined street where his parents lived. Wynton's oldest son was along, age three or four at the time, and Dr. Michael White, a New Orleans native who taught Spanish literature at Xavier University, where Wynton with his band and Michael had spent that day learning some King Oliver tunes. At the Chinese place Michael and Wynton had started talking about Sidney Bechet and I didn't know who that was.

"Don't matter," Wynton had said kindly. "I didn't used to know either."

That first tour for me had commenced right after we'd moved from the farm into the rented ranch house, which came with an enormous attached garage into which we more or less dumped all the stuff from the move that we didn't know what to do with. This happened in July, during a hot spell. On our final day at the farm when I had walked through the farmhouse that last time, its empty rooms already gave off a mustiness in the heat, and my footsteps had reverberated in the front hallway as I climbed its slippery wooden stairway.

At the top of the stairway, around the corner of the balustrade, there was a tiny room with two windows that looked out at the gentle valley below the house. For a time I had a desk there, but when Maren was born we made it her bedroom, the crib in the corner formed where the wall of our bedroom met the front of the house, above the porch. I looked in there that last afternoon, then slowly walked back through the hallway, past the other bedrooms and the upstairs bath with the Victorian bathtub we'd never replaced, and into the rear upstairs of the farmhouse that originally must have been where the hired hand lived. Except for one room I'd used as a study, we never got around to fixing this part of the house, though we had enclosed the hole at the end where the house used to meet the enormous barn, which we'd had torn down, partly because it was a fire hazard and partly because the expense of renovating it would have been so high. I stared out the back window to the ball field with the homemade backstop where Christian and I had played every night after supper, and then I walked down the back stairs, outside, where my children were waiting somewhat impatiently for us to get going. Having long before purchased a ticket to a summer dance performance, Bonnie had already driven off, leaving me to take the kids to our new place, which was only about half an hour away. Two or three days later I got on a plane for New Orleans.

"Dad?" Maren's voice startles me now. I was sure she was fast asleep. "We almost there?"

"There" is my friends' house, where we have instructions to let ourselves in so we don't wake anyone up, though I have a feeling someone will be waiting. We've turned off I-70 now, past the exit for Boulder to the north, and we're traveling south on I-25, actually the same road we were on two days earlier from New Mexico, the reverse of the route Wynton and I followed in that taxi the other night when he played at Chapultepec.

"I know that tune," I think, half listening to the radio, and then, "Yes, it's the first cut on the *Marciac Suite*," the piece Wynton wrote in 1999 for the small town in southwestern France where he's been attending the jazz festival every summer. I first heard this tune five summers ago, when Maren was ten, and a band that was composed partly of Wynton's old septet, augmented by a few more musicians, played a five-night engagement at the Iron Horse, two sets a night, every set a sellout.

Maren and Bonnie came to the club one night and Maren helped me take notes during part of the performance. "Pretty tune," she wrote in her stylish cursive. "Bluezy jazz." The rest of her notes are similarly cryptic, just little phrases:

> *Joking around.*
> *Wintin's playing,*
> *everyone joins*
> *quick, mellow tone*
> *and, upbeat!*
> *breaking into*
> *sudden stop*
> *talking*
> *Herlin fools around—*
> *on drums*

We were no longer living in the rented house then, but I could never forget that first fall there when the band came to Amherst for a gig at the nearby state university, and after soundcheck Wynton accepted my invitation to drive by and say hello to my family. Bonnie had thought we were going out and when we surprised her she was serving the kids supper. Wynton confessed he was hungry, and the only thing Bonnie had made because it was all we had in the house that evening was Campbell's Chicken Noodle soup with grilled cheese sandwiches. Wynton said how good it tasted and gave everyone a hug when he left, Maren only three years old then, Maren who came home from the hospital after her birth on a cold January morning, wrapped in a red blanket and a pink hooded sweater knit by her mother, who held her in her arms outside the hospital with our other two children standing by her, Anna gripping in one small hand the pink roses my mother had given her new granddaughter, and we drove home together that day, the five of us, back to our house on the hill, my family whom I later left all those days when I went on the road, and you never knew, could not know if you'd see the sun in the morning, "Will I See the Sun in the Morning Blues," sing them now, *Oh the memories that music marries, the voices of joy and loss that love leaves in our lives.*

5

Coming from Cardiff into London, Wynton dozed in the backseat of a Mercedes driven by an engaging, loquacious Welsh chauffeur named Roger, who freely dispensed geographic and linguistic information about his ancient homeland, rhapsodized about the quality of his automobile, which he proudly said he had traveled to Germany to pick up, and shared stories about previous clients, including Stephen Sondheim, whom he praised for his intelligence and thoughtfulness. That name got a rise out of Wynton.

"Yeah," Wynton said. "He's *great.*"

"Ran into the maestro yesterday morning at breakfast," I said. "'And what brings you here?' he asked, and I said something about the continuing challenge of getting on paper this elusive art, and I mentioned the gig on Friday in Birmingham. 'Yes,' Mr. Masur said, 'it is history.' Skain, you listening?"

"I'm here," he said, looking up from a paperback book of math puzzles he was studying. "Kurt Masur," Wynton added. This was the highest form of a compliment he paid: to say someone's name, just the name.

In Birmingham, Wynton had stayed late after the gig for an interview. Some fans had wanted to see him, too, a crowd of them by the stage door in the lobby of the atrium attached to the magnificent hall. Two were university students I had overheard as I was scribbling notes after the second encore, amazed, I heard one of them say, "to be standing by the expensive seats." I was able to get them backstage, where they had waited it must have been an hour, and when Wynton finally came through the doorway the words tumbled out of their mouths.

"Thank you, thank you," they exclaimed, and, "Did you hear me shout, 'Alleluia?'"

Now, we could see the water of Bristol Bay as we left Wales, somewhere past a sign for some Roman ruins. It was a cool, misty Sunday morning, the landscape green. Nearing London after a stop at a fast-food place for breakfast, I recognized the streets near Heathrow, not far from Windsor Castle, and remembered when I flew over here in '92, the time Wynton and I worked together on the "late night sound of the train" section of our book in the coffee shop of the hotel near Wellington Arch, started writing it actually, finished it in Nice.

Bonnie had driven me to Bradley airport for that trip, and because this was long before 9/11 she could walk me to the gate. Maren was along, too, still a toddler. I took one of those small prop planes on a connection to Boston where I was getting my London flight, and I remembered now, in Roger's Mercedes, the sight of my wife and very young daughter waving to me as the plane left the gate. There was something in that moment I had been fighting ever since, as if I were afraid of its power. "Going," I had such conflicted feelings, because I was certain as well that I was also actually "coming."

Quiet, calm streets as we entered London now, less than three months removed from the terrorist bombings in the city's subway system. What did he as an American citizen make of the war in Iraq? Roger had asked Wynton, tentative in his introduction of the subject, not wishing to provoke but nevertheless curious—and, it was clear from the way he himself spoke about Prime Minister Blair, deeply troubled. Wynton had responded immediately and emphatically with a stream of profanity, howling expletives directed at the incompetence and coldness of America's political leadership, shockingly on prominent display in the pathetic response to Katrina as well.

Just before we reached our hotel we passed Holland Park, and I recognized its name, remembered that was where my parents lived for several months when my dad had some kind of fellowship and a leave from his church. It was right after I was married, my wife and I living in a walkup in Providence, Rhode Island, while she finished college and I taught at a small public school. I remembered how filled with expectation my father was when they returned that winter; we met them at Logan Airport, went out to eat somewhere, and he talked glowingly about the future without once saying anything about the present.

There would be more of what my father invariably referred to in his letters as "new days." Right up to the morning that my mother drove him from the Berkshires to the airport in Albany, I think he somehow thought she would join him in North Carolina. Even after she had moved to Northampton, he was still writing her, begging her to change her mind, but by then she was beginning what became after much pain a new life for herself, and for us.

I had been thinking about my mother during the last encore in Birmingham, when Wynton played *Embraceable You.* Though she loved best the Rodgers and Hammerstein she used to sing with my father accompanying on the piano, my mother used to perform Gershwin, too. Having been invited after prolonged applause to the front of the stage by the maestro, who stood off to one corner, his hands at his sides, his body motionless, Wynton by turns soft and loud, high and low, always clear, cutting the air around him, then caressing it, *became* the music, which in turn became the comfort to someone's sorrow, the celebration of another's happiness, even or perhaps especially the other musicians also still on stage, who listened with a rare attentiveness if not awe.

Taking the train from London's Gatwick Airport up to Birmingham on the day of the concert there, I had gazed out the window at the farms we passed, people on the platforms at stations we sped through, rain on the streets and on the spires of Coventry Cathedral, which was bombed in World War II and then partially rebuilt. As I looked out from my hotel window the following morning, at what I could see of the old industrial city, and with the music from the night before still playing in my head, I thought also about my daughter and how she sounded when I called her before my plane left, the hope I heard in her voice. She'd finished her sophomore year of high school on the honor roll and over the summer had worked extra hours at the bakery where she'd been employed part-time, on and off, since eighth grade. She'd passed a very difficult figure-skating test and was, she said, "taking a break" from that longtime activity. She had learned to drive and earned her license on the first try, something she was very proud of.

Roger dropped us off at our London hotel with good wishes for the concert, which he regretted he would miss, he told Wynton, "but I hope to attend the one in Scotland," he said. Leaving tomorrow morning, I'd be home by then; tonight was my last gig.

My room wasn't ready, but Wynton invited me to share his while I was waiting. He also loaned me his cell phone, because it had an international connection, so I could call my family. There was a Billie Holiday tune he wanted me to hear, and he repeatedly played one phrase, *And when we want to dance, we dance.* Smiling, he sang the line himself as he hit the button on his remote to go back to it again.

"See what she does there, how the whole vibe changes," he said. Then he played it once more.

The hotel phone rang and Wynton took the call. I left him and used his cell phone to make another call. When I was finished I could not hear anything from his room, so I poked my head in. Wynton, it appeared, had fallen asleep.

"What you saying, Swig?" he said, without opening his eyes.

"I traveled with you all over the world to hear this music before I understood it didn't matter where I was."

"Y...yes," Wynton said. "I keep trying to tell the cats, the music's internal."

"Well, I don't think you can teach someone that, I mean by telling them. They have to discover it...Anyway, I thought I'd go check if my room's ready. I'll see you later."

Clearing, the London sky had invited the sun to make a rare appearance that afternoon, and around four o'clock, after a solitary lunch at an Italian place around the corner from the hotel, I decided to walk to Royal Albert Hall, where the chorus, augmented by additional singers for a performance in such a large space, was supposed to be having a pre-concert rehearsal with the composer. But when I arrived at the legendary venue the chorus was singing without Wynton—without orchestra or jazz band, too; the only accompaniment was from a piano, played by one of the singers who was reading off a roughly transcribed reduction of the instrumental parts. I took a seat near the stage, where one of the orchestra's percussionists was setting up the array of instruments she would be playing during the performance, and then I wandered out into the main lobby, separated from the auditorium by a carpeted hallway lined with photographs of past performers: Elton John, Liza Minelli, Rudolf Nureyev.

Through a glass doorway I could see across the street a restored monument to Prince Albert. The late light reflected off the gilded statue of the prince and the surrounding ornamentation.

I walked up a flight of marble stairs, where another lobby led to another set of stairs. I kept climbing, level by level, until I had reached the last, which opened up to a near ceiling-height area that all but encircled the perimeter of the huge hall. Wynton, I observed from my high perch, had at last arrived at the rehearsal. I followed along the rotunda-like walkway until I reached a kind of balustrade that prevented me from continuing around to what would have been the upper rear of the stage. From this spot I could see and hear the singers right below. Wynton had immediately gone to work with them on the a cappela section he had added after the New York premiere of the work, when *All Rise* had been a millennium commission of the New York Philharmonic. Then he moved to the climax.

"*Zum…Zum…*It's got to have a sound to it like a rattlesnake who just bit you, it's got to catch our attention," he said. Each time he stopped the chorus with another comment, he used some kind of similar analogy to make his point. He smiled when the chorus got it right, sort of shook his head and sighed when there was a mistake. He was dressed in a suit, not the one in which he would perform in a couple of hours, after a hurried meal in his dressing

room, where he also gave a young boy a pre-concert trumpet lesson, but certainly something appropriate if he were making a presentation somewhere, meeting the Queen perhaps.

*Look beyond, look beyond, higher. Look higher, look higher and
higher*...As the music echoed in the vast expanse of Royal Albert
Hall, I heard within myself a different note, far off and then closer,
like a voice coming from a well, and then other notes, coming toward me and then through me, off me, as if the sound were an actual thing, not simply resounding but rebounding. With my eyes
closed I tried to see the source of the sound, but only the reflection
of my eyes stared back at me, or so it seemed.

I wasn't there, of course, but when my parents lived those several months long ago in Holland Park, my father had talked his
way into trying the Royal Albert Hall organ, the pipes of which
now formed a backdrop to the scene before me. It was my mother
who told me about this years later. She and whoever let them in
were the only other people in the building when he played some
Bach, a little Franck, maybe some Buxtehude, she thought but
couldn't remember.

I closed my eyes again, imagining that moment. Once he was
at the organ bench, it was as if nothing else in his life really existed,
let alone mattered. All the things he could not control in his life—
lack of money, lack of authority, his children's ambitions, his wife's
needs, his friends' demands—were put in abeyance, subservient to
the seduction of those black and white keys and the magical buttons and knobs called stops that in an instant could change the
sound of a note from flute, say, to trumpet. At the girls' school
where my father taught music after he resigned his post at the
Buffalo orchestra, his students used to call him Uncle Hans, still
called him that when they had grown up and, getting married,
asked him to play the music at their weddings. There was one
march in particular, something he had written himself, that most
of them requested. Had he played it, too, that day here in Royal
Albert Hall?

As the chorus below me continued its rehearsal, I heard in my memory the notes of that march. With my eyes still closed, I saw the beginning of what I hoped was a smile on my father's gentle face. How I wished I had been able to reach out and touch that face a last time, after he fell that distant August night in North Carolina. Stern, his eyes were no longer light blue but green, then black like a thundercloud before a storm, followed finally by forgiving gray and then, once again, a tender blue. Suddenly all color left them, they were white, there was an intense white light obliterating everything…And now in my head I heard his voice calling my name from somewhere down in this very deep well, a long way down—a long way down from this high balcony where I stood. I imagined that depth as part of a line, in the way generations stand under or behind other generations, and when finally I opened my moist eyes, I felt momentarily dizzy and fell to my knees, had to use my hands to break the fall…*Look higher, look higher and higher*…And I said to myself, "How lucky I am! Now, at last, let me use these hands to make something, the echo of his ambition, accomplishment, heartbreak, and love, to share the feeling of what he heard that was beautiful, not somehow but triumphantly."

III

Walking Swig

1

TO HEAR SWIG TELL IT—as best as I can reconstruct from his endless digressions and many details—long ago, in his younger and more vulnerable years, on the day before he left for Phoenix on a magazine assignment, two people were killed and seven injured in a three-car accident. Recording these losses, Swig was able to list only the victims' names, addresses, and ages in the weekend roundup, because information in the police report was so sketchy. He had a question about whether one of the deceased, a five-year-old boy, had actually lived in the newspaper's circulation area. Nevertheless, when he had finished writing the roundup, Swig noted the child's name and a brief description of the accident in the year's Fatalities/Automotive log book. Later, he discovered that someone had crossed this out. Written in pencil in the left margin were the words, "Not local."

That afternoon in Conway, on a walk after work, Swig saw a pickup truck parked along the road. Two boys, standing on the other side, were removing snowshoes. They'd put the snow-shoes in the back of the truck by the time Swig reached them. One of the boys was now holding a rifle.

"Any luck?" Swig asked.

"Not us," said the boy with the rifle. "But my brother got one."

The others were coming down the hill—another boy and a man. They were both walking on snowshoes. The boy carried a rifle and a plastic bag. The man carried a camera, hanging on a shoulder strap. Before they climbed the barbed-wire fence, the boy stopped, opened the plastic bag, and dumped a rabbit from it, onto the snow along the road. The blood from the rabbit colored the snow red.

The next day, heading west, Swig's plane crossed the southern shore of Lake Erie, starting at the eastern tip, and below him, as far as he could see, the surface of the lake was covered with giant shapes of white ice, lining the American and Canadian shores except in the spot where the lake narrowed and formed the Niagara River. Next to the mouth of the river, with the lakescape of ice stretching before it and a white wisp of clouds obscuring the outline of its downtown buildings, Swig saw the place where he had grown up. The plane was quickly out over the middle of the lake, and he had to strain his neck to keep in view the image of the frozen city. The ice in the middle of the lake had broken in places, and the water in between the pieces formed irregular, bluish outlines. Soon, this was all he could see.

Swig looked at his watch. It had been his father's watch; his father's parents had given it to him when his father had graduated from high school, and Swig's father had given it to Swig.

"I guess I've got time to order another drink," he thought.

Swig liked to play mathematical calendar games in his head by computing a date as the midpoint between two others. He thought of each day as the terminal point of some previous projection and the germination of another. July, for example: equidistant intervals separated the present from the beginning and end of events whose time spans fell within a larger present, summer. Early the month before, the bean sprouts appeared in the garden, the following month there were still beans to pick; the first crop of hay was cut in June, the second in August; the water had been warm enough to swim in for several weeks and would continue to be so for several weeks more.

The contemplation of this seasonal myriad, on a hot, humid day in July, could be intoxicating and falsely illuminating. Upon this heady sense of ceaseless sun, Swig had, more than once, staked a private illusion of immortality.

"It's warm. When I got off the plane, everyone at the airport was in shirtsleeves."

"Amazing."

"And when you travel around, there are orange trees growing in people's yards. And along the sidewalks at the airport there were palm trees."

"How was your flight?"

"The leg to Chicago was smooth. And we went right over Buff. You could see the whole city, up against the end of the lake. Did my parents call?"

"No. But you got a postcard from your father."

"Saying?"

"Just a card—'Hi, How are you?'"

"Tomorrow morning I have the interview. And in the afternoon a ballgame."

"I miss you."

"Me, too. I'll call again tomorrow."

Waiting to cross the street near the motel, Swig saw a girl wearing a tee shirt, standing on the other side. The light changed, and they began to walk toward one other. As they came closer, Swig could see two words, printed in blue lettering across the front of the girl's shirt, the alignment of the letters changing as her breasts bounced while she walked. The two words were *All American*.

A woman entered the restaurant and sat down near Swig at the counter. She was about forty years old, had scraggly blond hair, was wearing black slacks and a red and white cotton shirt with a very low-cut collar, and in one of her hands she was holding a single red rose. A waitress, who looked about ten years older than the woman with the rose, placed a glass of water and a menu before the woman. The woman laid the rose on the counter, next to her glass of water. She studied the menu briefly, then picked up a black purse and took from it a small tin case. She pulled the top of the case off and, with a thumb and index finger, pulled out an unfiltered cigarette. She placed the cigarette between her lips, heavy with lipstick the color of the rose, lit it, and smoked.

"Funny," thought Swig. "She looks like someone I saw on the plane." The waitress returned.

"Poached eggs," said the woman, exhaling cigarette smoke.

"And how do you want them done?"

"I don't give a damn."

"Oh," said the waitress. Then, with only the slightest pause, "That's a lovely rose you have."

"Today's Phoenix receives part of its drinking water through canals built on the site."

Swig hated museums, and he found it impossible to concentrate on what the guide at this one was saying. He lagged behind the group and fought the desire to pick up one of the rocks from a ruined wall—an old cellar? a storeroom for maize?—and throw it into the canal. That canal couldn't be for drinking; the water was muddy. Crops, maybe.

On the other side of the canal, beyond a field, a water tower stuck up into the air. Next to the water tower was a factory. Swig could hardly believe they were almost in downtown Phoenix. Not many blocks away were the downtown stores. And over there was the airport—close enough that he could see, beyond the bank of another canal, planes the shape of gigantic arrows, taxiing on the runways.

Every person at the bar was drinking a margarita.

"What'll it be?" asked the bartender, who was wearing burgundy shoes, burgundy pants, and a burgundy shirt.

"What are they drinking?" Swig asked.

"Doubles." One or two of the dozen faces looked up. "It's a better deal than two singles."

"Guess I can't go wrong. A double."

The drink came in a glass large enough to hold a milkshake. Swig lit a Marlboro and studied the menu. Tortillas. Enchiladas. Hamburgers. Mexican salad with choice of dressing (French, Russian, Roquefort). No waitress appeared, so Swig opened the newspaper he'd bought. The Phoenix Suns were playing the Boston Celtics in Boston. Eleven men had been flown across the country to throw a ball through a hoop. *Many of the canals had taken years to build.*

"It wasn't like a regular game. When someone made an error, the game was stopped for discussion of the play. The weird thing, though, the place is almost a neighborhood park, and most of the neighbors are old. Bonnie?

"They live nearby, in these developments with ten-foot walls around them, and each single-story house has a double carport— one space for a car, one for a golf cart. And people drive them right into the ballpark. The field is below ground level, in a kind of a bowl, so the fans in golf carts park them behind the last row of seats, and that's where they watch the game."

"Do you have a Hertz Number One Card?"

"I do."

"How long will you be using the car?"

"Just today."

"And where will you be returning it?"

"Here."

Swig opened his wallet and took out the yellow and black card. He kept it below the blue Visa, above the gold Shell. As he placed the card on the counter, the Hertz clerk finished filling out the form, to the accompanying hum of a computer printer. Above the yellow and black of her blouse, in the V formed by the front of her collar, the Hertz clerk's skin, tan the color of the canal water, seemed to stare at Swig as though it were disembodied. Then the face that went with the blouse and skin looked up. A smile.

"Been to Phoenix before?"

"I wonder," Swig began to say, but was interrupted.

"Here are your keys. You have a blue Grand Prix. The car is in the lot off the door at the end of the building. Have a nice day."

A car was parked at the corner. Two children were playing near it, on a recently planted lawn in front of a lime-green ranch house. Unused and discarded construction materials were piled at the end of the driveway. Another house was going up next door. Across the corner, the street continued for another two hundred feet or so, then stopped. There was no line, no barrier—just scrub brush and dry, very sandy soil, stretching out unbroken to a hill, half a mile away. The hill was covered with the same kind of semi-vegetation, but there were paths that looked like playground slides crisscrossing it. Motorcycles? Dune buggies?

Getting out of his Grand Prix, Swig turned his head in the other direction, toward the city. He could see a sort of rim where the downtown was, and a few buildings higher than the rim. Beyond this, and to either side, forming a giant crater in which the city seemed cradled: more hills—mountains really, but from such a distance they appeared unforbidding. Swig had seen a postcard at the gift shop in the motel that depicted these mountains with snow on their peaks. No snow today. Hot sun and a wide sky and an insect buzz from the brush. Swig felt far from home—not local.

Back on a main road, Swig stopped across from a mall, at a place between a McDonald's and an Exxon called The Goods. A sign in the window said, SUNDRIES AND NECESSITIES. Swig bought a pack of Marlboros—his second of the week, but he'd stop again when he got home—and stood for a minute before the magazine rack. He wondered whether magazines were classified as sundries or necessities. The man behind the counter was waiting on someone else, so Swig ignored the cardboard sign on which had been printed in black crayon, "This is not a library," and opened a magazine.

Swig's concentration was broken when a voice behind him said, "You opened it, you bought it."

"Right," said Swig. "I was just going to get a couple more." He selected *New West* and *The New Republic*, put the other magazine between them, added a newspaper for good measure, and returned to the counter.

"Let me have a few of those postcards, too," Swig said.

"Which ones?"

"Oh, any. You choose."

Still dark and Swig was on the john for the third time during the night. What had he eaten? Each time he had awakened, the gas pains had worsened.

"Why didn't I remember the Lomotil?" he asked himself, and the medicine, the concept of it, took hold of his imagination. He could think of nothing else as he passed some more gas. Then, still partially stooped over and clutching his pajama bottoms—he'd lost the drawstring—he hobbled into the bedroom where, having miscalculated the time in the east, he telephoned Bonnie, who was fast asleep.

Renting a car again would be unnecessary; Swig decided to hitchhike. It was just after noon and, though he hadn't yet had anything to eat, he felt a lot better. He had slept until eleven.

Now, along the edge of the highway, Swig walked backward toward downtown, his right hand extended from his body with his thumb up. He walked quickly. A misty rain was wetting his hair and forming a filmy dampness on his sweater. Swig walked past a mall, its parking lot crowded with the cars of midweek shoppers and workers on their lunch breaks. When he reached the end of the parking lot and still had not received a ride, he stopped next to a sign for a bus and took the first one that came along.

Past stores and small factories, an occasional home and an exhibition hall for cattle shows, Swig rode into the main part of the city, where businessmen in business suits crossed the streets at corners and one man, wearing a cowboy hat, passed out leaflets advertising free drinks from four to six at the opening of the newly remodeled Cactus Show Bar. Even at this time of day, in the business district where Swig got off the bus, the city seemed only incidentally *there*. Was it the newness of so many of the buildings, or was it some expectation that Swig had brought, some sense that there ought to be a stagecoach coming in any minute from Wyoming or Nevada or wherever stagecoaches came from, and instead there were only these buildings with countless windows and the big cars and new pickup trucks?

Swig consulted the map that had come with the Grand Prix, pointed himself in the direction of the train station, and began walking again. By chance, after several false turns, he finally found the right street. What looked on his map like a large railroad yard with multiple spurs branching into a large station was in reality two lone tracks passing by one platform adjacent to a station of a size Swig associated with the scale of stations along the commuter runs into New York City.

A small, rectangular, red, white, and blue Amtrak sign was pasted on the entrance. The door was unlocked, but there was no one inside on the wooden benches. At one end of the waiting room a man in street clothes sat in a small, lighted office behind the ticket window. He was reading the newspaper. Near the ticket window was a sign that explained the schedule. One passenger train passed through Phoenix each day, one day traveling east, the next day west, the following day east, and so on. Curious—how long was it until that day's train came through?—Swig looked at the watch his father had given him.

The face and the watch mechanism were gone. What Swig saw was a watch band holding an empty watch housing. Swig looked below him, around his feet, then behind him, at the space between himself and the door: nothing. He ran to the door, opened it, and looked along, across, the sidewalk: nothing. He felt inside all his pockets, turned down the sleeves of his sweater, and checked inside the cuffs of his pants: nothing. Mentally, he retraced his day, trying to remember the last time he had looked at his watch: no specific recollection.

He began walking slowly to the place where he had gotten off the bus.

"It wasn't a very expensive watch," he said to himself as he looked at the sidewalk before him, along the curb beside him— looked with difficulty, the difficulty of seeing clearly through the wetness in his eyes that he could do nothing to lose.

"I called the bus headquarters. I even called the manager of the mall." Swig was talking at the pool to a young woman he had named Dulcinea, a magazine sweepstakes winner from Ohio whose group had just returned from the Grand Canyon.

"I'm sorry you lost your watch," she said. "I really am. But could we change the subject? I mean, what else is there to say?"

Nothing, Swig thought. Nothing at all. And he cursed his foolishness for having spoken. Nevertheless, though he did not tell her this, he felt less upset for having said something. What he felt now was an emptiness; then he would think about something else and be fine until, out of habit, he looked again at his wrist, and the emptiness would return.

"Were there cactuses at the Grand Canyon?" Swig asked, looking at the lone cactus. Pool patio, pale motel wall: what did it matter what her answer was? Swig turned and observed that, between the top of her bikini bottom and her navel, hair from her pubis extended in a narrow width. Sweat beads commingled here with suntan lotion, and the same on her chest, though there was no hair there. "It could have been your watch," he thought. *That's a lovely rose you have.*

That evening, Dulcinea said, her group would be visiting Scottsdale for an event listed in the Sweepstakes Winners' Book as Shopping Spree. Swig went to a last ballgame, part of his magazine assignment.

Friday, mid-morning: "Four hours ago I was taking a last swim. Four hours from now I will be halfway home." Good thing he had brought a coat; Bonnie said there had been more snow—the January thaw was over. Here, at the airport, new groups of sun lovers were arriving regularly, to cadenced announcements over the public address system.

Now—what was that music? Swig turned from where he stood at the souvenir counter—miniature cactus, miniature adobe homes—and saw, coming along the concourse, half a dozen unusually tall men. On his shoulder, one of the men carried a very large boombox. As the men passed near Swig's spot, Swig recognized the song, "Everybody Dance," nice chord progression, nice *do-be-do-be-do-be.*

A young boy at the magazine rack said to the woman next to him, "Hey, Mom, it's the Phoenix Suns!" The boy bolted for autographs.

Swig put down on the counter the watch he had been examining.

Before the mouth of the river, the lakescape of ice stretched out before it and a white wisp of clouds obscured the outline of its downtown buildings. Swig saw his father, sitting at the head of the dining-room table, reaching into his suit-coat pocket during noon dinner on a Sunday in July, saying to Swig and his brother, "I've got three box seats to the double-header today. Anyone want to come?"

Over the loudspeaker came an announcement for a flight to Chicago, boarding at Gate Number 2. By now, even in California, people were at work, while back east the work day was not yet done—in fact, the newspaper Swig wrote for was just being delivered, and Bonnie was teaching her last class of the day. A front-page, wire-service story in that day's paper, which Swig would not read when he got home because he had already read it in Phoenix, reported that over the recent holiday period there had been an increase over the same period the previous year in the national suicide rate.

Two boys, standing on the other side, were removing snowshoes.

Successfully, Swig checked in and proceeded quickly to Gate 2. In about the time that had elapsed since he had lost his watch, he would be awakening on a Sunday morning, a Saturday of being back in Conway already over, Bonnie still asleep beside him, his world in its familiar place—unless the plane crashed, he thought, as he said shalom to this city where, in just one morning, he'd seen seven suns, including the one that rose now—*her breasts bounced while she walked*—across the sky, and shone so brightly on the airplane's silver wings, on the runways and range beyond them, on the distant mountains, malls, cities, people…the distant, close land and life that he wanted so deeply to possess.

2

April at last! We've been doing errands and on our way home Swig has stopped at a cemetery behind a clapboard church. He parks our S.U.V. just off the street, by a driveway that appears to wander throughout the cemetery in a kind of rough correspondence to the outline of a stone wall that rims the irregular pattern of the cemetery's boundary. Swig opens the rear cargo door, fastens the leash to my collar, and out I jump, the latest story that he's been telling me in bits and pieces all afternoon very much on my mind. It's an April story, too, about a woman to whom Swig was first introduced when he was growing up and then didn't see for nearly forty years—and in all likelihood, now, will not meet again:

Stunned by the immense space and the eerie quiet on the empty highway, I passed a dirt road leading to a grain elevator, another to an empty farmhouse. In the distance, I could see a steeple. It was Sunday morning, and I had just left the Prairie Host motel in Stanley, North Dakota, where for less than thirty dollars I had spent the night in a very small, very noisy room (someone was having a party in a room on the floor above mine). I had been to North Dakota once before, as a high school student, hoping to change the world—or a tiny portion of it— during an era when many of my older, college friends were going south to participate in civil rights marches; with a dozen other teenagers, all from the New York City area except me, for five isolated, exhilarating weeks I lived in a tent on the outskirts of a very small town located adjacent to an Indian reservation encompassing land along the Missouri River. There, as volunteers, we attempted to rebuild an old, one-room schoolhouse for use as a community hall.

Usually on our own, we worked hard, if not efficiently, settling quickly into a routine. We cooked and ate our meals in the schoolhouse, where we also slept when rain leaked through holes in our tents. One day after breakfast we poured new concrete footings for the building, which had been resting on temporary blocks since being moved from its original location four miles outside town. We worked all morning—our regular schedule—and it was hot by noon (often after lunch we went on field trips or were driven to a larger town to do laundry or shop). When the finished footings had cured, a local man helped us move the old building onto its new, permanent foundation. Boards still covered its windows, and we laboriously replaced each pane; we also repaired the roof. The work went slowly; we made frequent mistakes, but daily progress...

It's chilly, that time of day when late afternoon is turning to dusk. The windows of a house at the other end of the cemetery suddenly flicker with lights; in another house through a glass door over its rear deck we can see a tree brightly lit with colored bulbs, as if it were Christmas.

"Looking for a stone heart," Swig says, as if I knew what that was, or cared.

...A path from our tents meandered by a shanty with some old cars rusting in its yard to a graveled-over place that was a parking lot for a diner. The diner was the only electrified building past our end of town, and most people drove to it when they came. I used to drink coffee there on breaks, sometimes with a girl I liked, but often by myself. From where I sat in the diner, I could see our small tents against the back-drop of the grain elevators. The schoolhouse looked small, too; it was white, and from the diner you couldn't see that the paint was peeling. That would be many days, I had thought—painting the building. The tents were dark green, the grain elevators were gray. I sat looking out the window through the smoke of one of the Kool cigarettes many of us favored (antidotes for the smell in our outhouse). Nothing in my vision moved but the trail of the smoke as it drifted to the ceiling, where a greasy fan quietly whirred.

From the diner parking lot I walked one afternoon to the side street, hardly more than a driveway, that led to Main. At the corner I turned left and continued walking. At the end of the street, someone had placed a pole in the ground; on top of the pole was a small rectangular sign that said, on the side I faced, "Leaving Parshall." On the other side were the words, "Entering Parshall." Persuaded under that seductive sky that I was on the verge of discovering a truth, I stared down the road, which bisected the plains of wheat stretching all the way to the mysterious, enveloping horizon…

Swig starts our search by following the driveway's path, but daylight is failing and he says he's afraid we won't find what we've come for. So we cut across plots, with Swig stopping occasionally to read a name or check a date, until we find ourselves in a section of the cemetery without headstones. Standing still, we can hear the steady, humming sound of traffic from the nearby interstate highway. Otherwise, quiet.

…Years later, south of Stanley, before driving the final few miles to Parshall, I could see Lake Sakakawea, which at a branching of the reservoir forms several bays. Anxious about reaching my planned destination, I made an impulsive stop after parking my rental car off an intersection on the highway near another of the many markers signifying that Lewis and Clark passed this way. I walked along a rutted dirt road toward the water. The sky was gray. The April temperature was about forty degrees. I could hear the lapping sound of small waves before I reached the reservoir; their gentle rhythm was soothing, like a friend's touch on your shoulders.

As I bent over to let my hand dip into the water I heard in my memory the plaintive, descending interval that opens Wynton's "Superb Starling."

Back on the highway, I soon saw Parshall, set in a kind of valley formed by the roll of the plains. I could see the sweep of the prairie in every direction, the grain elevators rising on the eastern and western sides of town. Following a sign, I was so distracted by the confluence of images in my view and my mind that I drove right by the turnoff for Main Street, which ran parallel to the road I was on. I was beginning to climb out of the valley, away from the town, when I realized I'd gone too far. Continuing a short ways, I turned around in a dirt driveway where I lingered for a moment, looking toward Parshall, which seemed a disappointingly small substitute for the exalted place I had nurtured in my memory…

I like going along on these field trips, even when I don't usually understand their purpose. I'm always wondering what is happening in Swig's life, I mean the parts when we're not walking, since of course he can't tell me everything, even on a long walk. Sometimes he gives me hints in something he's written that he tells me about or even reads, but the strangest thing is that, from what I've observed and pieced together, his version of a spoken story often varies from the written, or vice-versa, and *both* versions may be different from how he spoke or acted in an actual incident in his life. Though he customarily places a positive spin on whatever he's done, he can be hard on himself, too. This can be as confusing as it may also, in some cases, be revealing.

Something in the tone and timbre of his voice makes me pretty sure this story today is important to him. But to what purpose or point?

…As soon as I finally arrived in the town—no cell service here—I telephoned Celeste from what appeared to be the only booth in town. Celeste told me she was tied up with her family at the moment, but she'd been expecting my call.

"Why don't you come by after lunch," she said. When I pulled into the yard, a man sitting on the deck introduced himself as Celeste's son-in-law.

"Celeste is inside," he said, motioning me to follow. A large woman, with graying hair and a trusting face, sat on an upholstered lounge chair near a large console television, which was on without the volume. Next to Celeste was a young boy, nine or ten years old, and between them, on a stool, was a tape recorder. "This is my grandson," said Celeste.

"Make yourself comfortable, dear," she continued. "My grandson is interviewing me for his school project," she added. Then, in reply to one of her grandson's questions: "I was born in Elbowoods. Our family lived there on land along the Missouri River." Celeste smiled frequently and didn't seem distracted by my presence. Nor was she bothered by her

grandson's lack of skill with his tape recorder. He had a list of questions his teacher must have given him, and he stuck to their order, diligently asking the next question regardless of his grandmother's previous answer.

"Why do you live in Parshall?"

"Because I'm comfortable here."

There was a calming rhythm to Celeste's voice, and a conviction so palpable I was mesmerized by its spell. The simplest statement took on a special significance, and when she invited me after ice cream and cake to return the next day, I said yes as if her offer were a blessing...

In the cemetery, the dormant grass crinkles under my moving paws. It has started to sleet. Wearing a fleece jacket and no hat, Swig shivers, but the precipitation on my furry head feels good. Swig turns up the collar of his jacket. In one of his hands he holds a small flashlight that he brought from our car's glove compartment. The batteries seem to be dying, and he has to jiggle the flashlight to make the bulb shine.

"No directions," he mutters. "She didn't tell me where to find the stone, and I didn't ask.

"David is buried there," he adds, a little portentously.

"What's to fear?" I want to reply. "What are you really looking for, Swig?"

"His daughter was away at school when he died," he continues. "Must have been nine or ten. She must be out of college now." And he sighs.

It's a sad story. And creepy, when you think about it, I mean this business about being in a cemetery—not that I care, I mean it's a good enough place to walk, though too close to the highway for him to let me run free.

Swig shakes the flashlight again to make it work. Across the street from where we parked a man raises a garage door and comes outside to his truck. He looks up, in our direction. For a moment, Swig seems worried that the man might cross the street, wondering what we are doing, but he goes back inside his garage. Someone who lives near a cemetery must be used to intrusions at all hours.

...Quilting with some friends when I returned the next day, Celeste introduced me proudly as one of her friends looked up, saying, "I remember when you were here."

"What happened to the building?" another asked.

"You remember," Celeste said, "it burned to the ground. We were at a picnic when it happened, we were over at Newtown having a picnic. It was called Atinatawisa Hall," she added, for my benefit. "The name means 'corn mother comes.' That was my mother's Indian name. Now one of my daughters has the name. My mother gave it to her before she died."

Celeste took her time as she spoke, and she looked right at me. She gave me some scrapbooks about the hall to read, and while she quilted I learned that a community group had raised the money for the building supplies that we had needed. They raised over $1,260, and we spent $976. The year after we left, there were 83 meetings held in Atinatawisa Hall.

We were sitting in the kitchen, where Celeste was warming some stew. Gradually, the friends left; one of them lived only a few miles away, near Saddle Butte, but that was a two-hour drive around Lake Sakakawea.

During lunch, Celeste told me some more about her Elbowoods family, whose land was condemned even though it was well above the highest point Lake Sakakawea would ever reach. The day after that condemnation was announced, her father suffered a fatal heart attack.

"The dam construction was devastating because it took out the heart of the reservation," Celeste said. "We were viewed as just savages, we were in their way." The government maintained that the native people weren't using their land properly, she added. "But the Indians have a different use of the land," she continued. The whole idea of land ownership was basic to an understanding of Indians, she said, pointedly using the word Indian, which she said was no less politically incorrect than Native American.

"You learn to walk through it," she said, still talking about the land tragedy. "You know better who you are as an individual. Inside your heart of hearts, you know your ancestors owned the land. You release it. You let go of the trash. And you reaffirm the feeling, and say, 'I am.'

"Life is a rhythm. You start, you hit your high points, you hit your low points, you taper down, you stop. Basically, that is how we live—in a rhythm. It's a little like the seasons, or the wind. You listen to the wind, to different kinds of wind. One of the most magical things in summer when a storm gathers is to listen to the wind come up and then listen to it taper off. It's the same as grief. You cry your loudest and no one hears it, and as the storm tapers off, you taper off…"

"There it is!" Swig says suddenly, rotating his gaze from the man in the garage to a marker near the corner of the cemetery we just passed. Atop a rectangular stone a small heart looks poised to fall from its perch. Swig shines his light at the name below:

Mary Nelson.

Beloved wife, adoring mother.

Swig sighs again, shuts off the flashlight, and remains motionless, as if he were listening to his own breathing. A branch rattles in the wind. The wind makes some oak leaves whoosh. The dark branches of maple trees by the church create silhouettes against the sky. On the other side of the church, across Main Street, the lights from a general store and gas station shine strongly enough for the shape of the church to stand out as another silhouette. Swig bows his head. My paws are freezing.

"Come on, Jack," Swig says. "We'll have to look for David next time."

We walk back towards the car, Swig with his hands in his pockets. It feels cold enough to snow, as he continues with his story, something he wrote that he seems to have memorized.

…Turning onto Main Street from Celeste's house, I drove downtown one last time, past the gateway and the Redwood Cafe, across the tracks to the vacant field where our schoolhouse was. South of town, along 1804 Highway, I stopped at a place called Scout's Cemetery, located near a town named White Shield. Buried here were scouts who served in Indian wars as well as Indian veterans of foreign wars. I read the names on some of the headstones. Young Elk. Crow Bear. Lean Bear. Closing my eyes under this deep blue sky, I heard Celeste's voice again.

"Each generation has its own isolations and trials," she had told me, "its own loneliness." Getting to the next generation was a human need, she continued, a part of what she called, "expanding yourself." It was "a touchstone," she said, my coming here. "You got a little peek at it," she concluded—this part of the world that had such a hold on her, and me. "It's one of your threads."

3

Ouch! Hate that special collar he uses on me sometimes. Hurts my ears.

Walking early, we're taking a different morning route than our usual through the woods to the seventh tee with a cut to the third fairway. Instead, we go down the street and around the corner along the main road toward the eighth green. As a rule, that's our itinerary at night, before Swig goes to bed. He says we're going this way today because he's looking for the *Times* that should have been delivered to a house where the people are away, because ours didn't come. We don't find their paper either.

As we return back along the edge of the golf course behind the backyards of the houses on our street, the spring sun rises over the trees high enough to shine on the far side of the seventh fairway without shadows. I wonder if Swig has noticed this moment's beauty, or is he too upset about the newspaper's not coming, or whatever other little crisis or grand problem is on his agitated mind this morning. He's like that, I mean one day certain he's discovered some profound reality while flipping branches that were blown onto one of the greens in a storm overnight, on another occasion impatient if I start sniffing at something by the dumpster in the parking lot across from the clubhouse or just some other animal's scent in the woods.

"Let's go, Jack," Swig says, tugging at my leash. "Do your business."

"Right," I think, looking for a good spot, "like it's a switch you just turn on or off."

I'm a little worried about Swig, whose mother is not well. It seems as if he's been under a lot of pressure lately, like he's desperately trying to find something or magically "get" someplace, and it shows on our daily walks. When he's not out of town, there are usually three—this first early one, another, longer outing around noon, and then that last shorter jaunt in the dark; someone else in the family, almost always Bonnie, comes along for my run in the late afternoon, when Swig's finishing some work or doing an errand.

Going through his notebooks the other day, he found something dated January 1992 in Princeton, New Jersey, and one of more than sixty from his first year of extended touring with Wynton. Swig's agent wanted him to write a biography about Wynton, and Swig tried, but what he wrote kept coming out as something else. I'm wondering if that is partly what's bothering him, the perceived allure of something he has instead projected as a loss.

"He could have been anywhere, he'd crisscrossed the country so many times in 25 years of touring," Swig wrote in a recent sample of what his agent immediately noted was not a biography. "Wynton took yet another call on his cell phone," Swig continued, "rummaged through one of several opened suitcases in his already disheveled hotel suite, and cursed the persistent knocking on his hotel door before putting a hand momentarily over the cell phone's speaker and shouting, 'It's open!'" The full passage continued for a few hundred more words, which he shared with me after his agent called with some suggestions to improve the "arc":

Dark-haired and soft-spoken, into the room walked one of the many women who worked behind the scenes, to remind Wynton of a phone interview he had reluctantly agreed to do in five minutes.

"How long do I have to talk?" a very tired Wynton grumped.

"Not long," replied the ever-steady assistant, whose job survival depended in part on a remarkable ability almost never to let whatever

Wynton said get to her. He liked to kid people, but sometimes he wasn't kidding; the trick was to recognize the difference between a "Fuck y'all, with all due respect," and a "Goddamnit, why do they always schedule a reception before the gig." They *was usually a clue; they* sent the wrong shirts from the cleaners, forgot the piano he required at his hotel, wrote a negative review that he said he hadn't read, let him down when he'd agreed to compose the music for a movie and then submitted it late and they *told him it couldn't be used.*

Putting a hand on one of her shoulders, Wynton pretended to sigh, asked whom he was about to talk to, and what time was the gig tonight?

"Eight," she replied soothingly.

"I'm not making soundcheck," Wynton said. That meant he'd miss the backstage dinner, too, and instead order another room-service shrimp dish or steak that he'd eat part of while ironing his shirt and talking on the phone and hanging out with the student who called him. They had met last summer at a music festival somewhere—Wynton couldn't remember the place, but he'd given the student his room number when he called a few minutes ago. They'd talk while he ate and ironed and took a quick shower, put some cream on his scalp, shaved, played for the student the Coltrane tune he was arranging, got into the beginning of a long phone discussion with someone from New Orleans and told the person to call back later, after the gig—it happened every day, a constant bombardment of questions and requests.

One of his sons would call, too, just before Wynton headed downstairs at five of eight to the waiting limo, where he would sit in the front seat next to the driver and ask him about his family while he played some slurs on the mouthpiece of his trumpet, phrasing and articulating the slurs so they mimicked his response to what the driver was telling him about this town. It was called Shippensburg, a Civil War town in the midst of Pennsylvania's Civil War country, an Amish community, too, as Wynton knew, having observed the horse and buggies they passed in the Winnebago coming into town from Pittsburg earlier in the day.

And about ten minutes later he would say hello to the stage manager, greeting him as if they were childhood friends, take the custom-

made Monette trumpet out of its black leather case, pause, eyes closed, breathe very deeply, motionless, remain silent…and then walk ever so slowly onto the stage as the applause from another packed house filled the auditorium that Wynton's performance tonight was formally dedicating. And once again in a lifetime of performing Wynton would go inside himself, find a note, a sound, that someone hearing him for the first or fifteenth time might remember one day when he or she learned some bad news or was celebrating an anniversary or birthday. Wynton, in fact, regularly received mail from people who told him their first child was born to something he played, or maybe it was the music at a grandparent's funeral service or just the accompaniment to a long drive or a late night's embrace, an early morning's awakening.

I'm worried because Swig has always talked to me, but recently his monologues have become longer and more personal, often prefaced by the latest news about his mom, who's been in and out of a hospital in Maine, where she has been living for the last few years with Swig's sister. He shares secrets on our walks and frequently asks me something I wish I could answer or forgets to give me some crucial information, like who David was ("a visionary," he told me later; "he had a dream to create a kind of paradise in the wilderness—a golf course—and the dream lived, but he did not"). He tells me about his childhood, talks a lot about golf and music—strange combination—and is forever analyzing some "fine" distinction. I want to tell him to relax a little bit, not to think so much. I want to suggest he take it down a notch when he talks or writes about Wynton. I want to remind him to look around, to see where we are, to listen—this morning, to the crunch his footsteps make on the frosted fairways. I feel at such times that it's not fair that I can only bark or wag my tail and must play along with this fiction that *he* is walking *me*. Weird, that an illusion of such control would give him any satisfaction.

Whatever. As I've had to learn and relearn countless times to tell myself, "C'est la vie d'un chien."

4

Cloudy, gray morning. I'm ready to go out before Swig's finished the paper. We cut down across the lawn toward the woods and take the path along the seventh fairway. I do my stuff almost immediately, so Swig steps over some branches, jumps the trench that the former groundskeeper dug as a rainstorm runoff, and we're on the frozen ground just in front of the seventh tee.

Unlike yesterday, when it was so sunny, there's no wind, and soon Swig seems to realize he's worn too many layers. Nothing he can do about it, unless he strips, but that would be poor golf etiquette. And chilly for a human in this temperature. We walk past the seventh tee, around the tall pine trees where guys in the summer often take a leak, and continue down the rough that borders the third fairway. The grounds crew, still just two men until the weather warms, was working here yesterday afternoon, clearing winter debris, but there's no one out this early other than Swig and me. He picks up a few branches that the crew didn't get to, stops while I do a second pee, and we cut over toward the second fairway where I see another branch the grounds crew missed. Would make a good chew, but we keep moving.

Raw, cold wind in the afternoon, when we follow the evening route that we took yesterday morning, with Swig collecting random items of litter that "jerks" throw from their cars and trucks, some of them shouting, "Fore!," as they drive by. Swig mutters about this, though I've noticed he doesn't always do a perfect job of cleaning up a mess I've made. He carries a plastic bag for this purpose, but sometimes if no one's looking he just grabs a stick to poke the stuff under some dead leaves or a bush.

During the "off season," as the golfers call it, our litter patrol takes the place of our summer-long search for golf balls, which we find sometimes by the dozen on busy days, a habit Swig blames on the late, longtime pro at the golf club. At the age of 90, Swig says, and with a bad hip, the old man would have been out on a chilly day like this, even though it would have been hard for him to walk down the hill in front of the first tee without slipping.

The course, which Swig says the old man told him he first played in 1928, when he was eighteen, is empty today. It's been an open winter, with little snow, but the greens have been "off limits" since early November and the fairways are still thawing.

In the more than seventy years that have passed since the old man, just out of high school, first came here at the invitation of the previous pro and shot 66, whatever that means, there have been a number of changes made to the nine-hole course. I've gleaned that most of the improvements—the extension of the second and third holes from par threes to par fours, new bunkers on four and five, new tees for six and eight—took place under the old man's jurisdiction, because in 1943 he succeeded the pro who'd given him that initial invite. The old man kept the job for 35 years, until 1978, after which one of his six sons took over. That was more than thirty years ago, but the old man never really retired. Even after being told at the age of 87 or 88 that he couldn't operate the cash register any longer, he drove the fifteen miles or so from his home to the course, stopping along the way at a golf range a friend ran and another course where another son was then the pro.

Clean shaven, the thin, silver hair on his square head cut short, the old man at this time of the year typically wore corduroy or khaki pants (sharply ironed at the crease), a turtleneck, a bright colored sweater, and a golf jacket with the crest of our "semi-private" club or the exclusive Congressional Country Club in Chevy Chase, Maryland, where yet another golfing son was a member. On nippy days he might be carrying a pullover cap in one, mittened hand and a Callaway Great Big Bertha driver in the other. In his front pants pockets he would have stuffed a dozen yellow golf balls. One of the rear pockets contained a comb and a white handkerchief, the other an object he called his best friend. He was fond, Swig explains, of such expressions.

"Like I tell my son," he would say, "that's your best friend, what you keep in your ass pocket." He meant your wallet.

He never hit a ball from the first tee, even on a day when the course was closed and no one would have seen him do it.

"Christ," he would say in his squeaky, mellifluous voice as he shook his head, his smile changing suddenly to a frown, "that's for the members. I'm just out here having a walk, for Crissakes."

When the golf carts were in storage and he had to walk the course, he used the Big Bertha driver as a cane to keep his balance. It was a brand new Big Bertha, on loan from his son at the other club. He followed something of a path that cut diagonally across the hill in front of the first tee, and after reaching the bottom would stop by the wire fence that used to separate the right side of the first hole's rough from a small pasture not part of the course. He walked through an opening in the fence to the adjacent field, where he began the daily ritual of looking for lost golf balls and, in short order, working on his golf swing.

No one at the club, not even his son, knew how many golf balls the old man found in the more than two decades that passed after he relinquished his post as club pro, nor how many of them he had hit. But his legend lives today in the gossip of several generations of golfers. What Swig remembers is the old man's kindness to his, Swig's, children, two of whom received free lessons he hopes they'll remember for the rest of their lives.

Upon his retirement, the old man started playing golf every Thursday in a traveling foursome that visited courses where his PGA card got his group free greens fees. In return for sharing this perk, his friends were expected to treat him to lunch before the round. They also stopped for a drink afterwards, and the old man would order a Manhattan, his preferred cocktail and only indulgence since he'd given up dancing at nightclubs after his marriage.

As a young man he liked jazz, and he spoke with familiarity and feeling about his favorite musicians. Conservative in his views and outspoken about his respect for the often irrational rules of golf, he could be surprisingly progressive in his thinking about change in the game. Long before it became popular to say so, he was a huge fan of the pre-scandal Tiger Woods. But he could also be humorously profane at the club, cursing under his breath a person he thought had crossed him.

Practicing at this time of year in the fading light of a quiet afternoon, he would have taken off his mittens, reached into the pocket of his jacket, and pulled out a few balls. Then he'd have thrown the balls in the rough (so as not to take a divot in the fairway) and traded the mittens for a pair of thermal gloves. He'd make a few half swings with the Big Bertha, loosen something in his shoulders with a motion of his back and head, and address the shot. He would repeat this ritual until he'd hit about a dozen balls, and then, upon retrieving them, began the process all over again, going in the opposite direction, back toward where he'd started. It was never too early, he often said, to get a start on the next season.

"You ought to be practicing, too," he would needle Swig, whenever we saw him. "Here, let me see you hit a few," he'd add, handing Swig his seven-iron while I scrounged for some mulched grass to snack on.

"Christ, you're stiffer than a dead man," he'd say, as Swig tensed his forearms before taking his backswing. "Loosen up, for Crissakes."

It sounded a lot like advice I keep wanting to give Swig myself.

5

Away for several days a while back, ostensibly to cover a golf tournament at a famous place by the ocean, Swig quickly succumbed to the siren seduction of the sea air. I know this as soon as he begins talking about his trip, and it's not the first time this has happened. Invariably—inevitably?—he finds himself at odds with the stated purpose for his presence at an event or a gathering. Certain of his reason for committing to something, clear about the job he is to do, he time and time again takes a detour, confounding those around him and making things difficult for himself when he must account for his actions afterwards. As I understand it, this pattern of behavior began long before I came onto the scene, and it persists despite the imploring of Swig's friends and the demands of the presumably well meaning—he would probably say unimaginative—people with whom he has sometimes worked.

"At night, walking on the beach," Swig tells me about yet another, earlier trip this one has reminded him of, "you would have loved it, Jack. It was a short walk from the Days Inn, where I was staying. Across the dark tree-lined street, the lights from windows in the hotels and condos along the other side seemed beckoning, especially the brighter lights toward the newer area of town called Coligny Plaza, where there was a boardwalk that connected the sidewalk to the beach. College-age students played beach volleyball there in the daytime, the well-tanned guys mostly wearing bathing suits cut like boxer shorts and the young ladies in bikinis, most of them, though every so often there was one with a thong."

Swig seems a little tired as he talks; his flight was delayed, and he didn't get home until after midnight. The more he talks, the more I get the sense that he's practicing a piece on me, as if he's writing it while we walk, or maybe remembering one he already reported.

"Along the Atlantic Ocean in many towns they have bylaws now prohibiting thongs, or bylaws being considered for adoption." I have no idea what a thong is but let him continue. "In Palm Beach there are no thongs. In Palm Beach, someone told me, there was a woman who used to wear a thong and no top while she sold hot dogs from a cart at a street corner. So they banned thongs.

"You never see thongs at a professional golf tournament, Jack, only the suggestion of them, only the *promise*, as you walk along some well cut fairway at Hilton Head, with the leaves from the many trees so thick and expansive that they were recently trimmed back. Some of the greens had been getting too much shade and there was hardly room to shoot at the pins with certain pin placements, because of the trees that were also making the fairways very narrow.

"Walking along one of the fairways earlier one day, the South Carolina sun hot like our summer sun here and the flowers out, with palatial homes facing so many of the fairways, and everyone who walked by them following a group of golfers on the course, looking tremendously healthy in the sunshine, many of the men wearing Bermuda shorts and the women in pastel-colored short-shorts and sneaks and white socks with the tops turned town …*here* was a kind of promise, a silent pact that golf was being watched because it gave shape and purpose to this day-long prelude to procreation in paradise."

Swig says he knew this was not what his editor was expecting.

"Good," I want to tell him. "No one but the winner of the tourney really cares about the winner's score. Why don't you write *that*?"

I'm sure I would have liked the beach where Swig was walking—alone, he says, the water calm that night, tide out. If he had turned right and walked for several miles, he tells me he would have come, eventually, to the center of the resort, Harbour Town. But he had no idea what breaks in the beach there were, no certainty that the beach stretched without danger all the way to the resort's golf course. He walked a long ways on the wide beach, and the lights where he thought there should be condos by the shore were so numerous that he guessed correctly he must have come to the Hilton, "quite new looking, multi-storied, and laid out in such a way," he explains, "that from my perspective on the beach, it seemed all the rooms were somehow pointed at the water."

Walking toward those lights, Swig soon discovered the steps to a narrow boardwalk, really a maize of interconnected boardwalks that kept people from damaging the dune grass and took him, via several paths, past pools and outdoor bars, to the back of the Hilton lobby.

"It had been difficult to get a room at the Days Inn," Swig continues (as if anyone cared!). "But the Hilton did not seem at all crowded. In fact, Jack, it seemed empty. Perhaps it was the hour."

"What hour was that?" I wonder, but of course cannot say. In his oceanic reverie I realize Swig has forgotten the time, much as I understand golfers do when they are playing at the peak of their games in what some commentator once dubbed "the zone," a word now so clichéd that its use belies the very real, often very fervent inspiration for its continued employment. I think Swig gets the connection to his writing. But getting it and doing it aren't the same. Right, Swig?

"I was hungry, Jack," Swig says, continuing his ode to Hilton Head. "I thought I might have good luck in the lounge, where experience as a freeloader has taught me you can fill yourself with enough happy hour snack food to ward off stomach pangs."

Better yet are receptions, Swig explains, as if this were something I can relate to. Once at another golf tournament he ordered a mixed drink in the media headquarters hotel and the bill, he says, was $18.95, with tax and tip automatically added in. The next night, seeing an open door by a sign that said Sponsors, he sidled into a carpeted room filled with men who had been playing in that day's pro-am, for which they or their corporate sponsors had ponied up four grand or so per "am." Carefully unpinning his media badge, which to be cool he'd learned was ideally worn waist high, with the pin placed around a belt loop, he accepted a glass of champagne proffered by a welcoming waiter and then attacked the very succulent chicken wings arrayed on a nearby table, for the most part ignored by golfers whose sponsors would also be picking up the cost of their overpriced dinners.

"Those wings rank among the finest free food I've enjoyed on the road," Swig boasts, as he reaches for a golf ball that has emerged from the ground during this first warm spell, as if it had been in hibernation all winter. "But the prize probably will always go to the tenderloin I tasted in a corporate hospitality tent I once crashed in homey Endicott, New York, which the locals pronounce, 'Endeecott.'"

At the Hilton near Harbour Town, Swig took a seat at the bar in what the hotel had named Scarlett's Restaurant and permitted himself to order a Martini, a risky selection, he admits, when you are drinking alone in a strange town. But beer made him feel bloated and wine, he thought, would not complement the very enticing table of free nachos he says he passed as he came into the room, complete with a full array of condiments.

The Atlanta Braves were playing on TBS.

The attractive bartender, Dulcinea—not her real name, he adds, as if I hadn't guessed—told Swig she was an Atlanta Braves fan.

"I've lived here eleven years," she told him. Her husband was a carpenter, she continued. She was originally from Long Island. Since moving down there she was always having visitors from up north, especially in the winter. That was fine with her, made the time pass.

The previous night at TGIF's, Swig adds, there had been a wait for a table and the hostess had told him he could eat at the bar. The empty seat he took was next to a man whose suntan and dress made him seem a golfer, but he was too old, Swig sensed, to be playing on the pro tour.

"I thought I'd seen him around," Swig tells me. "But I'd never met him before. Finally realized he was a former caddy."

"Order the New York strip," he said to Swig.

"Yeah?"

"Yeah. Order the fucking New York strip. It's a good steak. Good price.

"So what else do you want to know? You ever go deep sea fishing? Ever need a boat? Here's my card. There's my phone numbers. You can do a day, half day, a week, whatever you want. Just call me.

"Now then, order the goddamn steak. What are you drinking? Mine's a Manhattan. A Manhattan for Chrissakes. Who the fuck even knows what a Manhattan is anymore?

"This one isn't bad."

At Scarlett's, Swig tasted the Martini that Dulcinea made for him. She'd even remembered to give him an extra olive. Swig asked Dulcinea about the snack selections listed on the small menu card perched on the bar. Were there really ten jumbo shrimp in the jumbo shrimp cocktail that was listed at only $8.95?

"Yes, there are. And they're good."

She was right. Swig ordered another Martini.

Jeez.

That morning at the pro-am, Swig tells me, an amateur in one of the groups had pulled out an unheard-of 15-wood on the last hole, and the pro in the group had said, "Calibogue Sound on the left," and then, mimicking the heightened tone of a television commentator, "condos and out of bounds on the right."

Then it was nighttime on Hilton Head, the second largest barrier island in the United States off the Atlantic Ocean coast, Swig said.

Dulcinea said more people would be coming in over the weekend for the tournament.

"Where you staying?" she asked Swig.

"Days Inn."

"How is it?"

"It's okay. Service was a little slow at breakfast, so I've been walking to Coligny. Went to that place that has the all-you-can-eat buffet."

"How was it?"

"All right, I guess. I ate too much, but I walked it off. Got tired of watching other golfers, so I went and played some myself."

"Where'd you go?"

"First at a place right down the road from Harbour Town. Sea Marsh, I think it was called. Played with a couple of guys from Boston here on vacation. Played pretty well. Then I went over this evening to the Fazio course. They were closing soon, but they gave me a cart and told me I could play until dark. I almost got in nine."

Swig said goodbye to Dulcinea.

"Hope the Braves win," he said.

Swig walked back along the boardwalk to the beach and continued walking without stopping until he reached the boardwalk to Coligny Plaza. There, he stopped for an ice cream cone and then cut across the main road that intersected with South Forest Beach, along which the Days Inn was located. On a shortcut he'd discovered when he'd eaten at TGIF's, he crossed the parking lot by the restaurant and entered an adjacent condominium complex that would lead him, he remembered, to the back of the Days Inn, where he thought he might take a quick swim before going to bed.

Within minutes he had lost his sense of direction in the darkness and did not know where he was. He followed a sidewalk left, toward some lights he felt certain must be coming from the Days Inn, but the sidewalk led to a driveway that connected to the entrance to another condo property. He decided to retrace his steps but all the sidewalks and condos looked so much alike he missed the turn he should have taken and found himself, instead, on a road he had not seen before. Would this road return to Pope Avenue? Or, if he took it the other way, would he reach Forest Beach?

The panic he was beginning to feel was similar, he thought, to the sinking sensation of a golfer who has just hit his ball out of bounds and, after assessing himself with the proper penalty—stroke and distance—proceeds to hit his next ball into a thicket of bushes from which he has to take a drop and another penalty stroke. The speed at which such a disaster takes place is always stunning, much as a person in quicksand must realize with alarm that his sure footing has instantly disappeared. Swig wondered if the old man would have looked at it that way, or was this kind of analogy another symptom of the tension he brought upon himself, something more than merely being muscle-bound?

Swig decided that if he simply continued walking one way or the other on the mystery road that he would eventually come out in a place that looked familiar. He had only to decide which way to go. That made him feel a little calmer.

Telling me about this, Swig then remembered a friend whose father once owned a share of an island south of Hilton Head. Attractive to paper mills, the island was assessed and put up for sale in the early 1970s. His friend's father's share was valued at ten million dollars, of which his friend would receive one-ninth.

"Then the Arab oil embargo began, the economy went slack, and my dad couldn't sell the land," his friend told him. "Eventually the state bought it and made a park."

With the park his friend's dream died like the fireflies on that warm night. A pipe-smoking, non-golfing, tennis-playing professor, his friend had maintained he was not bitter. It was a good story, like the same friend's tale about the therapist in his second marriage, a man about 70 who had fallen in love with a woman in her 60s and they made love, his friend said, several times a week, for three or four hours at a time.

Had he heard, his friend asked Swig the last time they saw one another, what Marilyn Monroe said when she was asked what she wore to bed? Swig had shaken his head, and with a smile and a sigh his friend had told him what he said was Marilyn's answer.

"Chanel No. 5."

Having reached the end of what he could see by the sign was Cordillo Parkway, which indeed intersected Forest Beach, just as he had hoped, Swig reversed the direction of his walk. It was not long before ahead of him he came to condos and ocean on the right, his air conditioned patio room with pool view, twin double beds, free cable and wireless Internet, home on the road safe harbor Days Inn on the left.

And so, at last...to sleep...to dream...

...how the wind sounds in the trees on the range, how it sounds as you wake up and the waves in the ocean with the balcony door open, how they remind you of something, someone, a lover, a father, a stone heart...and everything goes into your life that day—the conversation over breakfast with the cute waitress, the grizzled look on the face of the fellow at the bag room whom you talk to about the day's weather, and when you ask the man matter-of-factly how he is the reply shakes you momentarily out of your shell, "wife's got cancer, don't know how long she has," and then the smell of shoe polish in the locker room, and shaving cream and shampoo on the marble sink, cigarette smoke in the bathroom and ashes on the floor of the toilet stall from the last guy who was in there, the mist over those trees by the practice green, the memory of the flight to get here, and now another round, wonder whether "it" will be there, wonder if that little stance change will make a difference, can you keep it straight on the first, just get your par and be patient?

"Swig? Swig!" I want to shout but of course cannot. Wouldn't matter, he wouldn't hear me if I could. "Listen," I want to tell him. "Maybe you're taking some of this too seriously. Maybe you need to remember that first teaching job, the one you began right after you were married, you loved those little kids from Portugal that you taught, 'Mr. V.,' they all called you, like the way Wynton's band sometimes did later; and later after you moved, the kids in the Conway elementary school where you were subbing, how you loved the walks from the Harris farm to that school, the short cut on a dirt road, then past a brook, 'heaven,' you called it when you told me."

He started writing for the local paper after being the assistant to his friend the mason, a job he'd taken after the month or two he was the business manager of a children's theater and one night he was at the troop's farmhouse and slept over, it was on a hill just outside the next town from Conway, and the next morning when he woke up, having slept on the floor, there were all these naked people walking around. The things people do.

"True story," I can still hear him insisting, like the one about the sauna some other friends had and how it was "interesting," according to Swig, to see who would and would not use the sauna.

At the college library, where he often writes, I can imagine Swig at the corner round table, first floor, he says he prefers, said table facing several windows through which he can see a large part of the lawn that leads to the art building, where Swig became friends with a sculptor who no longer teaches at the college (but who did at one later point briefly become Swig's drawing teacher). And the whole time Swig knew him (two, three years), the sculptor was working on this life-size statue Swig in his memory calls... Dulcinea...that depicted a beautiful model who would often be there posing when Swig would stop by, probably on a rainy day like this, and the sculptor would bum a cigarette from Swig as they talked, and there would be Dulcinea during all this time as well, naked, on the floor, which was part of the idea of this statue, it was purposefully very provocative. You looked at it, Swig said, and wanted to embrace it (if you were a person, I wanted to correct him). And so they would talk, Swig and his friend, while it rained outside and Dulcinea would lie there, never herself talking, bored out of her mind probably, but who knows, as he likes to say.

"You never know," I want to tell him.

6

Halfway up I-80 from Reno to Truckee I saw the first snow, a light dusting on the trees above the Truckee River...

Nice lead, Swig. Keep going.

...I had flown into Reno the day before, to see this morning a fifty-year-old professional golfer, a longtime veteran of the PGA Tour...

A little awkward, but please continue.

...a past champion of the Senior Open, he was also a successful golf course architect. It was in connection with this last activity that I was driving to the site of a new course that was being built as part of a high-end real estate development off I-80 just before Truckee, and near an intersection for Donner Pass Road...

There was a time when Swig would have written, "and, incongruously, near an intersection for Donner Pass Road," but after decades of visiting and writing about opulent playgrounds, very little of what he encounters surprises him or seems strange or out of place. Something that is not incongruous might strike him, but he now *expects* to find a beautiful new golf course under construction a short walk from the site of one of the greatest tragedies in the history of the westward movement of pioneers in the United States in the nineteenth century, a disaster in which nearly half the men, women, and children who were forced by the weather to spend the winter of 1846-47 in the High Sierra—because they had mistakenly taken what they thought was a short cut en route from Kansas to Sacramento—perished, with many of the survivors allegedly turning to cannibalism to stay alive.

It's mid-June, May having disappeared in a blur of blooms— lilacs are my fave—and travels for Swig. He's been telling me about Truckee this morning, which has reminded him of the treatment for a television series, *Summer Lies,* a kind of Cheers set at a Caribbean golf resort, which he developed a few years ago with his son. He was reading it to himself, laughing indulgently at their purple prose, before he fell asleep last night in his clothes on the couch:

Immerse yourself in a sun-drenched paradise, steeped in the rich tradition of Caribbean luxury. Indulge in a lifestyle reserved for the privileged few, reminiscent of a bygone era when ancient royalty commanded the best life had to offer. The rarest of opportunities awaits you at Eagle Cove's astonishing Black Magic Club: heavenly views exploding over lush tropical landscapes, the hypnotizing turquoise waters of the Caribbean Sea, the exquisite feeling of a long drive carrying 300 yards down a pristine fairway. Relax, knowing the gated security and pampering amenities of a world class resort second to none are now yours, 24 hours a day. What place more perfect to reflect upon your lifetime of achievement than a custom-built architectural masterpiece, nestled amongst 36 championship holes of signature golf and the tranquility that only four miles of private beach frontage can offer. Life's odyssey takes us many places. Come home to the ultimate destination. Come home to Eagle Cove.

This was some puzzling poop, and I want now to tell Swig I was a little surprised. But he's preoccupied, prattling on as if he were pitching it to the producer of the pilot. He's got the damn thing down pat, like it's part of him, and when he gets to the riff about resort golf and its seductive lifestyle giving everyone a chance to conceal the contradictions of their crazy lives, I want to say, "Like golf, like writer?"

We've stopped at the pond in the middle of the farm next to the golf course. Swig takes a seat on a picnic table that no one else ever seems to use, and he talks on his BlackBerry and checks his email while I chase frogs. I rarely catch one, but the water on this hot day feels good. Every so often I come over to the picnic table, shake the water from my coat, and sit, waiting for Swig to give me a biscuit from the stash he keeps in the fanny pack he usually brings along on these walks.

Some life.

The grass in the mowing that borders the pond on three sides is already waist high in human dimensions. An early summer breeze makes the grass sway, and the trees in the woods along the golf course side of the pond, lush with leaves, cause a swishing sound when there's a gust. Across one of the mowings, in a field planted with flowers of all colors, a young woman with black hair wearing a light blue tee shirt and black shorts weeds a furrowed row of azaleas that will soon be for sale at our local farmer's market, which I pass every Saturday when Bonnie walks me into town.

Whatever could prompt Swig to flee this blissful place for the imagined seductions of other havens so far from his home? What did he think he would discover? How, especially when his children were younger, could he have left on another assignment?

After another stop for me to pee, during which Swig keeps on talking, he tells me I'm a good boy when I'm done. So condescending. And now I have to listen to Swig explain that summer lies is a play on a golf expression, winter rules, when you can improve the position of your ball because of the poor conditions off season. I want to ask him what gives, and instead he says, talking again about Truckee, "Just when I got there, to the course I mean, I had to take a shit, Jack, you know...do my business. What an inconvenience! Flips me out sometimes to think about everyone walking around with all that shit inside.  The sacredness of life. A strange memory from childhood, coming home after Sunday church, we would stop at the corner drugstore for some cigars for my dad and some Sealtest French coffee ice cream for dessert. This one time that sticks in my memory, when we got home my dad went to the bathroom, and I had to go upstairs later to get something and it seemed like the whole second floor of the house had that strangely sweet smell when someone has taken a shit.

"Why would that stick in my memory? The same bathroom he locked himself in years later, when he said he had a gun. I remember sitting on the porch there, after coming home. It was in September, same porch where my grandmother, his mother, had been sitting maybe ten years before that—no, more like twelve or thirteen—and I was upstairs on the upper porch and dropped a box over the railing for no reason and my father rushed upstairs yelling; he hardly ever yelled, hardly ever got angry. Did I know I could have hit my grandmother with that box? he yelled, and then spanked me, last time he did that, only did it a few times, cannot remember whether he spanked me on my bare bottom but probably, because that is the way the very occasional punishment was administered in our family. When he was a boy, his father whipped him and his brother with a belt and locked them in a closet.

"All I ever really wanted to do once we were living on that Conway farm, and long afterwards, when I wrote my first book and my editor kept telling me not to talk about myself, kept saying to me that I needed to realize everyone had their problems and my job was to write about them not me…all I ever really wanted was to be certain to include Cyndi Lauper and this club that I happened on near Worcester on the drive back from Boston and the connection to the ivy on the walls of Massachusetts Hall where the university president graciously came out to greet me from his office, to welcome me, when I interviewed him, and I was sure *all* that was my story, the rhythm of those times, the weather, the music, not just the president. But I never wrote that except for the first short draft that was killed.

"'This is not what I signed up to edit,' my editor told me over lunch at the Parker House in Boston.

"Sometimes when I was feeling low I concluded it must be because I was such a terrible writer, but deep down I was *sure*, despite also realizing how naïve I had sometimes been and probably still sometimes am, that I had simply not written the real story, the snow, the air, the way the water sounded in the brook by our farm, the smell of my father's shit, the sound of my mother's voice when she sang 'All praise to Thee, my God this night' every night when we went to bed. She would come into each of our rooms and sing it with each of us, then give us a kiss goodnight."

I'm told that well before my time with Swig he was on the road more than he was home. Kauai, Santa Fe, northern and southern California, both coasts of Florida, Mexico's Baja and Yucatan, the Carolinas, St. Martin, Jamaica, Puerto Rico, Barbados, Key West, London, Barcelona...this dude got around. He played Turnberry's Ailsa course in Scotland in a cold rain, repeating the ninth hole by the seaside ruins of Robert the Bruce's castle; twice he skied Mount Hood with two of his kids in July; he teed off alone, one glorious June dawn, on a windswept, mountaintop Donald Ross course in northern New Hampshire. And almost always on someone else's nickel. "America's guest," one of his old friends called him. But who knew what he was really thinking on all those trips?

On one of his travels a few years ago, Swig flew from London to Newark, New Jersey, where he met with someone at the airport in a conference room at a frequent flyers club before boarding a non-stop flight to Honolulu. There he made a connection to Maui, where he played three rounds of golf, was a guest at a luau, and explored a nude beach, before flying home little more than 48 hours since he'd arrived. He wrote a magazine column on the plane, filing it electronically after landing at the Newark airport, which he self-consciously calls by its airline acronym, EWR, and where he'd left his car for the long drive home.

Whether or not shit is sacred, I need to take one now, but everyone's asleep. Nothing to do but sneak into the laundry room and make a deposit on the rug by the storage shelf. Maybe I can con Swig into blaming himself for this transgression, because he forgot to take me out again after all that wine he drank with dinner.

7

Long before he and his imaginary buddies made birdies and bets on a mysterious Caribbean isle, Swig sang of glory one September afternoon, one sale down and another coming soon; glory of the smile and glory of the swoon; glory of the Cutco knives, forks, and spoons. But it was the same stylized story he'd continue writing in varied format, as if that shadow, the spell he could feel but some-how not understand, kept him still in its thrall.

He can still remember the first flush, the holiday feel of sales, sales, sales; he remembers the look on the face, the trust in the eyes, and all he could think was "sign! sign! sign!"; he remembers the thrill of the close and that transcendent moment when he could say, "Dulcinea, shake hands with Cutco"; and he remembers the closed doors, the shrill refusals, and the suitcase filled with blank order pads.

He remembers the noise! At the Park Street subway entrance, the squeal of the trains made him shudder. He listened: all across the city that subterranean sound could be heard by a myriad of strangers who called Boston home.

The smell in the stairway was of old cigar butts and urine. He praised the stench! He tipped his hat to the rotting apple! In the station, the air hanging over the concrete waiting platform was hot and dirty and the collective odor of food sold in little booths mixed with the redolence of human perspiration and electric engines. People were going home from work; students were going home from school; old men and women and kids with lollipops and shoppers with plastic bags were all going home. Jockeying for po-sition, stepping on each other's feet, swearing under their breath, the figures in the maze pushed toward the tracks.

There the doors of the cars creaked open, releasing one set of passengers and taking on another. More cars, more people—a surging, bulging mass, going together, their separate ways, home in the autumn night. Home—to Cambridge and Brighton, Newton and Brookline; to Dedham, Waltham, and Quincy; and, out be-yond the asphalt necklace of Route 128 (crowded with trucks and buses and commuters' cars), home to Lincoln and Lexington and other bedroom towns.

Oh, September…

…oh, Swig, so much rhetorical cleverness, but what were you *feeling* in this saga that you've retold so many times about your col-lege days as a salesman? Cut to the ending would be my advice…

...The first days of December fooled Swig. The weather was warmer than it had been in November, but the temperature finally dropped and snow came during the second week. Skipping an afternoon class, he took the subway downtown one very cold afternoon.

As he walked the Common, only the shadows of bare trees, sleek phantom shapes on the hard, white ground, accompanied him. Near the public men's room, the noise was nearly deafening as he waited to cross Charles Street. There were no swan boats—had been none since mid-October. He sat on a bench and counted peanut shells on the frozen pond.

Swig watched the night come on, the streets slowly becoming quiet, streetlights brightening, lights in windows on Beacon Street flickering. His ears detected the nearby ambulance of evening strollers, intermittent with the sharper sound of people hurrying home from work. Chilly as he was, he began to doze, and how quiet it was, how still, when, a little later, light snowflakes started to fall, covering.

Covering his city. For in a kind of euphoria he realized he had experienced before and, years afterwards, would recognize finally as familiar, he felt he owned at least a definable portion of it. He imagined young working women and men sitting down to a meal with those lovely forks and knives and spoons he had sold them. Families, too.

"Citizens of Boston," he thought, "can you hear me? How is your Cutco? Does it gleam? Does it dazzle? I miss you all so much!"

He was shivering now and getting hungry. He stood up and began walking.

Out on Boylston Street, a pretzel vendor was standing with his hands in his pockets, jumping from one foot to the other to keep warm. In the daytime, dozens of these men did a brisk business and strangers bought a pretzel or two to snack on. At this hour, Swig could see only a few, scurrying figures on the gray, concrete walks, some holding a pretzel in one hand and clasping a coat collar with the other to brace against the wind. He could see them disappearing in the snow toward the large, dark opening in the ground below the sign, Park Street Station.

Following, he descended the stairs, which had recently been swept. Wisps of snow dotted the entrance, and the doors gave with a sudden swish as the cold air from outside pushed against the hot rush from inside the huge cavern. The station was quiet—only a scattering of people were waiting for trains. Swig continued through the first level, past the closed florist and darkened food stand, down to the lower tracks, where the subway he wanted came in. Apparently he had just missed one, because the platform was empty.

Gradually, others joined him—a young man in a herringbone overcoat, a green book bag over one shoulder; an anemic looking high-school girl in a football jacket and jeans; two old men reading the paper, cigar stubs in their mouths; an elegant woman, perhaps 60, carrying flowers and staring at the ads below the ceiling across the tracks.

Swig stood on the edge of the platform and peered down the tunnel as a single, round, white light moved toward them. The walls of the station seemed to shake as the train roared in and, with a tremendous hiss of air, stopped and opened its doors, all in one blurred instant. The engines continued running while passengers entered the bright cars, and then the doors shut in unison. The train next stopped at Charles Street where, for a shorter interval, the ritual was repeated.

Majestically, they began to cross the bridge over the river. The snow was coming down hard and the lights in buildings on Beacon Hill beckoned like the ornaments on a Christmas tree. As the train reached the crest of the bridge, it clicked over a dead portion of the tracks and the car was temporarily blackened.

It all happened so fast. Had he fallen asleep during that split second? Visions of dancing flatware pieces seized his imagination and he felt he could have lifted Beacon Hill in the palm of his hand. He wanted to return to the coffee shop and find Sophie and they'd go to the bus station and buy two tickets for New Bedford. They'd ring every doorbell in town and give everyone free wild flower guides and all the water they could drink.

Someone pushed Swig's shoulder and said they'd come to the last stop.

"Farewell!" he silently sang. "If we're both around after the next verdure, I'll see you in September."

8

"Egypt?" I'm thinking. "You've got to be kidding me." But then Swig adds that it's been cancelled. Too dangerous. He's going to make a return visit to the golf school at Stratton, Vermont, instead. Or maybe not; his plans change as often as the weather, which today is fragrant and moist. Birdsong accompanies us on our walk around the field beyond the third tee. I'm hoping Swig will spend some time later at the piano he inherited from his father. Under his father's piano bench is a soothing place to nap when he's practicing.

Reminded of his father, I remember Swig telling me about the time, years ago, when he was watching Bobby Hull warm up before the Chicago Black Hawks played the Buffalo Bisons in a pre-season, exhibition hockey game. How Swig admired the ease with which Bobby moved between and around the other players, the total command of himself and the ice he possessed. How strong he was! And friendly, smiling at Swig when he signed Swig's scorecard. No one else's signature looked as Bobby's did, Swig says, the letters twice the size of the others, the bottom of the "B" and the "H" extending past the margin of blank space on the card, so that part of his name was written right over the list of his team's lineup.

Swig held his card when he and his brother and a friend took their places for the game, which the Black Hawks would win by the score of four to two. During the third period, a few of the people in the last row of temporary seats by the ice left early, and they moved to what was their favorite spot.

"Look out!" his brother shouted at him.

Instinctively, Swig covered his eyes with his hands, still holding the lucky card, so he was unable to see the puck that missed his head by no more than a foot. But he recovered quickly, pushing himself off the back of the chair to win the race for the prized piece of cold, hard rubber that had deflected harmlessly off the wall behind him and his brother. They telephoned their father when the game was over, and while they waited for him to pick them up played catch with the puck outside in the warm night.

"How was the game?" their dad asked, by which he meant, "did you have a good time?" The car was filled with the smell of cigar smoke, and Swig rolled down a window as he showed his father the puck.

Perhaps if he had been a hockey fan, his father would have understood why Swig kept running his fingers around the side of the puck, pixilated so a player could get better traction on it with his stick. His father might also have realized how one team or even one player could control the tempo of a game by controlling the puck. And he might also have discovered something else, which for Swig was a source of his fascination with the sport. When a person did something you didn't like, you knocked him down. When his dad received the personnel committee's letter that his salary was not being raised, he was very angry, but he took that anger out on himself.

"Bobby Hull shot this puck," Swig said. "Dad, it could have killed me," he boasted.

Except for the hockey traffic, downtown was deserted, so they stayed on Main Street, past the downtown department stores and movie theaters, before turning at North Street up to Delaware, where another turn brought them to the church.

"I left some music I need tomorrow morning," Swig's father explained as he pulled into the large lot by the parish house.

Leaves still covered the branches of the giant elm trees along Delaware and behind the church, next to the parking lot. The wind in the leaves made a summer sound, but a gust of wind blowing through Swig's sweater, causing goose-bumps on his arms, reminded him that winter and the real hockey season were coming.

Swig's brother and their friend remained in the car while Swig accompanied his dad on his errand. Swig had an eerie feeling at the church so late, with the rooms of the parish house dark. Inside the huge nave the street lights from outside shone through the tall stained-glass windows, not brightly but enough to see.

Swig had put his puck in his pocket, and he was clutching it there as he and his father walked up an aisle from the chancel to the choir loft. He pretended one of the pews was an opposing player, charged it, and checked the end of the pew as hard as he could with his shoulders.

Gently touching his son's shoulders with a hand, Swig's dad startled him with his voice.

"You're going to hurt yourself," he said.

"No, Pop. That was a great play."

"Well, come on then. It's late. You have school tomorrow. And we got a call from your uncle while you were at the game. He's coming to visit."

"When?"

"He may be here already."

"How could he, Pop?"

"How could he what?"

"How could he be here that fast, all the way from New York?"

His father fell silent, a habit that Swig feared. His father could be the most gregarious man he knew, talking animatedly with everyone he met, making friends with strangers after a service, never saying no to a request for his time or help. Then, just when you least expected it, he'd get a faraway look in his eyes and clam up, as if you were supposed to read his mind or something. It infuriated Swig's mother. They'd be discussing some problem—how were they going to pay for that car repair?—and suddenly his father would stop talking. You were stupid if you didn't understand what he felt and agree with it.

"You know something?" his father finally said to Swig, as he locked the parish-hall kitchen door on their way out. "You ask too many questions."

Years afterwards, Swig wrote a story that was kind of a reply to that miserable moment in the church. It didn't mention the puck, in fact it didn't even take place in the city:

Dad parked the Plymouth by the boathouse and we loaded our suitcases in the rowboat, which was powered by a small outboard motor. It took three trips across the bay to get us and all our things over. Stars were reflected in the lake as we crossed the water. The water was clean enough to drink.

The next day, sitting on the porch of the main cabin, with the blue lake visible through the white birches, we ate breakfast: scrambled eggs and large pieces of toasted bakery-bought white bread and strawberry jam that our parents' friend Margaret made. My father spent the morning writing letters and composing an anthem for his choir at a small table he had carried out to a clear spot among the birches, just like he did in Vermont where we also spent parts of several summers. Near the table was a hammock, strung between two trees, where I read after lunch until my mother said it had been an hour and I could swim.

Cloudy by sunset, it began to rain around nine, when my brother and I were supposed to "retire." It was Margaret who used words like that.

"Gentlemen," she would say, "I think the hour has come."

"What hour is that?" I asked, already knowing the answer. Margaret never said things twice.

My feet were wet after I had walked from the main cabin. I dried them and removed the pine needles from my toes and heels by rubbing them against the bottom of my blanket. The blankets on both beds were white woolen Hudson Bays, with red, green, yellow, and black stripes. I wasn't sure where Hudson Bay was located but Charlie had told us you could get there if you kept going north—maybe as far north again as we had already come to reach this lake?

"No," Charlie had said in his high voice that almost sounded as if he were singing. "Much farther. Canada is a big country." And a cold one, I thought.

"You going fishing with us tomorrow?" my brother asked.

"Nope," I replied. "Fishing is boring."

Fish gave me nightmares. My worst dream was to be in a bathtub with a live fish. Once I dreamt that I was in a tub and a fish came out of the faucet.

Rain dripped off the roof of the bunkhouse, which smelled of fish because Charlie kept his rods and tackle box in it. On the floor, underneath the workbench, the fishing equipment was stored next to a white enamel chamber pot. My brother and I never used it, but instead opened the door and peed onto the ground.

We slept with the window by the beds open. The air smelled of pine needles and fish, whose jumps for insects made ripple sounds in the lake. I slept in the top bunk. Our parents and sister slept in the cottage at the other end of the peninsula. Margaret and Charlie slept in the main cabin, near the point. When they woke up, Charlie would make a fire in the woodstove that was in the kitchen off their bedroom. There was no stove in the bunkhouse.

Old Saturday Evening Posts with "So you Think You Know Baseball" were piled on top of an old captain's chest, which stood under the window next to the bunk beds and was filled with extra blankets. Too tired to keep reading, I tossed the volume of Reader's Digest condensed novels I'd been thumbing through down onto the chest, reached overhead, and clicked off the light. A little of the ink from the book had rubbed off on my fingers. The sharp odor of the ink mixed with the mustiness of my blanket, which smelled like mittens when the snow was wet and my mother told me it was time to stop playing in our snow fort and come inside the house to help her set the table for dinner.

My brother and Charlie were already back from fishing when I awoke the next morning. To my great relief, they hadn't caught anything.

After breakfast, I found a canoe paddle in the bunkhouse, walked onto the dock, and turned the canoe over and pushed it off the dock into the water. Then I got in and started paddling. I paddled the way Charlie *had taught me, "Indian style," kneeling in the rear of the canoe even though my knees hurt touching the wooden ribs of the canoe's frame.*

I paddled through water lilies, staying close to shore until I rounded the point and was in the open lake. The shore dropped quickly behind me as I headed toward the island. The breeze off the water smelled of pine trees, and the water, when I put my hand in it, felt warm out of the breeze.

Without hitting any rocks, I guided the canoe into the shallow water of a cove that was at the end of the island nearest the peninsula. I had traveled about half a mile. I placed my paddle in the bottom of the canoe and moved carefully to the bow where, with a short jump, I landed on dry ground. I grabbed a rope that was attached to an iron ring in the bow, tied it to a tree, and started walking away from the cove, toward the other side of the island.

Hiking uphill until I reached a clearing in a ledge that formed the island's highest spot, I stopped there to catch my breath. Moss covered parts of the rock on which I stood, and in small cracks near my feet grass and juniper grew. The lip of the ledge blocked my view of the cove, but looking straight out through the trees I could see the lake and the peninsula. My parents were sunning at the point with Margaret and Charlie. Tiny and distant, they appeared only as splotches of color—yellow, maroon, blue, and green, the color of their bathing suits, and silver, the color of Charlie's and Margaret's hair.

"No one knows I'm here," I thought. "No one can see me."

Then I realized they could see the canoe in the cove.

"But they can't see me. I'm invisible."

For over an hour I explored the island. On the far side from where I'd left the canoe, I found the campfire site at which we had picnicked the summer before. It was on a low spot of ground, almost level with the lake, but, unlike the area near the cove, it was open, unprotected by trees and facing into the prevailing winds which now sent waves lapping onto the shore. A small circle of medium-sized stones, about twenty feet from the water, enclosed the charred remains of a fire. I picked up a few flat, smaller stones that lay nearer the water and sent them, one by one, skipping out into the lake. One stone skipped six times.

On my way back to the cove, I stopped again at the high ledge, but this time I walked out close to its perimeter so I could see the cove. The canoe was rocking gently back and forth on its rope to the push and pull of the water hitting the shore. I could see sand on the bottom of the cove, but when I looked to the other side of the ledge I was staring straight down a precipice that continued into the water and made the lake seem green rather than clear or blue. I wondered how it would feel to jump off the ledge here and land in that green pool.

"I'd try," I thought, "but there are probably a lot of fish."

I took the path through the woods to the cove, slipped as I was untying the canoe, then paddled back across the lake.

"You're quite the navigator," Charlie said at dinner, "taking yourself in the canoe out to the island."

Rather than pride at those words I felt a lingering fear over the prospect of my own near disappearance, mingled with a profound sense of my insignificance. I wondered if grownups ever thought about such things.

"I might have died," I thought, while my brother and I were in bed reading. "If I had jumped from that ledge, I might have hit my head on a rock."

I awoke the next morning to the sound of rain beating down on the roof of the bunkhouse. Out the window, I could see rain coming off the upside-down canoe in clear, curved sheets.

We ate breakfast in the kitchen, where it was warm by the fire, and then my mother said we should get started if we were going to the grocery store in Dwight. My brother, my father, and I made the first trip across the bay, keeping dry in the yellow slickers Charlie appeared with from the bunkhouse. Dad told us to wait in the Plymouth, but as soon as he left to get the others, I opened the door and walked to the boathouse dock. It was raining too hard for me to see across the bay. I watched the rowboat disappear into the rain and then I stood there for what seemed like a long time, watching the rain on the lake, before I heard the sound of a small outboard motor and saw the bow of the boat coming toward me.

"I am your oldest child," I said silently to myself as my mother and father approached the dock in the boat in the rain. "So, you think you know me, think you know my thoughts, my feelings. But my thoughts and feelings are not yours."

9

Warm this July morning, and foggy. Can't see across the fairway as we walk along the edge of the seventh, back toward the tee, but I can hear the grounds crew mowing from the direction of the first green. We cut over through some trees to the second, stopping to pick up some branches that must have come down in the rain two nights ago. Swig is silent as we walk, with a big day ahead of him, which I heard him discussing on the phone last night.

The concert is at eight, but he hopes to get there with enough time to see some of his friends. He'll leave his car outside the city at his brother's, where he'll change, and then take the train in. It's his first trip in many months to a place he used to visit weekly, back when Wynton's career was more localized and he was often either playing at one of the old downtown clubs or making another recording at one of the midtown BMG studios. One July week many years ago, Wynton played the Vanguard every night, three sets, all of them recorded, and the last set would go until about three a.m. The sky would be lightening as Swig drove back to his brother's—no train service at that hour—the Cross Bronx Expressway almost empty, the leaves at his brother's exit a deep green, gently moving and making a swishing sound in the early summer wind. He'd get to sleep just as everyone else in the house was waking up.

I'm glad Swig will be able to go this concert. Maybe it will take his mind off his memories, so many of which, like that story about his father or this one he just shared with me about an unnamed childhood friend who killed himself when he was in college, make me melancholy because they are invariably about someone or something lost.

*

Only a week before I had seen him at a Christmas party, Swig remembers, *the second time we had been together in just over a month, and practically the last thing he had said to me was, "Come down for dinner in January." We had drifted apart by then, but I had believed his invitation.*

My father sent me the obituary. The body had been found in a motel, the kind of motel which usually only gets into a newspaper nameless. A .22 caliber rifle lay near the body, according to state police. He had shot himself in the head.

The following spring vacation I visited his parents. I had been home almost a week before I went to see them. All the way over, the sound of an April rain, light touches on light leaves, and along the wet darkness of the quiet street, puddles by the curb.

Cordial, they went out of their way to make me feel comfortable. We sat in their living room, the floor of which was covered with soft, gray carpeting. Near his father's chair a fire burned in the fireplace; his mother was seated on a couch on the other side of the room. There was an awkward silence after drinks had been served and we had exchanged pleasantries, until his father said I could ask about him.

"It helps to talk," his mother said.

He'd been at a party his last night home. His family had been asleep when he returned, packed a few things, woken his youngest brother to say goodbye, and taken the gun from the case in his father's den. Two days later the police had called. His parents told me this calmly, but when I left, his mother insisted on walking me to the corner where, after thanking me for coming, she embraced me while the rain still fell, forming larger puddles from which our reflection shone because we stood near a streetlight.

I thought about that last Christmas party, how he had had all the moves down with his cigarette and drink and the right things to say. "Come down for dinner in January." I thought about the previous Thanksgiving when he'd driven up for a football game and we'd had a drink afterwards in my room. He was wearing a white and tan herringbone jacket and he chain-smoked Winstons the entire hour he stayed. He'd filled out a little, but he was still short. Still called me by the nickname, Earf, he'd given me when we first met and I'd signed my name in a fancy script which changed the first and last letters of my first name.

Somewhere in those inchoate recollections I kept hearing the sound of rain, no longer only in puddles along a sidewalk, but on the open highway as well. Other sounds mixed with that rainfall: a motorcycle engine, a voice, another voice, the two voices shouting to each other, trying to be heard over the motor's sound and the rain. Then, silence.

He had owned a series of motorcycles since he'd been old enough to drive. Each new one was a little bigger than the last, but I was never enough of an aficionado to know them by the number of cc's their pistons displaced, or however that worked. He had always been proud of his safety record on a bike (you never said "cycle" for short) and he could persuasively argue the practical purpose for owning one (good gas mileage, easy to take care of). I never quite bought those reasons, however. Nothing could beat pulling onto the grass by a tennis court on a summer evening and pretending you hadn't noticed that the game on court had stopped for a minute. We played tennis, too—he usually won, so I usually bought the beer, except the night we went to a "show bar," where the beer was a dollar a bottle and the go-go dancers' ankles were at eye level; I don't think it occurred to us that we looked like fools, sitting there in our tennis shorts, which strikes me as even odder now, since he was always very conscious of how he dressed, in a casual, tweedy kind of way.

On an earlier college visit one October weekend, he had arrived late Friday night. I prepared for his visit by stocking the refrigerator with extra beer. We stayed up talking about the courses we were taking and how life in our respective universities compared. I had already begun to let my hair grow, but his was still short, I think because a Naval ROTC scholarship was paying his tuition. He always wet it down before he combed it, but it stuck up in the back, where the part ended. His hair was a sandy blond and there were a few freckles on the skin below his light blue eyes. He had a scar on one temple, from a childhood accident with fire, I think. His voice broke when he got excited and his hands moved as he spoke, defining the empty space around him with the shape of each urgent point he made.

Nothing he touched just happened; everything happened to him, in him. He didn't know how to affect a disinterest; with his friends he was remarkably empathetic, but even with a casual acquaintance he was incapable of boredom, cultivated or natural. He had an innate, inward reverence for whatever meant something to other people, a trait which usually won him an immediate response. Gregarious by nature, he was capable of extreme seriousness when he felt some moral issue was on the line. This could seem, sometimes, pretentious, but he was so earnest that it was impossible not to respect his opinion. Once when we were kids and a girl in our class came down a slide in the school playground, he lectured the whole class on our thoughtlessness after we all laughed when we saw her underwear. Anyone else would have been ostracized for such a verbal performance, but we forgave his apparent hauteur: the next year he won a smashing victory in the election for student council treasurer.

Saturday morning of his October visit it was raining. When I woke up and struggled to the bathroom, he was still dozing on the couch in his tee shirt and white boxer shorts. We grunted a good morning and he turned over on his side and seemed to fall back to sleep.

We had coffee at a place called Hayes-Bickford and over second cups read the morning paper. Outside the big plate glass windows the street was crowded with Saturday shoppers and students and kids looking for something to do. There was a football game that afternoon, but neither of us had dates and so we had decided not to go. He suggested that we walk next door to Leavitt & Pierce, because he wanted to see if they still had a record of his father's pipe tobacco recipe. A man old enough to be his grandfather spent nearly half an hour looking for the mix. He spread an enormous log book out on the counter and we paged through it with him, skimming hundreds of entries, most of them in black ink and many with purchase dates noted in the margin.

At the dining hall for an early lunch, I went through the line twice, the second time as though I were getting seconds, while he waited at one of the large wooden tables with an empty plate I'd picked up on my first trip. He ate my firsts and I my seconds and then we both went for real seconds and afterwards smoked a Turkish Oval. One smoke led to a second and a second led to an idea—let's drive out to Wellesley.

"In the rain?" I asked.

"In the rain—how else? The brakes will hold."

I hadn't been on his motorcycle since the last time he'd driven me to work back home in August. The seat was just big enough for the two of us and I had to wrap my arms around his waist to hold on. We wove through the traffic in town fairly cautiously, but once we got onto the Massachusetts Turnpike he opened the throttle and we were sailing. I didn't know which exit to take, but we found the right one eventually and were pulling into the main gate at Wellesley by early afternoon.

Cars with college decals were parked along the curbs by all the dorms and we had to squeeze into a space between an old Mercedes and a new Volvo. He locked the front wheel of the bike with a chain and we walked across a driveway to Tower, its Gothic arches looking like an old castle on a moor in the rain. A girl we knew from home lived there— she was really a former girlfriend of his and would therefore be more surprised to see him than me.

During dinner we entertained an entire table with stories about that newspaper we'd printed together in sixth grade (lead story: "Editors' Minister Preaches in DC—Eisenhower at Service;" and the classified ad that a classmate "wanted a blond"). One story played off another and we were like two comedians, feeding each other leads and laughing at ourselves, at our guile when we changed a detail here or there to heighten an effect: that bedspread he and his date had ripped slightly, during the party when my parents were away, became now a total loss and how, we wondered, had I ever explained?

There was a movie later—Marx Brothers, I think, or maybe a Renoir. The rain was coming down harder around ten and I said perhaps we should think about getting back. On the highway the rain fell in sheets and the lights of oncoming cars were a white blur. He shouted to me that he was going to "let it out" and I shouted something back but he couldn't hear and then the machine seemed to take off from us, with us, and we raced back to Cambridge as the skies opened wider. We ran the toll booth and no one came after us. We ran the light at the Longfellow Bridge. We cut up through the houses and when we hit a snag in the Saturday night party traffic we drove up on the sidewalk and scared a slow moving couple huddled together under a single raincoat draped over their heads.

We dried ourselves by a fire in my room and when the beer was gone
we drank Almaden Golden Cream Sherry and late into the night we lis-
tened as the last MBTA cars made their run, right under the room it
seemed. He had changed into black woolen pants and a clean tee shirt
and was barefoot when he announced he was "stepping outside for some
air." I followed. The rain had stopped and the sidewalk was covered
with black puddles. From off in the distance music was being played in
someone's room. The sidewalk was lit by low lights, just strong enough to
show the way, and we followed the walk to the library where we climbed
the steps and sat looking out at the enormous stretch of dark, wet lawn
that bore the name of the college and was known as a yard. There, as the
skies cleared and stars showed and then were hidden in the breaking
clouds, we pledged to "do this again," for sure, because, we knew, and
never, we felt, for sure, and not forget, and how, and why...

Is Swig's memory for the people he loved a late imagination?
Or is it something else, too, that shadow he keeps trying to lose?

10

Outside at his favorite café, where Swig's supposed to be working
on revising an old essay of his, a young woman reading something
at the next table, leaning over, half her buttocks visible between the
bottom of her shirt and the open waist of her low-cut jeans, reminds him of a mermaid he once saw in Conway. He lived then in
a kind of perfection of place, he's told me over and over, with a
huge garden, a magnificent vista of fields across the river that
passed through the farm on the other side of the road, and a swimming hole beyond those fields, by a second farm his landlord
owned, at a big bend in the river that was hidden from the road, so
everyone who swam there skinny-dipped.

Across a corn field and through some brush, the naked ladies
would lie sleeping on rocks or talking with one another or with the
naked boys, and all through the long, hot Sunday afternoon various sections of *The New York Times* would be passed among them,
getting wet sometimes in the river but drying in the sun on the

small sand beach near the pool where trout were. Others came, shedding shirts and shorts and splashing in the shallow water near the beach or floating where the current carried them past the rocks. By evening the paper was read, and all the ladies and boys headed home.

Now, at the café, Swig gets up to refill my canvas water bowl that we keep in the back of our S.U.V. It's hot, mid-July. When he returns to his laptop he begins the essay, but he's still thinking about the mermaid. No mermaid, she!

Just a few miles from our former farm, in the middle of a cow pasture, a small growth of woods, not larger than a quarter of an acre, hid what was left of someone's onetime home. Other ruins lay close by other roads, but by far the greatest concentration of cellar holes in the town was located in a deeply wooded area called Cricket Hill.

One Sunday in mid-summer a middle-aged couple and their child arrived. They were each wearing cutoff jeans; in the father's case, that was all he was wearing. The father was the leader in taking them off, revealing ridges of fat that rivaled, below his navel, the corpulence above. The mother followed, first with her tee shirt (no bra), then her pants. She had large breasts, which sagged in a mimic of her buttocks' cheeks. Last to undress, turning away from the naked bodies near her, was the girl.

Dark brown were the eyes of the tannest swimmer, whose name Swig tried to tell me was Dulcinea, but I'm getting tired of that conceit. Her tan was the color of her hair, sandy brown. Her entire body was tanned; there was no lighter skin that showed where a bathing suit would have been before. She was lying on the beach, her hair tied back in a blue and yellow madras scarf. Near her, draped on the branches of a bush, was a white muslin shirt, with blue and red and yellow threads embroidered across the bodice. When the breeze blew the bodice billowed, and the sleeves swayed in rhythm with the pulse of the river's water as it rippled on the rocks.

*

Cricket Hill! Swig continues, and then quotes a reminiscence later published in 1917 in the town's sesquicentennial history. *"What a queer name to be linked in all its history to one district of the town just because some early hunters or surveyors were annoyed by crickets when camping for the night," wrote the Rev. William Fisher Avery in 1900.*

Taking the reader on a mnemonic walking tour, Avery went on to describe an area which, even then, was nearly abandoned. Cricket Hill had been one of the first sections of the town settled in the eighteenth century, after residents of neighboring Deerfield felt it safe to venture westward when the French and Indian Wars were concluded. By 1800, many men and women were heading farther west and Cricket Hill, like the rest of the town, witnessed a steady population decline.

Two of Dulcinea's friends sunned themselves in silence, while the middle-aged couple and their child swam, and another group—three young men, one woman—skipped stones around the bend, and a boy, standing on a large boulder at the bend, watched. Now, across the field, visible from the river until nearly level with the brush, came a blue van, music—*Rollin' on the River*—playing through its open windows, and a long-haired male head sticking out on the passenger's side. The van stopped next to the place in the river, upstream from the bend, where fill had been dumped so tractors and pickup trucks could cross.

"This is the place," the young man with the long hair said, intonating each word at a higher pitch than the last. And then, in a smoother voice, middle tone, he added a long, drawn-out "Hi," accompanied by a wave and a smile. "I brought some friends with me this time," he said, gesturing to the five others in the van. "Okay if we take a swim?"

One of the stone-skippers had walked back from the bend and was standing in shallow water, nodding to the long-haired visitor and his entourage. "Did you bring music," he asked, "or is that just the radio?"

"Hey, man, we are the music." And when no one responded: "Yeah, we've got a portable player."

One family that stayed longer than most were the Maynards, descendents of one of the first Cricket Hill settlers, a man named Malachi Maynard. "A daughter married Zelotus Bates, and lived long upon the old place," wrote Avery. "With them were two maiden sisters, Lucy and Anna Maynard. They were generous givers to Mount Holyoke Seminary at its very beginning. A dreadful calamity came upon this whole household. I remember it well, though a mere child. We were returning from church on Thanksgiving day, when, as our wagons came in sight of Mr. Bates' home, the flames were seen just bursting from it. A fire had been left to bake the Thanksgiving dinner, while the family were faithful to the public duties of the day. Alas, it burned down the house leaving little but some nicely baked potatoes in their large bin. A few silver dollars laid aside for the seminary were drawn out of the ashes, considerably marred. These two sisters went to work and patiently earned the remainder of the two hundred dollars, which had been subscribed, not permitting the proposed school to suffer from their loss. Those scorched coins were laid up in the archives of the seminary."

The Maynard place was rebuilt on the same foundation and Zelotus Bates lived to be almost 90. Later, the town purchased the property and for a number of years supported an unusual institution called the town farm, a place where anyone down on his luck could get a meal and spend the night. A daughter of the last man to run the town farm told me about her early childhood there:

"The main house had a big kitchen where we all ate, my family and the people who were staying with us. They slept in a separate building. If they were able, they worked on the farm with my father—we had some cows and grew our own vegetables. I don't remember the house that well because I was very young when we moved, but I go up there every year for picnics."

The house was torn down in the 1920s, soon after the town farm was closed, and all that remained were the cellar hole and the cemetery where Mrs. Bates and her two sisters are buried. You can find them easily enough, because the cemetery is marked on topographical maps of the area by a small cross; to reach the spot, all you have to do is follow the path of some abandoned roads, also marked on maps by dotted lines.

*

The van group waded around the bend, greeting the sunning women, nodding to the boy on the boulder, ignoring the middle-aged couple and their daughter. They waded until they reached another, smaller beach, where no one had been sitting, and there they spread out blankets and a basket with food and their music (Beach Boys, *Surf's In*). They swam before they ate, one of the women dipping the infant in the water. They did not share their picnic, but the long-haired man rolled some joints, and these were proffered. The only taker was the middle-aged father, who sat down on the beach with his new friends.

"That's a super recording you're playing, man," he said. "I've been a Beach Boys fan for a long time."

One of the women looked up and said, "Who are the Beach Boys?"

The air was thick with the sweet smell of clover from the pastures above and beyond the bend and, close by, of marijuana smoke. The grass in the pasture, like the foliage along the banks of the river, was a deep green. Sunlight shimmered in the shallow water where rocks stood guard, but in the deeper pools the reflection of foliage hid the darting shadow-images of trout. Into the deepest pool the boy threw a stone, and its splash elicited a shout from the long-haired man.

"Hey, don't throw the rocks. The baby's sleeping."

Shortly, from the first group—for they were together now, the three sunning women and the stone-skippers—came a second shout. "The farmer's coming!"

The boy dove into the water. The middle-aged father and mother stayed on the beach with the others. "He'll never see us here," the father said to his wife. "He's not going to wade around the bend." But he put out his joint, and the daughter went wandering in the clover. The male stone-skippers donned shorts, the women shirts and shorts, except Dulcinea, who looked up, rubbed her dark eyes, lifted her head, and then, removing her scarf and shaking her hair, lay down again.

The farmer—Swig's landlord, Mr. Harris—had reached the van and was about to ford the river in his tractor. He paused to survey his trespassers.

"You don't mind if I take my tractor over?" he seemed to ask, without looking directly at the naked woman back on the beach. And then he put his machine in gear, drove across the river, and nodded to the second group, whom he could see when he had reached the other bank.

Father, mother, and daughter left after that. The water, the father said, was "perfect." He said it three or four times, and he was having trouble getting his legs into his pants. Dulcinea, still resplendent beneath the muslin shirt, had sat up, cross-legged. She was now reading Section 2 of the newspaper, "Arts and Leisure." She seemed unaware of the eyes that were staring at her tan breasts.

"Perfect," the father said. "We'll come again if you don't mind."

"See you now, take it easy," someone answered.

I walked perhaps a mile, turning once at a lonely three corners, when, nearing the Maynard place, I saw the rusted frame of a baby carriage, leaning against a tree in the same place I had seen it on my last visit. I saw that someone had been cutting trees in one of the pastures, trees that had been planted too close together when the town farm was closed. I saw sleet on dead leaves, a deserted road rising to the west, then dipping past the family  *cemetery and disappearing beyond some birches. Jeep tracks, frozen in the ground, seemed to be following some footprints, also frozen. Looking from the rear of where the farmhouse had stood, I saw the meeting place of two stone walls, forming a cross. The house had been situated on a knoll and commanded what must have been an excellent view in all directions. Trees grew from what had once been the middle of the cellar floor.*

My voice echoed in the space between the trees, down the empty, hollow space kept open by the road. I heard a gunshot that seemed to come from far away. It was not loud; the predominant sound was still that of my own footsteps. There was no wind and the trees were silent. I stood at the graves of the two Maynard sisters and then sat for a while on the stone wall that surrounded the cemetery.

Dulcinea was standing on the sand, looking at her things as though she were getting ready to go. Near her feet lay a few sections of the newspaper and her clothes, except for the embroidered shirt, which she was already wearing.

She looked around her, and then began wading in the river. She walked slowly through the shallow water until she approached the bend; then she walked along the shore until she reached the large boulder. When she climbed up onto it, a few drops of water dripped from her legs. The fringes of her shirt were wet.

Having passed below the line of the tree tops, the sunlight did not brighten the bend, and the foliage, too, was dark. Dulcinea turned her back and looked into the trout pool; there was still enough light for a reflection, the rippled image of her shirt and hair, framing Swig's view of her bare ass.

Splash!

Circles of small waves moved outward from the spot where Dulcinea had dived, her figure moving underwater. When she surfaced she brought her hands out of the water and pulled her hair back. Then she swam out of the deep water and stood up, the white muslin clinging to her skin. Quickly, she walked to where her other clothes were and put on her jeans. She gathered the sections of the paper and slipped her feet into her sneakers.

A mist had started to come up over the meadow as Swig's mermaid disappeared into the flower-fragrant air of early evening.

11

He takes the long way over, he will tell me long afterwards, stopping for something to eat in Northampton, and then he will continue via the old route his mom used to follow when she met them halfway, leaving her car at a country gas station. They'd drive together, sometimes all of them, his wife and Swig with their three kids, and they'd have a picnic and sit somewhere on the immense lawn. Or it might be just his mother and Swig, and they'd get tickets inside, in the Shed.

His mother liked to sit up front, fairly close to the stage, where she felt more a part of the music. She loved everything about the experience, including the anticipation when you were waiting, watching other people looking for their seats, seeing the musicians come on stage one by one or in small clusters and listening to them warm up, and then how the house lights dimmed just before the door on the left side of the stage opened and out came the conductor as the applause began. His mother would relax her shoulders, clasp her hands and place them on the program cradled in her lap, and then maybe glance at Swig, a slight smile shaping her lips, and he would return the gesture by putting one of his hands over hers.

Rain soaks him as he walks from his car to a restaurant where he has brunch, something they used to do every Easter at a place called Sylvester's. The line there was too long so he has settled for Jake's, kind of a diner on one side of the Calvin Theater. Another place his mother loved, the Calvin is an old movie and vaudeville house that was completely restored a few years ago. Shortly after it reopened Wynton was in town on a beautiful fall day for an evening gig at the nearby Iron Horse. He spent the afternoon at the Calvin with his rhythm section, being videotaped while playing several old jazz tunes for a PBS documentary that was then in production. Swig called his mother and told her to walk over if she could, and she came right away, took a seat near the front in the empty auditorium, and stayed until they were finished, making a special point of speaking to Wynton afterwards.

A sign in front of his mother's former apartment building advertises that its units are being converted into condominiums. Otherwise there is no visible change from that bittersweet March day more than three years before, when the movers packed up his mother's stuff and she followed them in her green Tercel out of the rear parking lot to Bronxville, three hours away, into an apartment a mile from his brother's house. A ten-minute walk from the wooded campus of Sarah Lawrence College, her new apartment was even closer to the Bronxville hospital where she was admitted about six months after her move, with the first of a series of ailments that lasted until this summer, when her long glowing life came to a peaceful end in his sister's home in Maine, four days after her 87th birthday, which they observed together.

During many of the nearly twenty years his mother lived in her Northampton apartment Swig and his family were nearby, in Conway and then Amherst, where Swig's mother also briefly lived and worked when she first came to this area just before Swig's father died. His parents had been separated for a few years and officially divorced for three months when his father suffered his heart attack alone in his North Carolina apartment at the age of 64. A coroner called to inform him, and Swig then drove the few miles to the college where his mother had started working. He called to tell her he was coming, and she met him outside. He thought she knew before he said anything, though she was silent until he spoke.

"It's Dad," he said.

They were walking across the college quadrangle. It was warm out and sunny, an afternoon in late August.

Swig put his arm around her, on a shoulder, and said how sorry he was that he had to be delivering this news to her.

She stopped walking and looked at him, her brown eyes frozen as she stared into his, and he hugged her as they stood there. She did not sob, did not catch her breath, just stood still and finally said, "How?"

*

Swig's father, Hans, never saw where Ruth lived after her move to be near Swig. They had one final meeting after their separation, in a small Connecticut town south of the Berkshires, when Hans tried a last time to persuade her to follow him south. Swig was not there, and it was not until near the end of her life before his mother would talk about this moment with him. He can imagine his father's promising to stop drinking if only she would change her mind, but by then his mother understood that even had she wanted to go such an offer only worked the other way round. She would have listened, but Swig was sure she had already made up her mind as she said goodbye, never to see him again.

In her Northampton apartment there had been just one bedroom, immediately to the left of the rear door that overlooked the parking lot; the single, small bathroom was to the right as you came in, and a short hallway between the two rooms led to an equally small kitchen, which opened to a larger living room, with space for the tall, upright desk that had been made in the furniture company her father owned until the Great Depression. There were also two couches, one of which was also made by Swig's grandfather—by all accounts a somewhat distant, very religious man who doted on Swig's mother, the younger of his two daughters.

Named after one of his father's sisters who had died prematurely, Ruth was born at home, in the single-family house her parents had purchased when it was built on a tree-lined street in Queens, New York, not far from the West Side Tennis Club in Forest Hills, a place her family could not have afforded to join, but a sport she still played well enough to rally with Swig when he was a teenager.

Her sister was seven years older; a brother, born between the girls' births, had died in infancy and was never spoken about within the family. Swig's aunt married young, but that first marriage, which produced a daughter, ended in divorce. Swig thought of her second husband as his uncle. They lived near his grandparents, in an apartment across the street from the Esso service station his uncle managed. In an extended family that included several school teachers and a newspaper executive, his pumping gas for a living somewhat embarrassed Swig's grandfather, but being in the Esso station as a boy always made Swig very happy. Smiling as he wiped black grease off his huge hands, Swig's uncle would give him some change to get a snack from the vending machine, and Swig would stay and watch him change the oil in a car or replace some brake shoes or a muffler.

It was in his uncle and aunt's apartment that his grandfather died. Swig can still see him lying in a bed at the top of the stairs when his mother and he visited a few days before his grandfather's death. Swig was six or seven, just old enough to remember the Brooklyn Dodgers game his grandfather had taken him to before he had what was euphemistically called a stroke but was more probably what used to be diagnosed as a nervous breakdown. The Dodgers were his team, but Swig's mother's was the Yankees, and she and his grandfather used to go regularly to games at Yankee Stadium, where his mother's favorite player was Lou Gehrig.

After his grandfather's furniture company had collapsed during the Depression, he had become a coffee broker for the coffee roasting company his older brother owned in the Midwest. Every weekday he walked the two blocks from his house to Jamaica Avenue and rode the elevated train to Brooklyn. Weekends were devoted to his family, with a special emphasis Sunday mornings on church. For many years he was the superintendent of his church's Sunday school, which included some sort of a camp out on Long Island where everyone would congregate on frequent Sunday afternoons. Though Swig's mother invariably became sentimental when she started talking about the friends and relatives who attended those gatherings, it was clear from the way she described her father that there was something about his officious devotion that she found suffocating.

When she went away to college, first to Colby Junior in New Hampshire, and then to Mount Holyoke, where she transferred for her last two years, her father wrote her a letter every day. In 1940, after she graduated with a major in music, she moved home again. By then she and Swig's father were dating, though at some distance. They had met during high school, when Swig's father, who had grown up in the Washington Heights area of upper Manhattan, got his first job as the organist in the same Baptist church his mother and her family attended.

Then a teenager herself, Swig's mother was singing in the choir, and one Sunday after church her parents invited their new organist home for dinner. The romance that grew out of their meeting ended temporarily when Swig's mother went to Colby. It was reborn after her transfer to Mount Holyoke, because Swig's father had left home himself and was working in Great Barrington, Massachusetts, about an hour's drive from Mount Holyoke in South Hadley. They were married during World War II and lived briefly in Army housing in Texas and South Carolina before his father, an Army bandleader and warrant officer, was sent overseas for the duration of the war. Swig's mother once more moved home and took an office job in Manhattan, where she also studied singing at Juilliard.

When the war ended the young couple settled in a New Jersey suburb, where Swig's dad found positions as a church organist and choirmaster, and teacher at a nearby private school. Four years later Swig's dad accepted an offer from a wealthy church in Buffalo, New York, where he would also soon become the artistic manager of that city's symphony orchestra. Though she desperately did not want to leave the New York area, Swig's mother of course went along. It was the only thing to do.

The rain is coming down really hard when Swig turns around in the parking lot behind his mother's old building and heads west on Route 9. He passes the hospital where he had minor leg surgery the day his father-in-law died and where, just a few months ago, he rushed Maren to the emergency room for a mysterious abdominal pain that required minor surgery. Everything about the area is familiar with the aching exception of his mother's permanent absence.

The oldest of his parents' three children, Swig was his mother's constant companion as a boy. He did not attend school until kindergarten, staying home instead while his mother did her housework and going along with her to the grocery store each day and on whatever other errands occupied her time (this was before she began the first of many different music or teaching jobs). They made frequent trips to New York to visit her parents. It was about an eight-hour train ride on the New York Central, which left Buffalo from an enormous station that at one point must have been one of the busiest in the country. Swig's father would drive them over and walk them to their seats. In one hand Swig carried a little suitcase with some of his toys and in his other he pulled a string, a few feet long, at the end of which was an imaginary pet he called Gigi.

In New York they would spend time with his father's parents in Washington Heights and other relatives and friends in New Jersey, but they always stayed in Queens. As his family grew, with his sister's birth following his brother's, these trips became less frequent, but they still returned at least once a year until he was about to begin high school. By then the chief attraction for Swig of visiting his grandmother's house was the chance to watch a Yankees game on her large black and white television in the living room with its crimson carpet.

His grandmother had been a widow for several years, and she would live another ten, until the age of eighty, when she died shortly after his last pilgrimage to Queens, a daytrip his wife and Swig made with Swig's brother, who was still in college. It was the year after they were married in a ceremony his grandmother had attended, the only surviving grandparent in either his or his wife's family. Swig's mother admired her own mother for the brave way she had carried on after she was a widow, never moving from the Queens house, which she kept in immaculate condition, and never to Swig's knowledge putting pressure on Swig's mother or his aunt to take care of her. Within the rather confining limits of the times and culture in which she had lived, his grandmother was remarkably independent, though at what price of loneliness he could only guess. He remembers that when she was in her early 70s she went through a period of depression that was never openly discussed but, instead, became a poorly kept secret when she visited Buffalo one winter and was hospitalized briefly.

Swig's mother would have her own battles with despair when his father's habitual drinking became chronic after his uncle's early death and then again, years later, when his parents left Buffalo to start over again back in the Berkshires after his father had lost all his jobs. An old friend found work for Swig's dad at a private school, where they were also given housing. But the emotional difficulties that were either triggered by or were the cause of his drinking—no one could ever figure out which was which—led quickly to the same sad situation that had forced them to depart from Buffalo.

Before Swig's father made his last move to North Carolina, his mother had found a job as a guide at the Norman Rockwell Museum in Stockbridge. She continued to live in the apartment she and Swig's father had shared in nearby Great Barrington until the lease ran out; her own relocation followed. By the time Swig's second child Anna was born a year after his father's death, his mother had become a virtual member of his household, coming often for dinner, frequently spending Sundays with them, joining them on occasional vacation trips, including a happy fortnight one summer at Martha's Vineyard. Bonnie had started a new position at the same college where his mother would soon be working, and he was commuting several days a week to Boston to do research and reporting for his first book, so his mother volunteered to help with Anna's daycare. They were still living in the old farmhouse in Conway about half an hour from Northampton. His mother loved coming out there. Even after they had to sell the place, his mother still occasionally drove by. He can imagine her slowing as she came to the crest of the hill, stopping near the maple tree from which the kids' swing used to hang and pausing for a few minutes, deep in her own memories of their once-upon-a-time home.

Nearing Pittsfield, Swig remembers the turn for the shortcut to Lenox, past the museum that was created from Arrowhead, the house where Herman Melville wrote his epic. Swig once stopped there, and when he was told by the attendant that it was closed for the day he persuaded her just to let him walk upstairs to Melville's study, where the great man's desk looked out through a window toward the highest point in Massachusetts, Mount Greylock. From that vantage point, the mountain's silhouette in the distance appeared thrillingly to be shaped like a whale.

Now, not wanting to miss the beginning of the Brahms rehearsal he's coming to Tanglewood to hear, Swig barely glances at Melville's historic digs, takes a left at the signal where Holmes Road intersects with Route 7, and drives quickly to the turnoff just east of Lenox center that will take him via another shortcut he learned years ago from his father to Tanglewood's back gate.

He has been coming to this place his entire life. In a first-floor room of Tanglewood's original building—the main house of the estate from which the summer home of the Boston Symphony Orchestra grew—hangs a large photograph taken in 1940 in front of that very house, depicting the men and women who comprised the students and faculty of the first class in what was then called the Berkshire Music Center. Bow-tied, and seated prominently in the center of the photograph, is the man who became the most celebrated classical musician in the U.S. in the second half of the twentieth century, Leonard Bernstein. Far to Bernstein's left, seated in the second row, is a young man in shirtsleeves, the collar open; unlike Bernstein and almost everyone else, this man is looking not back at the photographer but, it appears, at something or someone off in the distance—a bird, perhaps, or a pretty girl, or maybe nothing at all. That person is Swig's father.

Even when they were headed elsewhere, his father would route them through the Berkshires, where in addition to his church work he also served as a rehearsal accompanist for the famed violinist, Albert Spalding (whose family started the sporting goods company of the same name), or the swimming spots where he used to go skinny dipping despite what Swig is sure were the admonitions of his father's loving but strict Norwegian mother. And during a short Berkshire visit, perhaps an overnight stay at the restored Interlaken hotel that his parents' friend (who was also Swig's childhood piano teacher) owned, they always went to at least one of the BSO's Tanglewood concerts. Sometimes his father would make arrangements with the orchestra's manager to get them into the Shed for a rehearsal, a practice that became routine during that iconic summer when they returned for two enchanted months.

One Friday or Saturday night that summer around the date of his mother's birthday at the end of July, they set out blankets on the lawn, just behind the row of benches at the rear of the Shed. The air was warm and the sky clear. During the second half of the program, the orchestra performed Debussy's gorgeous orchestration of Satie's glistening piano work, *Trois Gymnopedies*. Swig's father, as was his custom, found an empty seat in the Shed, but his mother and Swig remained outside where, listening on his back, he looked up at stars that always, afterwards, he would associate with that music and his mother.

On the afternoon of what even as it was happening Swig's siblings and he sensed was going to be her last birthday, their mother managed with his brother's assistance to make it from her bedroom in their sister's house to the porch. Their mother had been living in Maine almost three years, since her discharge from the hospital in Bronxville. She had long resisted moving into an assisted living place, and none of them had wanted her to die in a hospital, so Swig's sister had stepped in, offering not only her home but, it turned out, a large chunk of her life, particularly near the end when their mother needed round-the-clock care. Some of that was provided by a nurse, who came in each day while Swig's sister worked at the Portland store she owned, but there were still the nights, when their mother often had trouble sleeping, the visits to the doctor, the smallest events of the day that she needed help with—brushing her teeth or her hair, taking her medications, shuffling the cards with which she and Swig's sister played hearts every evening after supper, while watching *Wheel of Fortune*, their mother's favorite television program.

For this birthday, Swig's sister had suggested it would be overwhelming for their mother to have a large crowd. And so he drove up alone for the weekend from Massachusetts and his brother, Nils, from New York. Arriving in Maine on Friday night, he stayed only a short time before continuing on, with a stop at Bean's, to a friend's house where he slept. The next morning he visited with his friends before driving back to his sister's, again with a stop en route, this time to check his email at an internet café in the town of Brunswick, a routine that reinforced the illusion that all was well.

His mother's birthday was not until the next day, but they had decided to have whatever party she could handle on this Saturday. Sitting on the porch in her nightgown and robe, on a bright, mid-afternoon, she would seem to be listening as one of them told a story or shared a memory—about the time in 1970 or '71 that she'd been the soloist in Samuel Barber's setting of a text by James Agee, with his brother conducting a student orchestra at Harvard; or the golf they'd played when she'd joined the nine-hole course next to which we now live, the lessons she took there one summer from…who was it? Swig suddenly remembered, but looking over at his mother he noticed she had nodded off, so he didn't say the name, didn't say another word.

The time passed. Opening her eyes, Ruth indicated she wanted to go back inside. His brother helped her up, and Swig trailed the two of them, holding the tube that connected the oxygen tank in the kitchen with the device through which their mother breathed, a kind of tuning-fork shaped design in which twin, plastic prongs, emanating from the main tubing, protruded into her nostrils, the arrangement held to her head by another piece of plastic that went around the back of her tiny neck.

Even with all those tubes and her thinning, gray hair combed back, the lines and wrinkles on her face and the black and blue splotches on her delicate arms from all the places blood tests had been administered—even with, or despite, or maybe in part because of the central image of their mother's regal beauty—the glamour of her bearing, remained, indeed shone, just as the fact of her courageous life stood out, particularly the last 25 years, when she overcame cancer and dealt with an ailing heart.

Swig returned to the porch, where his sister had remained, while his brother poked about in the refrigerator for mayonnaise and a lemon to make chicken salad from the store-cooked chicken a friend had left earlier in the day. They opened a bottle of Chardonnay. Twilight comes earlier than elsewhere, there in Maine which extends out to the far eastern end of the Eastern Time Zone. Sitting on the porch in the gathering dusk, the air languid and warm, they ate their chicken salad and drank the wine, and one at a time went to check on their mother in her bedroom— really Swig's sister's living room, retrofitted for their mother as was the adjacent office space and bathroom.

Swig's mother opened her eyes when he sat on a side of her bed, then shut them again, but he was pretty sure she was still awake. He held her hand, listening to each precious, labored breath, and then kissed her face.

From far away, beyond the lawn to one side of the Shed and past the expanse of trees that separates the main part of the Tanglewood property from an adjoining parcel (the grounds of a second estate added since Swig's father knew it and with a newer hall standing near its far end)—from the parking lot there, near the rear Tanglewood gate, the sound of the orchestra is faint but distinct, the first strains of the Brahms concerto Swig has come to hear blending with birdsong and the light, persistent swish of damp, green leaves stirring in a damp, August breeze. He has parked his car close to an unoccupied ticket booth in this empty lot because that's what his father would have done—it was the way you did things when you were habituated to his father's backstage version of la vie bohème.

Barely two weeks had elapsed since he was awakened by a call from his sister late one evening, asking him what he was doing the next morning.

"The medics have just left," his sister said, in a voice that sounded an immediate alarm. "But the nurse cannot be here all morning, and I need to check-in at work."

After a quick stop in the center of town for coffee, Swig drove to Maine straight through, retracing the route by which he had returned from his mother's birthday only three days before. He arrived a little before one a.m., where he found his mother asleep in her bed, sedated and breathing now through an oxygen mask. The nurse wiped their mother's forehead with a washcloth while his sister and he embraced. Then they each took a seat on opposite sides of the bed, where they remained for nearly three hours, standing once or twice but never leaving her bedside, dozing off now and then, until a little before four a.m., when his sister startled him with two words: "She's gone."

Wondering if it were going to begin raining again, and aware that he has arrived at Tanglewood a little late, Swig nevertheless stands absolutely still, as if his body were literally unable to take another step. Then, prompted by the resumption of the distant music, he begins to walk, just as he did on his sister's street at dawn, before two men from the funeral home arrived.

It was already warm out that early morning, with summer sounds in the air—birds, bugs, and the occasional far off hint of a car—and he walked all the way to the main corner where a few shops stood, where on a summer walk two years before his older daughter Anna and he had pushed his mother in her wheelchair. He continued as he had then all the way down to the river that ran through the town and followed the path along the river where people hiked and jogged, again the same route as before, and he stopped at a waterfall where they had stopped back then, watched the water rushing over the rocks, and in that quiet dawn continued on to the school at the other end of town where he cut across the playground and walked back to his sister's.

Soon the undertakers arrived. His sister went upstairs so she did not have to watch as their mother's body was wheeled outside on a stretcher, less than two hours since the end of the all-night vigil. Swig followed the men and waited while they placed his mother's motionless body in the back of their van.

Opening a side door, he reached in and touched her arm. How cold it was! Then he stood in the driveway as the van left, and he didn't move as it turned at the end of the driveway and disappeared down the quiet street.

12

Misty, melancholy morning, windy and warm, with only a few of the maples just starting to show a washed, burnt orange. Where did the season go?

Swig says he will be traveling again soon. We've cut around the second hole of the course to avoid a group of old-timers playing in the September splendor. With the rail trail that runs along this boundary of the course empty, I'm not tethered to Swig with the leash, but I stick close by him anyway, in fact it's a little hard to keep up. Something in my hips has been bothering me since the weather began to change. But something else concerns me even more. How can I tell Swig that I think he may be trying too hard, like the match he wrote about in a golf memoir he thankfully never finished, as if he finally realized golf was just…golf.

He knew before the first shot he wasn't going to play well. All afternoon Swig had been thinking about the match with confi-dence, but when it came time to play he had hurried from the pro shop to the first tee because several other people were waiting to go out and he didn't want to be behind them. His brother and son had already hit their drives when Swig quickly took his stance, and sent the ball heading out of bounds. It actually landed in the first cut of right rough, but then took a terrible lateral bounce and disappeared in the direction of the woods that bordered the hole. Swig had to tee up another ball, which would cost him stroke and distance unless, somehow, that first one stayed in.

It had! (though he didn't discover this until he had played his second shot with his provisional, a nice three-wood that landed in front of the green). He found the original tee ball nestled by a root, right along the out of bounds line indicated by white stakes.

"It's okay," Swig shouted to his brother and son, who seemed oblivious to his narrow avoidance of golfing disaster.

Because the root lay between the ball and the direction of the hole, Swig had to hit his second shot sideways, chipping the ball back onto the fairway. He succeeded, leaving himself about 150 yards to a flagstick positioned in the middle rear of the green: an easy target.

Swig selected a 7-iron. Even with a mediocre iron shot followed by two putts he would salvage a bogey. Instead, he came out of the swing early and again pushed the ball right, where it landed in a deep bunker.

To be certain he got out of the bunker he took a longer than usual backswing, remembering then to hit the sand behind the ball. "Peel the apple," Byron Nelson had said in Swig's favorite instructional book, *Shape Your Swing the Modern Way*, one of more than a hundred he owned. It was a swing thought that usually worked for Swig in bunkers, as it worked here—but too well. The ball cleared not only the steep bunker wall but also the green, landing in the rough on the other side.

From there he used his new pitching wedge, trying to fluff the ball gently out of the thick grass, so it would land softly on the green and not roll downhill too fast. He hit the shot so well the ball actually stopped ten feet above the hole, something he would never have been able to do if that had been his goal. Now, with two putts, he was looking at triple bogey.

As he waited on the second tee to hit his drive—last, since both his brother and son had bogeyed the first—Swig began to wonder about the wisdom of this outing. Three years older than his brother, he had been playing golf with him on and off since they were boys. Having grown up in the middle of a large city, they had played only occasionally there, on an old public course in a park. But during summers in northern Vermont their father used to drop them off at the local nine-hole course, where kids were encouraged to learn the game, even receiving free lessons from the father of the coach of the Little League baseball team on which they both played. With a short, compact swing well suited to his small but muscular frame, Swig's brother soon developed a dependable game, which he used to beat Swig in the many matches they played on that scenic, mountain course.

How Swig loved those rounds of golf! Nearly fifty years later he could still see every hole in his memory, the blind drive on the first and second, the par three, straight downhill third, the dogleg left fourth and the well midway on the fifth with a hand pump that you used to get yourself a drink, the long sixth and seventh with the greens that for so many years had been kept roped off so grazing cattle did not eat the grass, the tremendous uphill eighth with the picnic area between the green and the adjacent, ninth tee, where you looked out at the mountains and the glorious, blue jewel of the lake below. How he loved the smell of grass there on a hot day, the wind rustling in the sweep of grass along the first and second and those hidden finishing holes where the cows used to roam. Hayseed and the smell of juniper, the feel of the hot sun on your neck and scratches on your legs and arms from looking for lost balls: that was their first real golf together, something that stayed with them when they began to play again as adults, first his brother at the college where he was teaching and then both of them when his brother visited—this was when Swig still lived in Conway and for a time had no modern clubs, so he borrowed first an old set of their mother's with her initials on them and then his father-in-law's set of Bobby Joneses with the steel shafts painted to look as if they were really hickory, and then finally a new set of Powerbilts, not a fancy model but new nevertheless and his own.

The par-four second hole, playing at 375 yards with a slight dogleg right from the back tees, was a pleasing sight, the setup of that shot, with woods framing both sides of the fairway and more

trees behind the distant sloping green. Swig hit a terrific drive after his brother and son and had only a short iron into the green.
He nailed it. Two putts and a par. Maybe the day was going to turn
out all right.

Swig had a decent bogey on the third, the hardest hole on the
course (though officially the seventh carried the number one
handicap, simply because it was the only par five). With the tee set
back on number four, a par-three, Swig chose a 5-iron to bring the
ball in high, over the bunker on the left. With a par here, on a hole
Swig usually played well, he might completely banish from his
memory that triple on the first. But it was not to be, and after a
break for dinner, the evening back nine was not much better.
Rather than a few disasters Swig had a sequence of mediocrities,
finishing with a 48 for an aggregate of 100. He could not remember the last time he had posted such a score at his home course,
where his handicap had been hovering around 13, perhaps about
to go down to 12 with that nice 81 he had shot only two weeks before.

Wearily he walked home, trying to make small talk. But he
was depressed, not so much at having lost to his brother but at losing control of his game and himself. How could he let something
he worked so hard at slip away?

"This is heaven," his brother exclaimed in the twilight, but
Swig barely heard him. His brother was referring to the view of
the fairway from the sixth tee, which they had just passed. Somewhere overhead in the darkening mist the moon was shining, so
the sky was lighter than it normally would have been at nine
o'clock. They were all of them drenched with sweat, and the mos-
quitoes were out.

A small dark shape flew nearby. A bat, Swig supposed.

"One more 9-iron," he said, putting his bag down in the sixth
fairway. His companions stopped as if on cue.

"How can you see?" asked his brother.

Swig did not respond. Setting himself over the ball, he began
his swing with his turn, the 9-iron feeling light in his hands, and at

the top of his backswing he must have started rotating his hips exactly when he should have, because when the club returned to the ball the impact was pure, and the ball, sailing out over the dark fairway, rose into the moonlit haze and before landing a foot from the pin hovered over the course, the entire sweet smelling languorous landscape, as if it were beckoning Swig to follow in its lovely thrilling flight.

13

A voicemail last night from Swig for Bonnie says he's left Las Vegas and is on his way with Wynton to New Mexico, with a stop en route in Arizona. He says he had been in such a hurry not to miss the bus the band travels in that he left his wallet on the counter of a coffee shop in the casino of the hotel where they stayed. Someone found it and gave it to hotel security, which traced it through Wynton's road manager to Swig, and the bus turned around south of Las Vegas and detoured back to the hotel so Swig could retrieve it. Nothing was missing, neither the small amount of cash or the credit and ATM cards.

While Swig's been away, I came across a box of old papers that he'd half hidden in a corner of his basement office, mixed in with bank receipts and tax records. I like to sleep down there when he's gone, and with my hips still sore it's more comfortable on his office couch than the carpeted concrete floor.

"I've long thought it a shame that more people don't take up jogging," Swig wrote in one of the stories I found this late October morning. "The waste of it all appalls me," he continued, in a style that immediately registered as a little arch, though the subject, naturally, struck a responsive chord with me. He must have written this many years ago. Substitute golf for jogging and it's essentially—though not stylistically—the same story he's still writing, like the change of register on the pipe organ his father used to play.

Oh, Swig.

*

"Night was coming on and you could feel a chill in the air as I stood on the green fairway of the seventh hole at La Paloma's Canyon course in Tucson," Swig wrote yesterday in another, older story I found. "In the lengthening shadows I could just make out the tall figure of my playing partner, a tall, athletic man named Robert, who worked at the nearby Ventana Canyon Resort and Club, where we played this morning. We'd played quickly, because there was a members tournament scheduled for the afternoon, and over lunch in the resort's dining room Robert had called a friend who ran the pro shop at La Paloma.

"Ventana Canyon. La Paloma," he continued. "They all sounded like soothing music to my usually frostbitten ears, accustomed as I was at this time of year to be checking the Weather Channel and ski reports. Here in Tucson, with the temperature in the high 60s, the forecast for the following week was: Monday, sunny; Tuesday, sunny; Wednesday...

"'It did snow once since I moved here from Texas,' Robert had told me earlier, before hitting another of his stupendous drives."

We've been having good walks, Bonnie and I, while Swig is traveling. She lets me off the leash, even with the golfers still on the course because winter has been so late arriving. Yesterday, it was cloudy, with geese heading north making a racket in the sky. A little ice had formed along the edge of the larger pond, where we saw a beaver trolling, but it has melted by today.

"Robert was good company on the golf course," Swig had continued in that Arizona story. "A self-taught golfer, though his brother was a teaching pro in California, he not only hit the ball far off the tee but usually kept it in play, and he had a super touch around the greens. Mostly, though, he knew when to talk and when not to, and what to talk about. Coming over to La Paloma this afternoon had been Robert's idea, but neither of us, I thought, had expected to keep going until dark. For a while we'd been joined by a doctor from Colorado, in Tucson for a medical conference and free just this one afternoon; he was playing with the husband of another conference attendee, and they'd caught up to us on a downhill, par-three that we had played twice, because the slow group in front of us hadn't let us play through. The doctor, it turned out, had once taken a lesson from a friend of mine.

Upon his return, Swig is still expounding on this trip and his game, as if I actually cared. Maybe this relieves his stress, to talk about golf like this. What happened to humor?

"Remembered how I played Woodstock, first time out in a couple of weeks; sunny, misty, empty…and for five holes I played without any sense of anything other than being within myself and that beautiful day, seeing the target, and—this was the really amazing part—swinging, I mean swinging freely, at the target, without thought of consequence, the way you feel when you are dancing well or other nice things; then, of course, I let thoughts creep in…but for that first hour it was truly glorious, and completely new and easy.

"Of course you've got to have the shots," he continued, "though there's always a new shot to learn. That's what makes the game fun. But when you're actually playing for something—a beer, a match, your career!—the most important part of your game is taking whatever it is you can already do when you're just hitting balls and pulling it off for real."

Has he forgotten I'm a dog? Sometimes I wonder.

"It sounds so simple, and in some ways it is! But then you've got a one-foot putt to win or a little 9-iron to the last green, and suddenly that little putt or that easy 9-iron feels like walking a tightrope high above the crowd under the big top, or landing a jet on a moving aircraft carrier, or going over Niagara Falls in a barrel. To make those shots you have to deal with your fears *before* you play. You have to prepare for your performance emotionally, mentally, psychologically the same way you practice your game, lift weights, eat well, get rest, take care of the rest of your life—*before you play*.

"Jack, I used to think the equation worked the other way, that if you could only pull off the impossible—win the Masters, beat the champion, whatever—then you could deal with whatever it is inside yourself that had kept you until then from achieving your goal.

"You learn this just like you learn to swing your driver. Or anything else in your game—or your life. It's not magic, though it seems like that that when you first experience it. Mostly, what I'm talking about is a matter of prior effort, and then repetition. The magic feeling, the sense of ease, comes afterwards. The challenge is to make this feeling a part of your life."

This has turned into quite a speech. And I'm not sure Swig's got it correct at the end there. Seems to me he's forgotten something he learned on another of his magazine junkets, when he spent a chilly weekend one January in West Palm Beach, Florida, with a famous golf teacher who told him, Swig said, that a golfer wanted to turn off his conscious mind and allow his subconscious to stay in control. Sounded to me a lot like what I keep hoping Swig will do with some of his stories…or maybe it's just the subject, though. I don't think so.

"Meant to add," Swig concludes, as he turns up the collar of his black fleece, "the doctor—the one who joined Robert and me at La Paloma in that story you read—was a former college basketball standout, a sport Robert had actually played professionally in Mexico and Europe. We played five or six holes from the back tees, even though the doctor's partner had just taken up golf. After we had finished our afternoon nine with the doctor and his friend, Robert and I had decided to keep going, without really any discussion, just a look and a nod and we were off like two kids. On the seventh at Canyon, I was so loose that I had almost been getting it out as far as Robert off the tee.

"I squinted at a flagstick neither of us could see.

"Had there really been something in this morning's newspaper about a snowstorm back east? I shook my head to myself as I watched the hills beyond the golf course change color, fading into a dark pink and then a gathering grayness as the sun set behind us, west toward California and other snowless locations. Winter was cool, I reminded myself; when I returned home I'd be able to ski or snowboard the next day if I extended this little break. On the other hand, if I stayed here in Tucson, where Robert told me it was often so warm in winter that he didn't need a sweater…

"'Good, good?' Robert asked as we drove up to the green, meaning that we agreed to concede one another's putts. We were unable to see where our balls had landed.

"'Good, good,' I replied."

14

Gone golfing on yet another assignment, at the induction ceremonies for the World Golf Hall of Fame, Swig experienced not only the sense of déjà vu that sometimes comes over him on such occasions but the nagging feeling that the golfing life, as he sometimes facetiously referred to it, was a giant foil. "Like golf, like travel?" I wondered, when I found some pages on his desk that appear to be a chapter of another book he started. Reading, I've been catching up on a few more of the musical adventures of my "owner."

Someplace past the Arizona/New Mexico border, as Wynton's band headed toward Albuquerque, Wynton walked sleepy-eyed into the front lounge of his tour bus. Leaning over the right shoulder of the driver, a middle-aged guy from Atlanta, he said, "Sorry, man, but the toilet's backed up again."

This was the least of the problems bothering the world's most famous jazz musician that Friday morning in November. As usual, he was behind schedule on numerous projects—the score for a soundtrack, edits for a new CD, plans for future concerts. Progress in his hometown of New Orleans was still painfully, maddeningly slow as the Crescent City rebuilt after Katrina. His oldest son, Wynton Jr., had been too busy to attend his dad's concert in Los Angeles earlier in the week.

We'd been traveling most of the night, having left Mesa, Arizona at about 2:15 a.m., a few hours after a gig the quintet played in a sold-out new hall. There were twelve bunks in the bus, four tiers of three each, located in the middle section of the bus, between the front lounge and the rear bedroom. About eighteen inches separated the mattress in the bunk from the ceiling of the bus, reason enough if you were at all claustrophobic to hang out in the front lounge. On all three television screens in the lounge a DVD had been playing soon after the bus left Mesa, though no one but Wynton's new young pianist seemed to be watching.

Wynton looked a little scraggly, as he poured milk into his cereal bowl and asked the driver (who had just pulled over so he could stop the bus for a moment while he fixed the toilet), where they were. Showing on the television monitors was CNN coverage of a car chase in California. Soon the bus, too, was moving again. It was a bright, sunny morning with fairly light traffic that the driver monitored constantly on his CB radio, all the while listening over and over to the same song by a country western singer for whom he'd driven a while back.

Dressed in sweat pants and a tee shirt, Wynton sat at the lounge's lone table and bowed his head briefly to say grace before eating his cereal. A loud ringing from the cell phone that he'd placed on the table by the cereal bowl interrupted the quiet of the moment. The phone was perhaps the only piece of contemporary technology he had embraced; he still couldn't turn on a computer.

"Damn it, I don't give a fuck who they think they are," Wynton said within seconds of answering the call, which was from one of the minions back in New York who were making the first of what would be several reports this morning on the planning for an upcoming concert and the slow progress of ticket sales for another. Ever since the most recent administrative head of his jazz organization had left several months ago, the ritual of these phone calls had become a daily occurrence in Wynton's road life. Somehow, the more contentious the issue being discussed the more enjoyment Wynton seemed to take in the conversation. Instead of tiring him out, the experience had the opposite effect, energizing his sense of the day's beginning and preparing him for the battles ahead—with a band member who needed a kick in the butt, a friend waiting to play basketball that afternoon, the arrangement of a new tune he was composing, the trumpet that he'd been wrestling with since he was a little boy, coaxing it to purr, to sing, to stun, to celebrate...to move.

Having recently observed a birthday with a gig in Victoria, British Columbia, Wynton still possessed the soft features and smooth skin of a much younger person. His natural exuberance was youthful, too, though that quality had always been mixed with a seemingly oracular wisdom that especially in his 20s and 30s belied his age. He moved from one mood to another with lightning speed and sensed in an instant the feelings of someone he was with, but his countenance did not always register his own. He could be circumspect, only to follow a question that he chose not to answer with a confession or an outburst that was as open—and sometimes abrasive—as it was unexpected.

He was relieved that the chest pains that had sent him to a hospital emergency room in California had not returned, more or less confirming the doctor's diagnosis that the problem was simply gas. He'd been lucky so far with his health; the only real issue had been the cyst on his lip that he'd finally had surgery on. He was still getting back his endurance and range, though he'd admitted one night in his New York apartment before playing a program of Louis Armstrong classics that physically the lip was now fine; what remained, he confessed, was mostly psychological, the fear that if he attempted something more than he should he might be dealing with the same problem all over again. For a trumpet player, this kind of talk was uncomfortable, like a movie actress discussing her face or a pilot his or her vision.

Between bites of his cereal and sharp, staccato questions about a promoter during another cell phone call, Wynton remembered how on another tour someone had told him he had to see the Northern Lights. And so that night he had done just that.

"And what did I see?" he asked rhetorically. "A huge horizon. A whole lot of lights!" And he laughed.

"But then I heard about a six-year-old who went to Alaska on a trip with her family. And at night she went outside and came running back to tell her parents about all the different kinds of cut-up ribbons she could see in the sky. Cut-up ribbons. To that little girl, the Northern Lights were a phenomenon."

As he said that last word, it was as if he were also recalling the older Las Vegas couple who'd come backstage after the gig there earlier in the week, a man with a black toupée wearing a purple suit and a woman with her hair in a pompadour and a greatly augmented chest showing off in a gown with a décolletage that went down almost to her navel. They worked the room, too, speaking with each person in the band and then posing for pictures with the obliging star, who draped an arm around each of their shoulders.

Or Wynton might have been describing the soundcheck the afternoon before. The band had driven most of that day from Las Vegas to Arizona, and didn't arrive at the Marriott in Mesa until the afternoon. Soon after checking in everyone had left for the Mesa Arts Center, Wynton in a black BMW convertible driven by the concert's promoter, an old friend, and the rest of the band by van or foot (the venue was only a few blocks from the hotel).

The languid Arizona air late in the day was still warm, and the street from the Marriott to the theater was quiet, crossing one busy intersection but otherwise devoid of cars or pedestrians. But the quiet scene was no reason to take it easy.

"I learned hearing Miles and them," Wynton would say, "I never was going to not really play because I didn't feel like it. Some people last night paid a hundred dollars for their tickets. There was a couple at the gig who said they'd waited eleven years to hear us. They don't care how you're feeling."

No one, of course, had bought tickets for the Mesa soundcheck, a ritual before each gig that Wynton sometimes skipped (if the band had arrived late at the day's destination, or if there were a crisis elsewhere he had to deal with on the phone, or sometimes simply because he was too tired or maybe someone he knew from his last visit to wherever had called). A soundcheck—at least the formal part of it—might only last a few minutes, after which the rhythm section usually kept playing just for fun. Or it might end before it ever really began, as happened in Los Angeles at the beginning of the week, when the usually mild-mannered saxophonist Walter Blanding had packed up his instrument and walked off the Disney Hall stage because, he said, "we're just bullshitting."

Not that day in Mesa. Without so much as a, "let's go," Wynton took his place near the front of the stage, stood very still, and started playing a ballad. All the while he played, a local crew worked with the lighting. And then it was over. Wynton put his trumpet back in its case and disappeared, back to the hotel to shower and change, but he'd return for some of the good food the caterer had prepared, including a killer meatloaf that Boss Murphy remembering it from when Wynton's big *band had played here the year before, specially requested. What wasn't finished was saved for the bus, where, about twelve hours after the Mesa gig ended, another day in the life of this band was beginning as we pulled into the parking lot of a Cracker Barrel on the outskirts of Albuquerque. It was a bright, sunny morning, chillier than in Arizona but still comfortable, and the restaurant was packed. Ahead was an afternoon and evening off, and then two weekend gigs here in New Mexico. The actor Jim Carey, who'd met Wynton earlier this week in Los Angeles, was flying in on his own plane with his daughter and bodyguard for the Saturday night performance in Albuquerque.*

Wearing the suit he had performed in, Wynton would be deep in another chess game with Walter while all around him people in his dressing room fawned over Carey. Unassuming, and smiling constantly, Carey would be posing for obligatory fan photos when the subject of hip-hop came up. Carey's daughter would quote a favorite, and Carey would say something about not necessarily approving of certain lyrics, "but I admire, say, Snoop's production values." And all this time Wynton would be staring intently at the chess board, as if he were unaware of what was being said in the room.

"Man, look it," he suddenly said, raising his head and looking directly at his new acquaintance, perched in designer jeans and leather jacket on a coffee table next to him. The room would become quiet except for Wynton's passionate, mellifluous voice.

"If I'd known when I was growing up in the '70s…I mean if I could have imagined, that a day would come in this country when one black person said to another on television or in a recording, 'Hey, nigger,' and people would be saying how this was an empowerment thing…it's not. It's a disgrace. It's minstrelsy is what it is.

"You know, I got hold of some of the old minstrel lyrics and read them to my sons. Check it out. It's practically the same words they're using now. It's degrading, man." And he would look around, wait for someone to respond, respond himself with a handshake, leaning across the space between him and Carey to find Carey's hand, shaking his head, offering also a smile, returning his gaze to the chessboard and after straightening his posture make his next chess move, listen as Carey offered a more general comment about music that would lead to a related

but altogether different kind of discussion about other musicians and where might Carey start, he was just learning the music, and, "Let me send you some things," Wynton would say, "here, call this number and tell her your address," he would continue, but Carey would already be writing it on part of a paper napkin.

That was ahead, Saturday night in Albuquerque; on Sunday morning the weekend's promoter—Bumble Bee Bob!—would pick up Wynton in a white Lincoln town car and they'd drive together to Santa Fe, an hour or so to the north, where the band was invited for a picnic at yet another friend's home before an evening gig at the historic Lensic Performing Arts Center.

In Santa Fe, they would set a blistering pace in the last tune they'd rehearsed at the Mesa soundcheck, and then the rhythm section came up with a melancholy opening to another new Wynton tune, and this was followed by a version of an extended recent piece, the title track of Wynton's first CD with Blue Note, with the different segments of the piece turned around so even their usual order was changed, and there was a kind of magic to that...like those lights high in the immense nighttime sky above Alaska, a wildness and beauty within a form...and before dawn the next day the band would have scattered, most on their way to the Albuquerque airport for early flights home, Wynton en route to New York by bus. By mid-morning that Monday, when the rest of the band was changing planes in Houston, they were crossing the Colorado plains, where Wynton worked on the final edit for one of the tunes on the upcoming CD.

Someone calling him then might be welcomed with an excerpt, which Wynton might whistle or sing, just as at home in New York he often answered the phone by playing on the piano whatever he happened to be composing, making the moment a kind of call and response. Many times at gigs he had done something like this when a child in the audience cried or laughed or in response to the rumble of a subway underground or whistle of a train that was passing outside, and in places as disparate as King of Prussia, Pennsylvania and High Point, North Carolina Wynton would move toward the side of the stage while he hit more of the high notes at the top of his final phrase before sliding all the way to the bottom in the same breath, in a technique now perfected to the point of his being able to replicate not only the timbre of someone's voice but the sound and feeling of a person's breathing, hushed sometimes, then panting, finally yearning, each such performance made with the same passion regardless of occasion or venue or audience.

"You never know when something's going to end," Wynton once said at a New York City rehearsal for his big band before it went on the road again. Wynton had just stopped his musicians after the introduction to an Ornette Coleman tune and said in a voice barely louder than a whisper that they sounded complacent, too used to playing with one another. Some seat shifting and murmuring followed before Wynton continued, this time to dutiful if perhaps annoyed attentiveness.

"Your job is to make the person next to you sound great," Wynton said. "Maybe this is the last day we play together. You need to play like it might be that last day."

Hopefully, this wasn't his last day in the world, but if it was he could say he'd had, "one glad-assed time, yes indeed." A smile crossed his lips as he spoke, remembering the places he'd been, the musicians he'd met...the women whose company he had enjoyed, and who had presumably enjoyed his. For all the so-called normal things he might have missed, the ups and downs of a typical daily life—the welcome home at day's end from family, misunderstandings between husband and wife, a last-minute trip to the grocery store for a gallon of milk, worry about an electric bill that seemed too high, the compliment of a boss that came with a raise—for all that he could say what few men and women could, that he'd done exactly what he wanted to do, every single minute of every single day...hadn't he?

15

Pressed for an answer or explanation about a tardiness or postponement, Wynton—so Swig tells me—invariably replies, "I take my time." Though an instrumentalist, he will sing a blues on the occasion of an alleged missed opportunity or failed initiative, concluding with the refrain, "I takes my time, baby. Baby, I takes my time."

Would that winter had heeded such an admonition this past weekend, Swig thought, when he found himself not on a mountaintop up north but coping with the ice and windblown drifts on the single-lane Massachusetts Turnpike during a long, slow drive back from Boston at the height of the storm. Or am I forgetting something? Hard to keep all these dates straight.

The irony of the situation struck me, too, as I reflected on our venture out into a snowy world on a day Swig had been expecting to ski Mount Tremblant in distant, French-speaking Quebec. Done in then by the weather as well as by an illness in his family, those plans were rescheduled for later in the winter.

Back when he first got the ski bug and thought nothing of leaving the city where he lived at five in the morning to be on the lift when it opened four hours later, he would have known the answer. But that was before the era of all-night snowmaking and corduroy-perfect grooming, made possible by the advent not only of technology but—gasp—the $80 holiday lift ticket that one of our local playgrounds is now charging.

Tempus fugit: these days, even at the beginning of a ski season that has started later than in recent years, Swig tries not to hurry. Enjoying the routine, he still packs his stuff the night before and likes to make a lunch to bring. He still gets up early and if he's in luck stops on the way at a diner for the world's finest ham and eggs (the cook, a die-hard Yankees fan, carves the ham to order). Depending on where he's going, he may avoid I-91 and take a shortcut on some back roads, though the last time he tried that on a trip back from Bromley he got stuck on an unplowed dirt road south of Grafton. Had to retrace his steps and stop for some Grafton cheddar.

At his destination he no longer puts his boots on in the parking lot but, instead, leaves his skis or board outside the lodge and then carries his clothing bag inside. There, thanks to the best ski tip he ever got, he even changes into a pair of dry socks he's remembered to bring. What a dry toe-comfort difference that makes on an especially cold day!

At Stratton, where he always makes the resort's cozy Sunbowl area his base, to avoid the crowds, he walks to the bottom of the six-seater Sunrise Express, unless, as was the case a year ago April, the snow is too deep. Ditto at Mount Snow, where the Carinthia area is always a good bet for parking and ease of access. He's looking forward this year to exploring the possibility of this kind of option at Okemo, the third of his trio of usual places for a daytrip, where the newer Jackson Gore section of the privately-owned resort is open.

Swig says he's thinking about Okemo right now, the last time he went there with Maren, the dinner they had the night of their arrival at a small, family restaurant on Ludlow's Main Street. It was snowing lightly after they ate and they walked along the street counting the snowflakes in what may be the most quintessential ski town in New England. It was quiet there, and even quieter in the morning when they awoke to several inches of fresh powder that they could see on the hill between their condo and the lift.

So much for resolutions: he was in such a hurry to make first tracks that they skipped breakfast. Sweet were those early morning descents through tight glades and over slick straight-aways. With only a brief break for some of Okemo's famous french fries, they continued their search for the perfect run, and when the midday sun had softened the snow into something more the consistency of chilly mush they had long ago lost track of the time. When was that?

This afternoon, walking through the woods behind our house and then along a winter path that crosses the neighboring farm before we return on the deserted golf course—a kind of circle Swig and I make each winter day when he's home—Swig tells me about a recent conversation he had in New York, when he spoke with the artist Drue Katoaka about the Japanese enso, or circle, which Swig says he sensed is like the creation and then the publication of a book.

A chapter of such a book, Swig says, as we pick our way through a slushy, muddy path…a chapter might be titled "30" (the chapter, not the book), might track Wynton through a frantic fall and early winter, when he was straining to complete a long composition on time for a Brooklyn premiere, then move to Princeton (where Wynton was recording what turned out to be one of his last classical CDs). Swig remembers a moment the following spring, when Wynton was pushing to finish another long piece (much of which he wrote on the bus and in hotel rooms as his septet played gigs all across the United States), when he looked at Swig and, shaking his head, said, "Thirty." That was the only word (not an uncommon occurrence; he did the same thing with names, still does, so that a sign of affection when he sees someone is simply to say his or her name, or nickname, and then maybe repeat it after a pause, as if the name carried some special import—which, in the world according to Wynton, it does).

"Such a chapter," Swig continues, "might link in a larger narrative arc to some of the events of this past year with others, longer ago, like that already distant time in Princeton, and I don't mean only musically (though, my, how he played the chorale of the Hindemith Trumpet Sonata, the dark tones echoing the dying winter light outside Richardson Hall, or the poignant affirmation of Ravel's *Habanera* in a ravishing arrangement for trumpet and piano). Wynton alternately praised and questioned his friend and veteran producer about the recorded sound of his trumpet. He cajoled and flirted with the pianist, who had been his piano teacher at Juilliard. Often he broke into a blues upon the completion of another take, one time improvising upon the nickname Swig had been awarded the month before during a gig at Blues Alley in Washington D.C. ('I've got the Tre Swig blues,' Wynton sang with a false tremolo. 'They called me Tre Swig, they called me Tre Swig all night long.')"

The inclusiveness Wynton created with that small gesture was soon followed by another, Swig remembers, with three total strangers (to Wynton). One of Swig's closest college friends had lived in Princeton, and the previous summer had died tragically, leaving three kids, the oldest still in high school. Swig had called their mom, after driving that morning to Princeton (where he also took a call from Wynton, wondering where he was supposed to be—a typical question whenever Wynton was on the road, which was most of the time back then). After explaining to her what he was doing, Swig had asked about her children and impulsively invited them to come by Richardson Hall after they got home from school. Around four o'clock, that is just what they did. They were each musical, and Swig knew that her son had recently started playing jazz piano.

"During another break between takes I introduced them to Wynton and mentioned that one of them played piano," Swig tells me.

"'Play something for me,' Wynton said.

"Shyly at first, the boy took a seat at the piano on stage and started a blues. Without saying anything further, Wynton sat down next to him on the piano bench, then stood up, then sat down again and finally joined in, adding a little descant.

"'That was cool,' Wynton said. Looking over at the boy's two sisters, Wynton continued, 'And you've got your cheering section with you.'"

He didn't know the word then, Swig says, but that moment, like certain relationships in his life, his family, friends, the constant evolution and echo of work and play…love…was the completion of an enso…and in New York, Swig continues, as he looked out at the sunlight on the leafless trees in Central Park, he wondered if, as Wynton's friend remarked, the two ends of your enso are the points both furthest from one another and closest, then what bridges the gap, what enables us at certain times if we only dare it to take the "short" route, face to face, note to note, across that space that is so close yet so far, deep, dangerous, and yet, finally, strong?

It's a question, he tells me, that he faced again in a story he leaves out, as if for me to read, soon after a New Year's overnight trip to Chicago…

…that somber city, cold and snow-swept, summoning ghosts after twilight along the lake, the wind off the lake howling like the faded roars for old hockey stars, the screech of the elevated at Adams and Monroe mimicking the long-gone grooves of Eddie, Bix, Benny, and Louis. Bundling himself in extra layers for the short walk to Symphony Hall from the gilded Palmer House, now a Hilton, Wynton all but ignored a compliment about his massive work for jazz band, symphony orchestra, and chorus that was about to receive its Chicago premiere.

"Where's my horn at?" Wynton asked. "Do you see it?" And then he remembered he had left it after the rehearsal at the hall. Time to go.

Walking quickly, impatiently waiting for the elevator, he focused now on the music, not its ability to contain a sense of each place in which it had already been presented but, rather, on what he himself would be doing tonight during the two-hour concert. As he cut across the back of a parking lot to the stage door, Wynton gave no outward indication that he was thinking about anything other than who might win the Bears-Saints game on Sunday (he'd played The Saints Go Marching In *at the conclusion of the final rehearsal that morning). The placid look on his face was not a pose; unlike so many performers who became anxious before a performance, Wynton eagerly awaited the moment when the house lights dimmed and the audience hushed. He'd prepared his whole life for what followed; to play the trumpet then, he said, was his power.*

"All right, now," he greeted the female guard backstage and kept walking, around two corners and then down a flight of stairs to his dressing room. Removing his overcoat and woolen cap, he opened the black leather case on the chair next to the couch and took out his trumpet. Unpolished except for its gold mouthpiece, it looked old but was actually a new prototype model that Dave Monette had given him in Washington state when his quintet performed there in the fall. Weighing less than most of his previous horns, it incorporated a breakthrough that Monette might have explained to him, but Wynton paid little attention to such details. The horn could either play or it couldn't; this one could. He'd known that before he tried a note.

Holding the trumpet, idly pushing its finger buttons, he sat now on the couch. He'd neglected to turn on the light when he came in; no need to. Someone brought him an espresso from the machine down the hall, and he sipped it, making a little face, but said nothing. He was wearing a black tuxedo, white shirt, and light gray silk tie with a design of small red squares and smaller white ones. Cradled in his long, thin-fingered hands, the trumpet seemed a physical extension of himself, just as the notes that started to come out of its bronze bell when he blew into its other end instantly became the feeling of this early evening, the crowd of people in the lobby of the venerable building across Michigan Avenue from the city's art museum as they removed coats, picked up tickets, moved toward the inner doors, everywhere a palpable sense of anticipation, a collective murmur in this grand space, the human noise of shuffling feet, coughs, whispers, and soon it would be his time to walk slowly upstairs, wait for his cue from the stage manager, then take his place with the rest of his band, seated in the midst of the great orchestra, and he would wait with eager anticipation for the chorus to sing the notes that began the piece, notes he'd written down in a little notebook while sitting at the piano in the living room of his New York City condominium but truly, if someone asked, he'd first heard them long ago, the echo of the horn on the New Orleans bus his mother had to ride in the rear, the song of the bird in the bush that summer night in Massachusetts when he sang to it in return, the voice of his second trumpet teacher, sternly telling him to leave when he'd shown up unprepared for a lesson, the lonesome distant train whistle he heard through the open window one fragrant early spring night in Columbus, Mississippi, the cry of his first born when he came out of his mother's womb and when…when had he ever heard anything more beautiful?

The story makes me think of Swig's nearly one hundred-year-old Vermont friend—and Wynton's—Blanche Moyse and her rapture over Bach, which began when she was a girl in Switzerland and first heard the *Saint Matthew Passion* at the age of ten. "That summer, in the mountains, I knew by memory the passages I loved," she once told Swig. Given a score by a teacher, she learned the work, she said, "by singing to myself, crying all alone." Before rehearsals for a new performance of the *Saint Matthew* she still relearned the piece by singing it to herself in her head wherever she was—in the bathtub, cooking. "I go from number to number," she explained to Swig in her mountaintop Vermont home, "and when I make a mistake I work on it." Each time she conducted the piece, she said, "I see, I hear it better. It's like the mountains. You see the summit. Then, when you reach it, you see more summits."

As an "artist-interpreter," Moyse defined her role as "someone who falls in love with beauty, who cannot create it himself or herself. It's fantastic, like a photographer in love with nature, so excited about fantastic sunsets that other people are able to enjoy them." Diminutive in physical stature, Blanche presided on the podium with an authority that stemmed in part from the feeling she conveyed of sharing a momentous discovery. "I'm just like the person who opens the door," she said. "What moves people in my performances is what Bach did. I feel especially clear it is not me. I'm not there. The *way* we do it is mine, but the greatness is the music. You are illuminated by the song, but it is the song that is incredible, not you."

On a January night several years ago, over dinner at her daughter's New York City apartment, Blanche met Wynton, who as long as Swig had known him kept on the wall by the desk in his study a friend's color photograph of her beatific face as she led a rehearsal of Bach. "Generosity of heart," she told Wynton during dinner, saying she was quoting her late father-in-law, the flutist Marcel Moyse, "begets beauty of tone."

As they left, Blanche asked Wynton how she could stay in touch with him, and he invited her to attend rehearsals in New Haven. Her daughter drove her there, whereupon Blanche got herself a hotel room and announced she was staying the entire week.

"I can't hear everything you are saying," she told Wynton at the first rehearsal.

"Then sit up here on the stage," he said.

And she did, between two of the saxophonists in the band; she was still sitting there when a CBS television crew arrived to shoot footage for an interview.

"I'll move," Blanche said.

"No, you can stay right there," Wynton said.

And so, when the interview ran several weeks later, there in one shot of the band was white-haired Blanche.

16

Not Bach but Mozart has been the composer of choice for Swig of late. And he doesn't just listen constantly to Mozart's music; he's started talking about Mozart all the time, telling me a story that sounds so authentic I'm beginning to think it must be true.

Pawing at the basement door before, I'm ready for my noontime walk before Swig's finished zipping his jacket and grabbing his gloves. A gust of wind sends snow flying into our faces as we step outside. It's mid-March, and the second storm in as many consecutive Saturdays has yet to subside. The snow in our backyard is nearly a foot deep.

"An intimate tale of passion and creativity set in late eighteenth-century Vienna," Swig describes his Mozart story, "which presents a riveting portrait of one of history's greatest composers and dramatically decodes the dynamic relationship in Mozart's music between technique and emotion, particularly that of longing." Pretty cool, I wanted to compliment him, but don't get carried away with cleverness, I wish I could add. "Narrated in the first person by the ravishing…Dulcinea Anders (a piano pupil of the legendary man she comes to call Amadé)…the story will also depict a clandestine couple's ecstatic exploration of paradise found and lost."

This is actually pretty nice right here, I want to remind him as we set off. Such vistas. Fresh air. Memories.

One of the neat things about snowshoeing, Swig has figured out immediately, is the learning curve: instantaneous. The only thing he has to remember is not to follow me over every fence or under a fallen branch, or he'll catch the tip of a shoe. And he needs to find a good rhythm, I realize, brisk enough to keep me from getting bored but steady so he doesn't suddenly get out of breath.

"Fiction with a basis in expert fact," I overheard Swig telling his agent on the phone this morning, "*The Breathless Present* takes place during the mysterious summer and fall of 1788, about which very little in Mozart's well documented career is known. No Mozart letters from this period survive, except for one to his sister and repeated entreaties to a Masonic friend for money. Mozart was 32 then, with three years of his short but hugely productive life left; his father had died the year before, a six-month-old daughter borne by his often infirm wife Constanze would not live, and he was broke, which among other things obliged him to move from one Vienna suburb to another. Facing the abyss, he had never been more alone."

Phew.

"Throughout this period," Swig continued, "in order to support his family and their relatively lavish lifestyle, the most accomplished figure in the history of Western music continued taking in pupils." Perhaps immodestly, he added: "*The Breathless Present* will imagine such a student, a young woman who is as beautiful as she is talented. Smitten, the charismatic Mozart begins to explain to his protégé what he has been working on, sometimes with music at the piano, occasionally with talk at his own billiard table, eventually in bed. Dulcinea Anders' education, within the story's narrative, will become the reader's."

Soon we're on the snow-covered, seventh tee of the golf course. No foursomes in sight! I bound over to the adjacent third green, while we continue down the third fairway toward the third tee. The empty sheep pasture beckons on the other side of the tee, and we head toward a knoll I can just make out in the blowing snow. We stop when we reach it, and I look around in the silence, staying at Swig's side because he has bribed me with a biscuit.

"Ten years younger than Mozart," Swig said on the phone, reading from something he had written, "Dulcinea has a premonition he is going to die soon, and recognizes finally—fatefully— that his only enduring attachment can be with music. But Dulcinea also realizes that Mozart's ability to take his listeners to a sense of the infinite, to rejoice and to comfort, comes from her mentor's—her lover's—intimacy with every aspect of human life. Most importantly of all, she begins to see how life's vicissitudes, large and small—both the big crisis and the day to day—bring each of us full square to face a much more terrifying truth: the answer to the question, 'Who am I?'"

He was on a roll by then and kept going.

"Sensing something from the very start, Dulcinea records her encounters and observations, and by early autumn, when her lessons and affair come to their inevitable conclusion, she has written a musical memoir unlike any other. Dulcinea's diary, complete with a cache of explosively revealing letters Mozart wrote her and several she wrote him, remained puzzlingly unknown until just recently, when a stagehand in the basement of the Vienna opera house found all the material.

"Emerging from the pages of Dulcinea's diary, the mythic figure of Mozart becomes a man as vital as his life-giving, gorgeous music. Dulcinea helps Amadé get through his grief over his daughter Theresia's death, talks to him about his larger-than-life father, comforts him over the chilly Viennese reception to *Don Giovanni*, cheers him up when a summer concert series is cancelled. As their duet plays out through stories in which Mozart looks back at his work, most of which he had written by the time of this 'lost' year of his life, Dulcinea's whole approach to music—and love—has changed, charged with the energy, the *chi*, of his creativity.

"'What a rake he is!' she thinks initially, unaware that the man who composed the sonatas and concertos she is practicing once confessed in a letter to a cousin that he hoped to take a shit on her nose. 'How does his celebration of the physical nurture his creation of something so spiritual?' she wonders, not without daydreams of her own. After only a few lessons, Mozart leaves his fly unbuttoned; one day Dulcinea forgets her underwear! Finally they plunge together into a four-hands piano transcription of *The Marriage of Figaro* he has arranged for her.

"'Now,' he urges her, 'play each note as if your life depended on it.'"

Is that a voice we hear? From the woods? Or long ago?

17

Coming home from an assignment in Newark, Swig hadn't planned to take the back roads through the Berkshires. But after several detours because of flooding, he found himself late on that rainy April afternoon in Great Barrington, near the old movie theater, across the abandoned train tracks, a block from Main Street—down which in one direction was his father's first church and the other way his one-time apartment, and at the bottom of the hill on which the local hospital stood, where after his parents came back to the Berkshires Swig spent so much time visiting his father after a Thanksgiving car accident.

Swig's memories knit themselves with downtown Newark, where he reminds me he'd been that morning, also in the rain, the old buildings there, the fat white cop at Starbucks who told the old black guy selling newspapers in the rain to keep the change, the delight of the man he was interviewing when Swig said the name Louis Armstrong, the memory of that man's childhood love of jazz, which he said had sustained many people in Nazi Europe. The mention of that horror, he says, reminded Swig of Ellie Jewel Dahmer, the Mississippi woman whose nightmare he documented in a magazine story that was a decided departure for him. What, he still wondered, had sustained her?

Several miles north of town around a big bend in the road after the pavement changed from asphalt to crushed stone and the land opened up on the western side, Ellie Jewell Dahmer kept her cows in the fields once farmed by her murdered husband. She could see the cows when she was outside taking care of her flowers, under the shade of one of the four, giant, flame-scarred oak trees planted by her husband's forebears; another oak, on the other side of the driveway, stood near the concrete foundation of her husband's store, destroyed in the fire. Behind the house, pine trees rimmed the small field, the last place on earth her husband, Vernon Dahmer Sr., ever walked after the Ku Klux Klan assaulted his home and his family. But the man responsible for orchestrating the crime remained free for more than thirty years, living in a predominantly black, poor neighborhood in the nearby town of Laurel, Mississippi, where he owned a vending machine business called, incredibly, the Sambo Amusement Company. Vernon Dahmer Sr. was 58 years old when he died. Four of his sons were on active military duty at the time of his death.

Every day when Ellie Jewell walked down the hallway in her one-story ranch house, she passed the spot where the picture window in the family's home used to be. The glass in the window was shattered by gunshot the night of the Klan attack. Then the Klansmen threw gasoline bombs into the house, which caught fire. When Ellie Jewell was awakened by the smell of smoke, the first thing she saw were the eaves of the house in flames.

"Wake up, Vernon," she said as she shook her husband in panic. "They got us now."

They were the same Klansmen who had been threatening the family since Vernon Dahmer Sr. had started speaking out on behalf of voting rights for Hattiesburg blacks.

Everyone in the community knew Vernon, who ran a cotton farm, and owned and operated the area's only general store and a planer mill. He was born in a house down the road from where he lived with Ellie Jewell, his third wife. One of twelve children, he was the only male in his generation in his family who did not migrate north.

A leader by quiet example, Dahmer was known for his kindness and generosity. He regularly gave help to travelers who ran out of gas on the highway, despite the danger that one of them might be a member of the Klan. Neighbors who didn't have enough money to buy food for their children could shop at his store and pay later (when he died, many people owed him money). The pond in the middle of the pasture across the road from his home was open to everyone as a place to cool off on a hot day. Vernon also liked to go fishing there, a pleasure he shared with Ellie Jewell. He even kept a little boat in the pond; it had to be little in a pond that small.

Despite his lack of free time, Vernon Dahmer Sr. became involved in the activities of the local NAACP. When in his view the NAACP moved too slowly to make voting rights a reality for the black citizens of

Hattiesburg, Dahmer invited organizers from SNCC (the Student Nonviolent Coordinating Committee) to live in his home while they did voter recruitment work. They stayed for the better part of a year, moving on to another area of Mississippi well before the Klan attacked Dahmer and family.

"*We got calls," Ellie Jewell recalled. "Always had.*

"'*Nigger, you're going to get killed.*'"

By then, Ellie Jewell had lost her Hattiesburg teaching job and been forced to find work elsewhere. Vernon's insurance policies were canceled, and the couple could no longer borrow money from the bank. Klan threats were repeated.

"*They didn't say it to me or the children, but when he picked the phone up they would say it to him:*

"'*Nigger, you want to be white, you want your children to go to school with white people.*'"

Ellie Jewell and Vernon had to sleep in shifts.

"*I would sleep the first part of the night and Vernon would sleep the second part of the night," Ellie Jewell remembered, in the strong, calm voice with which she narrated her memories. "I would go to bed as soon as we finished everything. And I would go to bed early, especially during the school year, because then I could sleep from about five or six in the evening until about one or two in the morning. And then Vernon would go to sleep, and I would get up, and start making preparations for the next day—dinner, ironing, whatever I could do to keep myself from going back to sleep.*"

Fear became a constant part of the Dahmers' lives, governing their view of the world. But fear did not dissuade Vernon Dahmer Sr. from acting according to his principles. He and his wife continued to sleep in shifts, while the pressure on them increased.

Nigger, you're going to get killed.

"*The latter part of 1965, in December, we stopped getting calls," Ellie Jewell explained. "We thought everything had quieted down.*"

In the false sense of security created by a lull in white response to the integration struggle, Ellie Jewell and Vernon had thought they were safe.

"*We made it through Christmas of '65 and then it happened to us on the tenth of January,*" Ellie Jewell continued. "*We had our guard down. Because if we had been sleeping in shifts, I probably would have been up.*

"*They hit us somewhere between 1:00 and 1:30, because when I looked at the clock at the hospital it was near 2:00 when we got there.*"

The house burned quickly. Where Ellie Jewell sat as we spoke in her rebuilt kitchen was a bedroom then. During the frantic flight to save the lives of her family, she did not have time to get dressed. She ran to find her ten-year-old daughter Bettie and shouted down the hallway to her son Dennis, who was twelve. Vernon rushed to the living room and started firing his gun through the shattered picture window. Ellie Jewell opened a window in the rear of the house so she and Bettie could jump out.

"*I hit the window so hard I fell,*" she said. "*I heard shots coming in before we left the house.*"

Another, older son of Vernon's named Harold fled through a different window with Dennis. Harold, who was 25 and just home from military service, then ran to the carport to rescue his father's pickup truck before it caught fire. The family's sedan was already burning.

"*Where's Aunt Rainey?*" one of the family called out in alarm.

Eighty-year-old Luranie Heidelberg was Vernon Dahmer's great aunt. She lived in the back of Dahmer's general store, where she also worked. The store was across the driveway from the house. The store was also on fire.

"*I'm okay,*" Aunt Rainey's voice came from the rear of the yard, where she had hidden in terror.

Shadows created by the light of the fire outlined the shapes of trees and people. In that frightful light, the family made its way to the hay barn at the farthest edge of the yard, by the woods. Over the rustle of dead leaves and the creaking of branches, amidst their own panting, everyone listened.

There was the sound of a car driving up the road, away from the house. The family could hear a tire rim scraping on the road. Someone must have shot out a tire—either Vernon or, in their confusion, one of the Klansmen.

None of the Dahmers knew if the Klansmen would return to attack them again. It was cold in the barn. Bettie was crying hysterically, her arms and her face burned. And Vernon was having difficulty breathing. His lungs could not inhale enough oxygen.

Harold raced up the road to a neighbor's for help. The rest of the family waited, watching the remains of their home and the store disappear in the smoke: the paneling in the rooms that Vernon had planed himself in his planer mill, Bettie's and Dennis's toys, everyone's clothes, all the family photographs, furniture, food. Everything they owned.

"They wanted to destroy us," Ellie Jewell remembered. "They didn't just want to kill my husband or burn our home, they wanted to get us all."

That afternoon, in a hospital room with Bettie, Vernon Dahmer lay in bed, his lungs mortally seared from the fire and smoke. Bettie's arms and face were bandaged. Miraculously, the other members of the family were physically all right.

Vernon Dahmer Sr.'s wife sat at his bedside. She placed her hands on one of his.

"Jewell," he said, and died.

Farther up the hill from the hospital in Great Barrington was the Lord's mansion, the place where Fritz grew up, singing all those years ago in his dad's junior choir, Fritz who eschewed his family's real estate business and in the '70s lived on a beautiful old farm with his kids and wife, and who after that marriage ended went off to Harvard Law School from which he graduated at around the age of forty, Fritz who led the memorial service they had on Mount Everett when they scattered his dad's ashes and who, Swig learned after her own death, was his mother's close friend following his dad's move to North Carolina, without her.

"On a summer afternoon, Mrs. Dahmer and Swig climbed into her pickup truck and drove across the road, where Swig removed the barway from the pasture fence while she drove the truck into the pasture. They then drove slowly over the bumpy ground past an occasional tree to the pond where she and her husband used to fish and where her

children and the neighbors used to swim. Her cows had beaten them to the spot; it was a hot day, and the animals were trying without much luck to stay cool.

Mrs. Dahmer's dog, Heidi, rode in the rear of the truck. Whenever they passed a cow, Heidi stared at it and seemed to think about jumping out. Finally, when Mrs. Dahmer parked the truck near the pond, the temptation for Heidi was too great and she did jump over the side. Swig had to chase her and call her back to the truck.

It was hot—probably a hundred degrees in the sun. Not until around Thanksgiving does southern Mississippi get its first frost, and through the fall the temperatures are apt to remain in the 70s. In late August, the trees were still in full leaf. The air smelled of pine needles and cedar.

They drove back across the pasture to the house and Mrs. Dahmer parked the truck in the carport. Then they walked around to the front of the house, where a ditch had been dug to lay pipe for a new connection to the town water line.

"I pay $22 a month for water," Mrs. Dahmer lamented, though she used the water mostly for her flowers. There were roses here, Queen Anne roses and others.

"That's a pin oak," she said pointing across the yard. "The leaves stay on the longest." These were old trees, probably seventy or eighty years old. A wisteria bush stood nearby.

Inside the house, the phone rang. It was a neighbor, telling Ellie Jewell that one of her cows seemed not to be well.

"Uh-huh," she said as she listened. She prefaced many of her answers to questions with that word, as if to give herself a moment's pause to think through what she wants to say, as if she were reminding herself that she lived much of her life in a society where a black person might be killed for making the wrong reply to even the simplest of questions. Generous with her time, she was careful with her words.

They went back outside, got into the truck again, and drove to the field where the sick cow was. After looking at her for a moment and talking briefly with the neighbor who had called her, Mrs. Dahmer returned to the house and immediately telephoned the veterinarian.

"This is Ellie J. Dahmer and I have a cow that is sick," she said. She gave the vet directions to her house. While she was waiting for him to come, she complained about the poor economics of raising beef. "Yesterday, the price of cows was at an all time low at the auction," she said. "Two hundred and forty-one dollars a cow was the average."

After the vet examined the sick animal, he reported that the cow had "blue tongue," and he gave Mrs. Dahmer some medicine to cure it. Shaking her head over the potential cost of having to treat all her cows for the disease, she wrote him a check, and he left.

Up Monroe Road, Ellie Jewell's daughter Bettie wondered who had been visiting. She would give her mother a call. They talked often. Every morning at six her mother called her, usually to chat about the farm, or Bettie's work for the state employment security commission. And sometimes they talked about what happened years ago. The memories were always there, still fresh and unspeakably painful. But they were, if not balanced, assuaged by other, happier ones.

"I was terrified that night," Bettie said. "I had no idea what was going on. I was very very bitter for a long time toward anyone who was white, because of what happened. I'm still very bitter towards the persons who were involved in the death of my father. But at least I am able to distinguish between the two. I have more or less come to the realization that you cannot live off anger. It will destroy you."

She lived in a stone ranch house built by one of her older brothers.

"It's peaceful here," she said. "You know, even though we have had a violent past—a tragedy occurred—it's peaceful here. I feel safe here. We don't have a whole lot of money, but we live pretty good. This is still a community, we all know everybody. People still check on each other."

Bettie loved to read. She had happy memories of the times she used to spend in the library in downtown Hattiesburg, "a beautiful building" (a new library has since replaced it). She used to go to that library "and sit in one of those comfortable leather seats and go off on my trip, wherever I was going that day."

After the fire, when Bettie first went back to school, she was still bandaged. She could not use her hands. Friends had to help her, just to open a door.

"I do not physically remember being in the fire," she said. "I remember the intense heat. I remember Daddy having skin hanging off of him. I remember the intense heat and fumes, skin just literally hanging off Daddy, but he never complained, he never complained. I didn't understand how what had happened could happen. I was just a ten-year-old child."

Bettie's father adored her, and they spent a lot of time together, much of it working. They'd go fishing, too. They'd walk to the pond and fish for bream, bass, and some "huge" catfish. But mostly they worked.

"We worked from can to can't—from can see to can't see. Yes indeed, Daddy believed in work." And she laughed.

It was a busy life at the Dahmer farm. Everyone was expected to help out.

"Get up and get it," was Vernon Dahmer's philosophy, even when the person who had to get up and go get it was a young child. Bettie Dahmer remembered learning to drive a tractor almost before she knew how to ride a bike, so she could help her father in his cotton fields. Nights when they were harvesting cotton, Vernon would come in for a late supper and then head outside again, working in the dark with his tractor lights on. Even during the school year, Ellie Jewell helped out on weekends, in addition to doing the family cooking before she left for work and after she got home. There was little time left for play. But there was always time for church. Vernon was superintendent of the Shady Grove Baptist Church Sunday School, and the family attended church very Sunday, usually not returning home until well into the afternoon, the one time during the week when Bettie and her brother Dennis could also play with their friends.

An attractive woman who smiled readily, Bettie never flinched as she discussed what she remembered about the night of January 10, 1966. But she didn't want Swig to take her photograph because she hadn't yet put her makeup on. The makeup covered the disfiguration of her skin, from the burns she suffered in the fire.

Later, at a candlelight memorial service for her father, Bettie joined her family and friends in the Shady Grove Baptist Church, next to the cemetery where Vernon Dahmer was buried. Just before the service was to start, it began to rain, so the congregation had to move inside.

Bettie sat in the front pew, next to her mother. The minister leading the service had asked for a family member to read one of the scriptures, and Bettie had volunteered. When it was time to do so she read from Saint Matthew, in a voice that was so gracefully inflected she might have been singing:

"Blessed are they which are persecuted for righteousness' sake: for theirs is the kingdom of heaven."

Then she took her seat next to her mother, and the Mount Carmel Baptist Church Inspirational Choir sang.

"Oh, freedom," the voices sang. "Before I be a slave, I'll be buried in my grave."

After the anthem, everyone joined in singing Amazing Grace. *Then the minister prayed aloud.*

"What's been done in the dark will be brought to light," he said. And some in the congregation responded aloud, saying "Amen," or "That's right."

Speaking in a booming voice, the minister concluded, "If justice doesn't get you here, *it will get you* there."

Upset by the memories that had been stirred yet again, Ellie Jewell kept her eyes closed. Tears formed in the corners of her eyes and she let them come. Her head bowed in prayer, she wept. Finally, she stood and walked outside to greet people, to speak one at a time with each of those who had come to see her.

From the movie theater, Swig returned to his car, thought about calling Fritz, changed his mind—he would do that next time—got out of the car again and walked back past the theater and toward the train tracks that cut right through the center of town. Was this, he wondered, where his father used to take the train on trips back to New York to see his parents, or had he driven first to nearby Hillsdale and taken the train from there instead? What was he still looking for?

18

Another summer. Swig's just back from a magazine assignment that took him out west for a long weekend, during which he interviewed another famous athlete, someone he liked.

"And what a deal it was, to arrange it, I mean," Swig says. He seems bothered again by the nagging sense that what was really interesting to him was not the athlete's fame or the athletic achievement that drove it but a series of seemingly random little events that transpired while he was traveling. And he ticks some of them off: the Korean owner of a dry cleaners at a strip mall by his motel who fixed the zipper in a pair of his jeans; the bartender at the steakhouse who didn't question his request to have his wine put on a separate check; the waitress at another restaurant who'd never heard of Wynton and so after dinner he bought a CD at an adjacent Barnes & Noble and returned to the restaurant to give it to her...and I want to tell Swig it's more than fine, these anecdotes about the human music he hears, they *are* the story, his story.

What else could he have been thinking when he decided several years ago today to jettison yet another rewrite of the very long book proposal he'd spent much of a year writing and rewriting, and deciding instead to write his "own" book (damn quotation marks)? How, sitting in a Starbucks in Boston, late on a December afternoon, trying out the new wifi card in his laptop, did he realize that an email he was writing to a friend about a musical rehearsal he'd just attended in Boston's Symphony Hall—an email in which he not only described the hall, the stage, the players, and the music, but also began making connections with his dead father, his ailing mother, his youngest daughter—how at that exact moment could he have suddenly recognized what began to grow then and sustains him still?

"Found my way back to some work," Swig wrote another friend, in an email I peaked at. "Completed it in town outside at a cafe, and then came home and kind of punted my way through the pre-dinner hour and dinner itself and then I was really up shit creek—haven't used that expression in maybe 35 years—and walked Jack early and came back and got ready for bed and poked my head into the den where Bonnie was watching TV and finally said goodnight, it wasn't even nine yet, read a little more of a new translation of *The Odyssey*—enthralling—and was soon asleep; forgot to mention, have my first poison ivy of the season, on my right forearm; anyway, when at 1:15 a.m. or whatever time it was I suddenly had that panic feeling I've had off and on these past months, but mostly gone recently, I focused hard, thinking about a biography of Mozart I found from stuff my mother had saved, a biography I had read as a child and in the flyleaf is a bookplate with my name on it and an image of a boy sitting on a rock looking out at the sea and a distant enchanted island."

He was still "there" this early morning, on his way to the airport to pickup Maren, who had been visiting her brother and was flying in from LAX on a Delta redeye; he was thinking about this, he says, as he drove at dawn through Holyoke, an old mill city south of the town where we live, on a route he has taken countless times on his way to another writing assignment (on his way to the airport, that is): what he *knew* this morning after a record-breaking walk around the golf course—we found 35 balls, nine of which were expensive Titleist Pro V-1s (most of them lost, Swig guessed, in a charity tournament held yesterday)—that prompted us to take a field trip to Conway, where Swig and Bonnie used to live. Not a long drive, maybe half an hour, but in terms of commerce and local culture it's worlds away.

"The musical world," Swig tells me on the way there, "is shocked when the sensational diary, more than two hundred years old, of a pupil of Mozart is found in the basement of the Vienna opera house and authenticated by a panel of musical scholars." Right away I realize we are back to the story I overheard him talking about in March. "Johann von Englewood, the esteemed chair of the panel, explains the context of the diary's chronology in the 'lost' year, 1788, of the great composer's late period. But he is unable to fathom the frank language that animates the diary's entries, which are organized chapter-like by date and explicitly convey the composer's celebration of human sexuality. In fact, Professor Englewood confesses, there are several passages he would rather not have had to read. What could Mozart have been thinking?"

I'll be damned if I know, but Swig seems certain he's figured it out.

"It's spring, 1788, and 22-year-old Dulcinea Anders, a Viennese beauty ten years Mozart's junior, arrives at Mozart's home in early May for her first piano lesson with the man she will soon address as Amadé. Anders lives with her father, Josef, a prosperous merchant, who has never remarried since his wife, Dulcinea's mother, died of consumption when Dulcinea was eighteen. Technically very talented, Anders makes a poor first impression on her new teacher, or so she believes, in the diary she begins immediately to keep. Caught off balance by the invasiveness of Mozart's questions and the physicality of his manner, she is flattered when he invites her to attend a rehearsal for the Vienna premiere of his new opera, *Don Giovanni*. Afterwards, he uses material from an aria in the second act to illustrate the difference between playing notes and making music. But Dulcinea ponders Mozart's true motives. What is the real reason for the extra time he gives her? Why does contemplating this excite her?"

Think he's leading me on here, as if I was born yesterday.

"All is not well in the Mozart household, Dulcinea realizes by the beginning of June. Still grieving over the death the year before of his father, a fierce man whose legacy, in a sense, is his son's career, Mozart seems preoccupied with worries that are certainly not Dulcinea's doing. Little by little as he works with her on several suites by Bach, Mozart shares information about himself. His daughter, Theresia, born the previous December, is sick. Though Mozart does not mention the correspondence he initiates with his fellow Mason, Michael Püchberg, asking for money, the Mozart family is about to move again to save on rent. Perhaps he will be able to pay Püchberg back with the proceeds from some concerts to be given later in the summer, for which Mozart composes the first of what turn out to be his last three symphonies. He completes this piece, his Symphony No. 39 in E flat, on the 26th of

June, the same day he tells Dulcinea he has written a piano sonata for her. Three days later, Theresia dies, the third of Mozart's four children not to survive.

"By now, Dulcinea's personal rapport with her teacher has advanced even more rapidly than her musical education. Over the summer, Mozart continues composing, including two of his greatest masterpieces, the Symphony No. 40 in G minor and Symphony No. 41 in C. Dulcinea records the musical details in her diary, with an increasing confidence about her ability to understand the nuances of all that Mozart has explained, particularly insofar as they shed light on how the music achieves its effects —what, in other words, makes the music work. Fascinated as she is by these astounding music lessons, on a deeper level Dulcinea is intrigued by the hints and declarations through behavior and words of what beyond the practical necessities of earning a living moves Mozart.

"Lonely when she first comes to Mozart, Dulcinea begins to discover her teacher is, too, though for very different reasons; he is always working, obsessed with his music, and the breaks he takes are also obsessive. Nothing in their conversation—nor, soon, in their relationship—is off limits. Candid is as candid does. Though devoted to his wife Constanze and religiously conscientious in his conduct, Mozart can't seem to help himself.

"And Dulcinea? Recognizing early on the impossibility of a long-term relationship, given the constraints of family and society, Dulcinea is nevertheless galvanized by her encounters with a man she comes to believe is a genius at life as much as at music. He does not manage his financial affairs well, he may not be an adroit schemer behind the scenes, he will, to borrow a phrase, soon be dealt the worst of hands with his health. But Mozart is in all ways *alive*, embracing if not celebrating every aspect of what that means, not just spiritually and emotionally but physically.

"For Dulcinea, this reality triggers an awakening of her sexual self in a series of increasingly bold meetings. Ever since her mother's death, she has fought a kind of self-induced fear, as if by refusing to act on her impulses—for example, with her friend

Gustav—she could control not only her behavior but life itself. Mozart, who guessed as much after only a few minutes of listening to her play the piano at her first lesson, knows better than to jeopardize his marriage over a flirtation. But Dulcinea's empathic response not just to his music but to his voice, his gestures, his presence embolden him to trust her. That decision leads him into a liaison that he knows must end, but not before Dulcinea has learned something more important to her—and us—than another melody or song."

Just as we're coming down the hill into Conway, Swig finally changes the subject, mentioning a poet he knew as a young man, a famous someone with whom Swig corresponded over the last ten years of the poet's life.

"Once I sent him a letter that his wife, Ada, returned to me, explaining that it was something he said I should keep." Not until we return from this outing will I learn what the letter said, because Swig will leave it on his desk:

Some of the meetings I cover for the newspaper are a kind of Walt Whitman Kiwanis. There are times when I feel discussion on some point in a meeting will never end, and then there are nights when each chair, the calendar on the wall, the pencils on someone's desk, the different ways people hold cigarettes, the little interchanges that take place between people over sometimes the slightest point (a new coat of paint for a fire truck), the way the air smells outside after a meeting, the cars parked outside a town hall, the pickup trucks, the street lights, a light in a window on the second floor of a house across the street, a person walking down the street, so many things—everything—explode in a kind of inward chain reaction that can go anywhere. I think of Thornton Wilder or Sherwood Anderson in this country, but there is a certain craziness, too, that underlies what can seem from the outside an incredibly tiny public gesture, one small town's lights in the midst of a dark night, nothing and everything in the way the Sunoco sign hangs outside Weeks' Luncheonette as you come around the bend in Rte. 116.

Now, however, Swig wants to share the ending of *The Breathless Present*. "Over three years have passed since Mozart gave his last lesson to Dulcinea, a concert pianist famous through Europe, newly married and the mother of a boy named...Wolfgang. Ten days after Mozart's death at the age of only 35, Dulcinea has traveled to Prague, the city of Mozart's most ardent admirers, where Nicolai Church is filled to overflowing with men and women mourning Mozart. Writing that night a final entry in her diary, she describes listening to a large chorus and orchestra perform a Requiem. And she remembers the day Mozart asked her to play the scale of C and all that followed, 'the eternal harmony and counterpoint of a man and a woman, the anguished mystery and ineffable beauty of the world that this man put into his music, *made* into his music.'"

Once a prosperous farming community, Conway has been in transition for a number of years, with new families moving in, building new lives on old farms, so in some ways the place has the feeling of a museum. With its sleepy Main Street and barns scattered orphan-like in the surrounding hills, much of Conway still looks in wide angle as it must have generations ago or even when Swig still lived there. But up close, in zoom focus, what's missing—livestock, farm equipment, new fence posts, tilled fields, a tank truck stopping at a farm's milk-room for fresh milk, a man in a blue shirt and blue overalls opening the bar gate in a pasture as he calls his cows—becomes apparent.

After our last visit, Swig included me in a sestina he revised about some Conway cellar holes.

I

Under the moss, beside some still,
Gray, somber stones, set slightly back
From the road, Jack finds a rusted, old,
Dilapidated baby's carriage,
Lying alone. We sit near the leaves
Of sugar maples and listen: no wind.

II

Throughout these woods, stone walls wind,
And, after years of ruin, still
They separate: the trees, the leaves,
The former pastures gone back
Full cycle, save for a carriage.
Even the shaded sun seems old.

III

Across the road: the graves of old
First settlers. (Now, is that the wind?)
Long ago, the stage coach carriage
Came through; the old dirt road is still
Intact. We wander further back,
See broken glass among the leaves.

IV

Stumbling from where a path leaves
The road, we find foundations: old,
Neat, chiseled stones, with soil piled back
Behind, supporting only air, the wind,
Wild vegetation, a dream: still-
Born dream of a child, a carriage,

V

A home, a name, a farm, a carriage
Barn (the Sunday rides…). The rotting leaves
Rustle where the root cellar still
Gapes, earth encrusted: earth, that old
Impartial welcomer. Then the wind

VI

Back to the vanished time, back
When one said not "posture" but "carriage,"
When these fields felt August's wind
Sweep over corn and hay, not leaves
Of second growth, and when the old
Headstone names were young, not still.

VII

We hear the wind in the summer leaves;
We look back the abandoned road: old
Carriage, its secret hidden still.

It's been terribly hot all week, and the first place we stop is a little turnoff by the South River, actually an old tractor crossing with a waterside gravel space wide enough for Swig to park. Without a leash, I bound out of the vehicle as soon as he opens the door. I can hear the water in the river gurgling as it flows over small rocks, but I nose around in the fishy smelling sand along the edge before putting first my paws and then, wading further toward a deeper pool, my torso into the chilly, clear, heaven-sent stream.

"Come on, Jack," Swig says, as he stoops to take off his socks and shoes so he can cross without their getting wet. I follow, waiting on the other side as he uses one of the socks to dry his toes, and we are soon on a path through an empty pasture, walking towards a corn field that lies on the other side of a small marsh created by the backup of water from an old beaver dam. Swig stops while I do my stuff, and then calls me again, as if to make certain I don't decide to snack on my own shit, a dog delicacy he's never understood. Nothing makes him angrier than when I disobey over this issue, and I can still cop a treat by pretending to mind him. Imagine what he'd say if he knew what I think of his stranger habits, like checking the messages on his cell phone in the middle of a long hike—something he probably won't be able to do here, I gather, because Conway's cell phone service is so spotty.

Ahead, on the other side of this field, a gap in the barbed-wire fence opens to a much larger expanse, once also used for corn, Swig says, but now what the few remaining farmers here still call a mowing…a hay mowing, that is, a hayfield. The grass, rolling over and beyond in two directions, is a deep green and fairly short, indicating that it's been cut and baled at least once this summer. A well fertilized field, Swig says, may yield three cuttings if there's also a good amount of rainfall, but two is more typical, with the first in June and the second, called rowan, in September.

A kind of path—really just tractor tracks—follows one side of this immense area, near the edge of the South River on our left. We take it, quickly climbing to a ridge that overlooks in the direction we've been going some wooded hills beyond the end of the mowing and yet another adjacent to it. I charge ahead before I realize Swig has stopped and turned around to face some trees bordering a bend in the river and, up and beyond a small field on the other side, he tells me, there was once an enormous red barn situated between a smaller, brown tobacco shed and, somewhat hidden behind two maples and set back from the road farther than the barn upon a little rise, the old white clapboard farmhouse that is still there, though empty.

"That's where we lived," Swig says, as if he were addressing a crowded theater from the stage. But there is no one with us, of course, as he stands still in calf-high grass, gently caressed by an afternoon breeze, the only other sound the persistent staccato of invisible cicadas.

"Of course, back then, everything was different" Swig continues. I'm like, "of course?" But…of course…I let it go. And let him go, too, as he recalls what he says was a hillside pasture behind the barn, completely covered now with trees.

"Amazing that they grew in so quickly," he says. "It can't be more than fifteen years since the last of the cows were sold. I used to hike that hill, Jack, sometimes to the top, where there was a hidden apple orchard, but usually up and across, to the next farm, where I once followed a small stream—really little more than a rivulet—to its source, a spring that started somewhere underground and then surfaced amidst some rocks below an old gravel pit, no longer used.

"Who knew," Swig goes on, lost in his reverie. And at first I can't figure out where this is leading. Then he completes the thought. "I mean, what brought us *here*, now?"

It's the sort of question I often ask myself, but I sense he means something different, crosscutting the tall summer grass by the river with the June rain when he was off to meet his son in New Mexico, where a year later he would travel with Maren, but on this trip his son and he drove from Albuquerque to Santa Fe, where they stopped to say hello to some friends, the family Christian had lived with between high school and college, and then they continued onto Colorado, where they played golf at a new place high in the mountains and then at the Broadmoor in Colorado Springs and finally near Denver where he could see the plains from the second-floor bedroom window of the friends' house where he stayed, the lights in the distance as he looked west and in the morning the mountains would come into view and, he says, looking out, he thought about Bonnie, that very early morning years ago when they almost turned around at that corner near the river in Deerfield, and how clear the air was then, slightly fragrant of spring, slightly chilled, still dark, quiet, calm, their lives suspended as if it were in the turning of the earth, that moment in the dark moist dawn just before Christian was born at the hospital to which they continued driving, finally, when Bonnie's contractions resumed.

Now he begins to gesture with his arms, pointing toward a place below the level of the road that runs somewhat parallel to the meandering stream, another tractor crossing, the place where Mr. Harris who used to own these fields would go on his way to spread manure or chop corn.

"My mother used to wade there with Christian," Swig says, as if he knew I were looking that way, too. "It was just after my dad left, and she had moved nearby. She would drive out on a hot day like this. We were in our own house by then, on the other side of town, but we'd come over, leave our car in the turnaround by the milk room, and walk down to the river. I can see her in her bathing suit, sitting in the stream, the shallow water running around and over her legs, and she'd be holding my son, who was a year old, his small naked body dripping, his blond hair wet, and how he'd holler in delight each time she dipped him in the water. She was my age now."

I can sense we're not going anywhere for at least another minute; it's truly as if Swig is hypnotized. In fact, he hasn't moved since we reached this ridge. I wonder what other memories are on his mind, what people—real or their imagined surrogates—in his heart, as if his entire life were contained in this single moment that itself is becoming part of his past even as we stand here together, just the two of us.

"Where does everyone go, Jack?"

Maybe on the way back Swig will tell me a new story, something that happened or that he'll make up. Or maybe we'll just resume walking. Except for his breathing, Swig doesn't move as he continues to stare across that field, across those years.

"Among the things my mother left was a little cardboard box with her initials written on the top, and then an 'X' and an 'O.' I wrote those initials and the two letters—a kiss and a hug, they symbolized—when I'd given her another of the lapel pins I collected for her when I was away. I'd just come back from somewhere and I'd put the latest pin in that box when I gave it to her. After she died, when I found the box among her things and opened it, every pin I'd given her was inside.

"The first one I took out was circular and depicted some kind of white bird flying over an old ocean-going vessel, and along the bottom portion of the pin was the name of the place I'd visited, 'Bermuda.' Another white bird decorated the next pin, which was from a place called Bodega Bay. I had to think for a minute before I remembered where that was—the northern California coast—a beautiful spot where I saw a whale offshore from the hilltop golf course I later wrote about. Anna was along with me on that visit; I'd picked her up in San Francisco, where she was in circus school, and we'd had a picnic on the drive.

Valérie Remise

"The next pin, in the shape of a small flag, was from the Bahamas, and then I pulled out a pin that said, 'Yankees, 1996 American League Champions,' and then a pin with no words, just a howling coyote and a lone cactus under a crescent moon, and then a small circular design with a flowering tree arching over the name, 'Princeville,' which is a resort in Kauai, and then a star that said, 'Hollywood,' and...oh, Jack, I couldn't keep looking, there must have been four dozen pins in that box, my mother had not only kept them all but every time I used to see her she'd wear one of them, and we'd talk about what fun it would be...would have been...for her to have come along on whatever trip it was, an impossibility for many reasons but we would always say it, dream it, like the last round of golf we were always going to play, how she loved when I was home and she still lived nearby to go out on the course with me, we'd rent a cart and she'd drive and keep score, applauding even my bad shots, and out where the course makes its turn, farthest from the clubhouse—you know the place, Jack, where we were walking just last evening, when that breeze came up and for a moment you could feel the distant approach of autumn even though it's two months away—anyway, we'd stop, and I'd help her out of the cart and give her my 7-iron, and choking up on the handle she'd take a swing and tell me a story I'd already heard about a time she'd played, years before…"

Silence suddenly. Swig has stopped speaking, and I know better than to bark.

Finally he bends down and pats the top of my head, reaches with a hand to stroke first one and then my other ear.

"Where…," he repeats himself before once again pausing. "All the people you love…where do they go?"

IV

The Breathless Present

HALLOWED GROUND OR REFUGE FROM THE REST OF MY LIFE,
Tanglewood this late summer morning is sunny and warm. Parked
my car far from the Shed, something my dad would have done.
Think about him now, sitting in a seat in back, waiting for the music to begin.

"Hansie," Josef would address him. To my knowledge, my godfather was the only adult who used this name of endearment to
write my dad. "Please reconsider," Josef wrote after he left his

manager's post at the orchestra in a letter my father kept that I found among his papers after he died.

One by one now, or in clusters of two or three, the musicians begin to come on stage, but in my memory I see Mr. Bishop standing off to the side, as if he were taking attendance, Mr. Bishop whose teaching studio was located above a store that sold pianos, electronic organs, and television sets. Sitting here in Tanglewood, I remember watching the World Series on a floor model at that store, after my lesson, when Bill Mazeroski hit the home run that beat the Yankees in 1960. That was the year I played Grieg's *Wedding Day at Troldhagen* at my June piano recital. How nervous I was!

A young man—actually a student still, as are most of the musicians in today's group—taps on a drum, with an ear bent down, close to the drum's skin, while with one of his hands he makes tiny adjustments to a kind of lever that tightens or loosens the skin's tension, changing the drum's pitch. Watching him, I see Mr. D'Anna doing the same thing when I was a boy, and I remember my anticipation—always rewarded—of hard candy he would proffer when I visited him onstage, after the concert, as he was covering his drums with pieces of canvas cloth colored a muted beige, suggestive of, but hardly synonymous with, the brass splendor of the drums' outer shell.

Like most of his fellow players, Mr. D'Anna, a short man who sported an immaculate brush of a moustache and spoke in a high voice that belied the stern visage with which, during a piece, his squinting eyes watched Josef for his cue, was a friend of my father's. Sometimes, waiting out the minutes until we could go home, I thought it seemed my dad knew everyone. That was neither true nor possible—the hall sat more than two thousand people, the orchestra was comprised of about a hundred mostly men—but my dad did know more people who worked in or for the orchestra or attended the concerts than I saw in my school life during the two-week intervals between concerts.

We knew the old man with a cane behind whose house we parked our car. We knew the women who sold tickets, whom my father always spoke to, though we had season seats and didn't need to wait in line at a box-office window. We were greeted by name by the white-haired gentleman who took tickets at the door we always entered, unless we had come in backstage that day, where elderly Miss Lattimer zealously guarded the stage door. We knew, too, the women in muted dresses who handed out programs and showed patrons to their seats. We didn't need their guidance, of course, but, when I'd become separated from my parents before the start of a concert, I occasionally indulged in the ritual of presenting my ticket stub to one of them and being ushered to "my" seat (really a lounge chair almost, with a thick cushion and a fuzzy back; not at all conducive to attentive appreciation of the music, but I was more interested in counting the recessed light bulbs in the ceiling or trying, in the darkness, to read the ads in the program after the first piece had begun).

Mr. D'Anna liked to tell jokes. Sucking on a butterscotch lozenge or a peppermint life-saver, which he'd just given my brother and me, we would listen to him ask a riddle, the delight of which, though we didn't fully understand that then, was the way he immediately gave the answer, always in a high voice, and with a smile that seemed to say, "isn't this fun?" Unlike the other musicians (or the audience, for that matter), he didn't have to sit during a piece; he could even walk around a bit. Whenever he played his drums, the success or failure of a particular passage hinged partially on his ability to come in at exactly the right time; I suppose this was just as true, in a way, of a second violinist, but Mr. D'Anna was all by himself. The pressure, I thought, must have been enormous. Hadn't I heard, from my father, the story about the drummer who lost his job because of the mistakes he made during Ravel's *Bolero* when Toscanini was conducting? Yet Mr. D'Anna was cheerful, suave, modest, and self-demurring. He would rather tell jokes afterwards than talk about himself. During a piece his hands moved sometimes with lightning speed. When the sound he had unleashed was supposed to cease, he would muffle it with a quick, hands-down gesture, all the while watching the conductor and keeping count.

"Here, look what I've got," he would say afterwards, as he reached into a pocket to produce a licorice, or one of those fruit candies with the soft insides, the kind I didn't like though I could never tell him and would wait until later to spit it out.

My mind drifts back to the present and I check my pocket to be certain my notebook is still there: *Cutting back from the corner of the farm by the exit to the bike path, Jack and I run into the groundskeeper's son, ten or eleven years old, who is teeing off on the third hole, the only person playing this early, and we walk with him to the third green, where his mom, who now works here in the summer, is doing the bunkers while his dad disposes the grass clippings from the fourth green he just mowed.* Time to move upfront with my score, a reporter's trick I learned at a spring training baseball game in Florida on my first trip south more than thirty years ago: dress the part and look like you know what you're doing. I did that then in Tampa, where I walked into the ballpark with the other reporters with only my notebook as identification, and I do the musical version here, brandishing the score of today's work so anyone looking over my shoulder could read its cover, which says in large letters, "Gustav Mahler, Symphony No. 3." And if someone stops me, I can add that I have an appointment to greet the conductor afterwards, which I do; the truth never hurts.

Waiting for the music to begin, I am still thinking about the farm, which is called Bramble Hill, where Hans the foreman with the ponytail was fussing over his tomatoes when we saw him while his dog Bracken watched Jack warily. In Mahler's summer days he too would have awakened on a morning like this, had breakfast before walking to the little cabin where he wrote this symphony, and then gone hiking late in the afternoon. It is what we do in the world when we are not sick or fighting a war or braving rough seas, and every single note he wrote was written against that same backdrop of all our lives, what also came over me this gorgeous clear morning, that someday my daughter whose growth I embrace will be an old woman, someday her beauty, too, will die, all these people, Bonnie, the superintendent's son, my other children, the passing of this time and these lives, and I tried then and I do now to imagine the enormity of this going on around the world in so many lives, and it is so incomprehensibly vast that I come back to just what is here in my mind and memory. What will survive us?

Wynton and I were on our way back from a gig in Troy, New York when I asked him the same question. It was a warm, spring evening, and the band was leaving by bus sometime after midnight on a long drive to Pittsburg. No longer touring regularly, I was about to drive home, just two hours away. Instead of responding directly to my question, Wynton answered one I had not asked.

"Don't forget the sword," Wynton said in the chauffeured car as we returned to his motel. "It's the source of the music's power." Then his cell phone rang, and we never finished the conversation.

A year passed, and I was in New York for a meeting and called him afterwards.

"Come by in fifteen minutes, I won't be home long," Wynton said, and so I kept walking to his apartment, crossed the plaza that I had crossed on my way to or from countless concerts and rehearsals. The doorman whom I know let me go up the elevator to Wynton's floor. Not until I knocked did I realize Wynton had been saying to me he was not there yet but would be—but only for a short time, because he had a date with someone. And so I waited in the hallway, my knocking on the door triggering an older man's opening his own door a few apartments around the hall corner, and he offered to call downstairs to the doorman who informed us Wynton was on his way.

"Swiginski," was the new variant on my nickname, and then, "hold on a minute." And so I went to the piano, where I found a score of his on a shelf filled with scores, his own mixed with others, mostly Bach, and opened to the place near the end of my favorite piece where the band starts a syncopated clap that audiences at premieres in Spain and Italy and Cleveland, Ohio have picked up in their applause. I sight-read the chord structure on the piano, and then he emerged and lay down on the bed in his bedroom, called my name, we talked for a minute, I mentioned something about the Gershwin encore he had played at a recent gig in Pennsylvania, said, "Let me get some of those grapes in the kitchen," came back to the room and thought he had fallen asleep. Wouldn't have been the first time.

"What you doing, Swig?"

"I was going to read something, but I can see you're tired."

"No, please read."

So I started reading, and at one point I was quite sure because he seemed to be snoring that he was in fact asleep, but I kept reading. And just when I was positive he was asleep I realized from the way he turned his head that he was listening to every word…

…I had driven into Boston in a snowstorm, so much snow the turnpike was deserted. I should have turned around, but I kept going, parked in the garage I always parked in, where my friend Bobby used to work, used to let me park in one of the reserve spaces if the garage were full.

No Bobby that night, wonder whatever happened to him. Strange vibes still here in Boston, not that long since I met another Boston friend also named Bobby. Bobby Joe Leaster. In the 1980s he had been picked up by the police two blocks from Symphony Hall after a store clerk had been murdered. It was fifteen years before Bobby Joe Leaster left prison a free man. He was on death row many of those years for a crime he did not commit. In Boston then, not Mississippi or Alabama but Boston, being black and unemployed and hanging out on a street corner had been proof enough to be sentenced to die.

Bobby Joe works for the city now, works with kids in the neighborhood not far from Symphony Hall, where many of the seats were empty the night of the last performance of All Rise, *even though the concert was a sellout. Because of the snow many folks stayed home, in fact there were several members of the chorus who didn't make it and even a few players in the orchestra, not the Jazz at Lincoln Center orchestra, which was staying at a hotel only a few blocks from the hall, but the Boston Symphony Orchestra, some of whose members commuted from the suburbs.*

I reached the hall just a few minutes before the concert began and poked my head in Wynton's dressing room.

"How's our girl?" he asked.

Just before he left the dressing room and, holding his trumpet, walked onto the stage, he talked with Maren on the phone for a minute.

"You know I love you," he said to her, "me and you, we go back a long way..."

...Standing up, Wynton said, "Hold on," and he called the restaurant where he was meeting whomever.

"Sorry, Swig, can you keep reading while I shave?"

"No prob, have done that before," and I picked up my reading.

Finished shaving, Wynton moved to his closet to iron a shirt. His assistant Gen, perhaps the only person in the world who at any given moment might be able to answer a question about his whereabouts, called from his office. Caring and intuitive, she talked with him on the speakerphone while he continued to iron, and she mentioned a chorus she was singing with later.

"What time is it? I might come," he said to her. And then, to me, "I have to go, get your stuff."

I grabbed my black leather bag, and soon we were in the elevator.

"Where are you going?" he asked.

"Home," I answered. "I have my car here. Do you want a ride?"

He thought for a second as we walked outside.

"Thanks, but I should take a taxi. You want to ride along?"

I answered with my feet. We were at a corner on Broadway and, as if commanded, a taxi pulled up to let someone out and we got in and the driver, an older man, said, looking back, "Are you...Marsalis?" and Wynton of course said, "Yes, I am," and we started downtown and he urged me to continue.

Arriving at the restaurant, Wynton opened the door and reached for his wallet.

"No, I'll pay the man," I said. "I'm going to ask him to drive me right back to where we began."

"Okay," Wynton said, and got out and stood for a moment, looking at me through the window of the cab before it started moving again, waiting to catch my eye, and I looked, and he motioned with his arm and fist, up and down, a kind of variation on the old power salute. He did it a second time and I returned the gesture as he smiled, nodded his head, and disappeared.

A few months later, mid-summer, I was in Maine to see my mother, who since her last hospitalization was again living with my sister. En route afterwards to a friend's new house, where I would spend the night, I called Wynton from my car.

"So, what did you mean that time, when you started to talk about the sword?"

He paused for a moment, and I continued driving to my friend's, looking for the exit off I-295 that would take me towards Brunswick and then, with another turn, the ocean.

"You know when someone or something has truly hurt you?" Wynton said.

"Yes."

"So when that happens, you are completely vulnerable."

"Yes."

"But you must go on. So you create a kind of hardness around the hurt, to protect yourself, to face life."

I listened.

"The music takes you there, takes you back to the place within you where you were hurt, takes you to that tenderness. That's the sword, Swig, because of where the music comes from."

At almost that exact moment in our conversation our cell phone connection started to breakup. We had been talking for about thirty seconds.

"I'll call you back," I said, but I never did, not then, not about that.

In a dream last night, I was traveling with the happiest family as my father used to call us, and I was sure, looking out the window, that we were going in the wrong direction.

"Hans," my mother exclaimed. "Hans. This isn't the way."

Dad kept on driving. He was smoking one of his cigars. The smoke from the cigar filled the car, but no one said, "Put it out." We were used to it.

"Dad," my brother piped up. "Mom's right. This isn't the way home."

Our father had stopped talking. He seemed very intent on the road. The car began to accelerate. Where were we? Why was he doing this?

At a corner we'd come to, the car stopped. My heart was beating fast. I looked at my brother and sister next to me, our mother in the seat by our father in the front, and I opened the door.

"Come on," I said to my brother and sister, "get out."

They followed me to the curb.

"What are you doing?" our father said, raising his voice. But he stayed in the car. Our mother had now joined us on the side of the road. We were holding hands, the four of us, staring at Dad.

Then the light changed and the car left without us. It soon disappeared in the dusk as we watched. Then we began walking slowly in the other direction. No one said anything for the longest time. We never saw Dad again.

Thinking of him now, here in the Tanglewood Shed where he was a conducting student nearly three-quarters of a century ago, I see him at the organ at Easter, I see a hundreds of people in the church turn their heads as he begins the breathtaking arpeggios of the Widor Toccata; soon the brass enter, and the moment comes when, with full organ, he ascends to a climax so loud and powerful that some in the congregation have to cover their ears.

The church is empty another day at dinner time, when my brother and I find him sleeping in the choir loft. Cradling his head in my lap, I try to make a joke about the accommodations, while my brother shuts off the organ and turns out the light on the console.

I see myself talking with him on the front porch, a hot night long ago in mid-September, and there are tears in his eyes as he says to me his dead brother's name, over and over, and the next day we fly to Boston, where he is admitted to Massachusetts General Hospital and sedated with a drug that makes him slur his speech and stumble when he walks. Later, he lies in a hospital bed, unshaven, wearing a white gown, his hair mussed, tubes connected to various parts of his aging body.

"You're going to be fine, Pop," I say.

"No," he answers, "I'm not."

I remember the summer we spent two months in the Adirondacks in an old boarding house that we rented with my father's brother's family. The house was a big clapboard Victorian, with a porch that went around three sides and a double-decker porch in front. Downhill and through the woods was Lake Pleasant, and the nearest town was called Speculator.

Usually my father had one month for vacation, but that summer he took both July and August. We left Buffalo soon after the last Sunday in June. Our Plymouth station wagon was packed full, and I remember that my brother and I made little "forts" in the luggage space. We took the new Thruway, exiting at Utica, and arrived in Pleasantville an hour or two before our cousins, who also brought a teenage babysitter named Ottie with them. My father's brother was working then for *Colliers* Magazine and only came on weekends except for one two-week stretch.

The bedrooms were on the second floor. The center one in the front opened onto an extension of the porch and looked out on the lake. That was my bedroom. There wasn't much in it—a brass bed, dresser, musty wallpaper. One night that summer I was reading in bed and a bat flew into the room. My father and uncle came to my rescue, using brooms to chase the bat away while I hid under the covers.

Downstairs was a large living room and an even larger kitchen. We used to play cards in the living room on rainy days and at night. I remember a sun porch on the west side of the house with a hammock. That was where I stepped on the ukulele that had belonged to my grandfather. I was afraid that I had done irreparable damage, but my uncle was able to get a violin maker in New York to glue it back together. At a party the weekend after my uncle returned, the grownups stayed up late playing poker. There was an old piano in the house, and my father accompanied my uncle on the repaired ukulele. Everyone sang old songs and the house echoed with their voices.

For some reason we didn't swim directly below the house but instead would drive a mile or so to a beach shielded by pine trees that gave off a strong scent on hot days. We'd change behind some bushes before walking into shallow water with a sandy bottom. Once I was caught spying on a young visitor as she changed into her bathing suit. Shame! We built great sandcastles. I remember a warm afternoon when Ottie offered to help me and I refused. She was very upset and cried. My aunt had a talk with me and I apologized to Ottie, but I felt guilty about it the rest of the long summer.

One rainy day in the Adirondacks my father helped us make a scale to weigh the stones we were selling in our pretend store in the carriage barn across the driveway from the house, near a meadow where apple trees grew. Another day, I hiked with him through the meadow and he showed me how to stick an apple on the pointed end of a birch sapling and pull the birch branch back, with the apple still on the end, then let go and watch the apple fly across the meadow toward the house.

There were tears when we left. Returning to Buffalo, I remember how the city seemed strangely foreign, with the late August breeze blowing the leaves in the elm trees along Richmond Avenue. But it was exciting to get back for the end of the Bisons' baseball season. Even going back to school was interesting for a few weeks. Seeing my friends, riding my bike, playing catch with my best friend down the street, wiffleball in the back yard with my brother. Our parents seemed glad to resume routines.

But there must have been nights when my parents reflected. My uncle was healthy then. My father was well established in his work but not so entrenched yet that there weren't still new things each year. It must have been around then my mother began leading the freshmen glee club at the private girls school where my father had become the one-person music department since resigning his position at the orchestra. Or maybe she started a year or two later when my sister went to school. Money was a concern, if not an anxiety, but there was apparently enough to live on. Even with bargain rent, the summer in the Adirondacks must have been expensive.

We never returned to the Adirondacks as a family. Indistinct and blurred not only by the passage of time, those two months are mixed in my memory with the recollection of other summers. In my mind I hear imagined calls for dinner, requests to do a small chore, invitations to play more poker (my father was an expert who enjoyed teaching others) or catch or go swimming or to town or walk back to the apple trees to shoot apples. I smell the pine trees by the beach and the meadow in the afternoon by the hammock on the porch. I hear the rain on the roof late at night when we kids had gone to bed and I'd finished reading and downstairs I could hear the voices of my parents and aunt and uncle and whoever was visiting (from among a constant stream of guests), playing cards or singing or just talking or perhaps sitting on the porch in rocking chairs, listening to the rain or the crickets and thinking about how their children were all asleep and healthy and maybe we'd all go to the double feature in Pleasantville tomorrow. I touch the grass outside in the front and see the paint peeling on the porch and feel wet sand in my hands. I see the white house as you'd see it from the road, much larger than it actually appeared years later when my wife and I went back to look, and though there were trees by the drive as we went up to the house, what I see most clearly is the sun on the south side in the afternoon, making the green grass look almost yellow and lighting up the porch with shadows cast in long, strong shapes from the pillars and railing: the incredible ease with which all those phantom shapes move inside and outside with time to spend—two months!—time that seemed so long then, an entire summer.

Four years after the Adirondacks, our family began spending the month of July in a rented house on a lake in Vermont. For my father, our vacations there were everything his childhood summers in New York were not. He liked talking with people at Willy's General Store and at church suppers, and he was excited when he caught a glimpse of one of the community's famous summer people, who included the author, John Gunther, and, it was rumored, Greta Garbo.

"She bathes nude every morning in the lake," Dad said he had been told.

He took great pleasure—greater, I'm sure, than my mother, for whom it meant extra cooking and an intrusion in her routine—in welcoming overnight visitors from home. They included a couple from our church who were on their honeymoon. The bride, whom my father had known since she was a girl in his junior choir, was a "knockout"—his word, which he used with delight. Her husband, a lawyer, drove a Corvette, which made him an idol in the eyes of my brother and me. Another visitor was a young musician, one of my father's best organ pupils. How my father loved telling the story afterwards about the night they all went skinny dipping and this man had insisted on wearing his bathing suit.

"So I asked him, 'What do you think you have to hide?'" my father said. "And he answered, 'The body is a temple.'"

Laughter brought tears to my father's eyes, and my mother had to beg him to stop. Wearing a short-sleeved shirt with an Hawaiian print and baggy Bermudas, he carefully filled his pipe with Dutch Amphora, lit it, and clenched it in his teeth so that his lips formed an almost perfectly horizontal line. Then his eyes widened and he grabbed the pipe from his mouth as the affectionate laughter began all over again.

Our rented house, with its fieldstone fireplace and wicker furniture, its small kitchen and smaller, second-floor bedrooms, was empty most of the day. Only at night or when it rained did we spend much time there. In wet weather we played Monopoly and poker or we read, unless we took a trip—to Craftsbury Common, where my parents shopped for antiques, or to St. Johnsbury, where there was a coin-operated laundry. On Sunday nights there was always a concert of classical, recorded music, played over speakers from the porch of a house about halfway between ours and the public beach. People went out in their boats or canoes and, on the lake, listened to Rachmaninoff and Brahms.

We bought our Sunday newspaper at the gas station in Greensboro, which was always a busy place, because the owner was also the town's main real estate agent. Crossing the road to Willy's, we waved to passersby, most of whom we didn't know. The store smelled of sawdust, sprinkled on the floor behind the butcher's counter. There was a penny candy counter near the cash register, where long strips of red and black licorice competed for attention with Tootsie Roll Pops and miniature Mars Bars.

Up the road from the store, past a series of white frame houses with large porches and larger lawns, was the golf course where my brother and I played. From where we lived, it was a two-mile drive to the course, on which my brother and I rarely broke 50 for nine holes. Though he was always happy to drive my brother and me over to the course and pay our greens fees, our father never joined us for golf. He did come to our Little League games, though. He was too unathletic to help with the coaching, as some of the other fathers did, but he more than made up for this with his enthusiastic cheering.

My brother and I were among several summer "ringers" who played on that team. We practiced on a hayfield and played games against teams from nearby towns, including cheese-famous Cabot, where each July fourth there was a fair. Cabot had a real baseball diamond, with a backstop and outfield fence, and the stands were filled for the game. The starting center fielder, I'd never played in front of so many people. I made eight errors that day and have never forgotten the feeling of helplessness as ball after ball fell out of my glove. On one line drive, I tried to redeem myself by making a shoestring catch and ended up trapping the ball in my glove on one bounce. There was a runner on third who broke for the plate, and I came up throwing. The ball sailed straight home, about fifteen feet too high, and cleared the catcher, the umpire, and backstop.

Our coach was a medical student from New York City. Why didn't someone good enough to coach want to be a major leaguer? I had frequent talks with him about it, at my parents' suggestion, and I asked him—this was after the Cabot game—if he thought I'd hurt my chances of making the Yankees. He said there were other things in life besides baseball. Shagging flies one warm evening during practice, the smell of clover and the sound of crickets in the air, I wondered if he knew what he was talking about.

Roger Maris was chasing Babe Ruth's record for home runs that year, and I used to walk up the driveway to the mailbox every morning to get the *Buffalo Evening News*, which was mailed to us from home. I'd turn immediately to the sports section and check the box that compared Ruth's 1927 statistics with the progress of Maris and also Mantle, who had a good chance at the record, too. A friend who lived on our Buffalo street sent me clippings from *The Sporting News*, and I'd sit in the hammock on the porch and study them, while my mother made the beds and swept the floors and my father worked at a small table he'd place on the shaded lawn between the porch steps and the water's edge.

Our second or third summer in Vermont, my uncle rented a house there, too, and that was the last time both families were all together. My uncle's height was no longer imposing but awkward; when he had on a bathing suit you could see his ribs stick out and, after exercising, his breathing was labored. He had started to get the shakes. Our house came with a rowboat, and he liked to go out in it with his young son; my uncle rowed, the muscles in his back bulging, and I watched them at twilight from the shore.

My uncle's modern house in New Jersey was located in a small development near the center of a formerly rural town. I remember an evening in April, when we were visiting during school vacation, and my oldest cousin and I walked to the station to meet her father, who took the train home after having crossed the Hudson by ferry. He was wearing a suit, a trench coat slung over one arm, carrying a leather briefcase. He bought us candy in the store across from the station and smoked as we walked along shaded streets past the older houses. He took long strides, and we made a game of jumping to match them.

Later during that same visit, my uncle invited me to tag along while he walked Sheba, the family dog.

"My mom told me you were in a tank in the army," I said as we headed downhill.

An ashen look came over my uncle's face. He said nothing for several minutes while we walked. Finally, he changed the subject to my school work. I never asked him about the war again. Years later, talking with one of my cousins, it finally occurred to me that this moment was a revelation of what today, given his experience as a prisoner of war, would be diagnosed as a symptom of post traumatic stress disorder. Might not my father have suffered from the same thing? We would never know.

The last time I saw my uncle, deep furrows marked the hollows under his bloodshot eyes. His breath smelled of nicotine. His handshake was firm, but his hands twitched when they were not occupied. Flakes of dandruff were scattered on the shoulders of his suit-coat. The skin around his chin and cheeks seemed stretched, so that the bones protruded, while his shirt collar fit loosely around the tendons in his neck. He spoke in a quiet, slow voice, sometimes not completing his sentences. Keeping his eyes on the road ahead, he did not look at me as he talked. He asked simple questions about my father and the rest of the family, and how was I doing in school. He said nothing about himself or the circumstances under which we had met at his home in that New Jersey suburb.

Having the day before attended a conference for high school yearbook editors at Columbia University, I had taken the bus from Manhattan to visit my cousins, whom, I discovered, my uncle was also visiting, because he lived now in a hotel in New York and apparently saw his family only on Sunday afternoons. I accepted his offer of a return ride to the city. Soon we were crossing the George Washington Bridge in a long stream of car lights, which shone in the rear view mirror, so my uncle's figure appeared somewhat in silhouette. He sat well back from the steering wheel, and his long arms looked disconnected from his body. His head nearly touched the ceiling of the car. He lit another Viceroy and took deep gulps of smoke, exhaling with a hiss, his lips barely open. When he stopped the car to let me out, he put a shaking hand on my shoulder and saying, "Give my love to everyone," squeezed until I could feel each finger.

Less than a month after my return from the journalism conference, my mother woke me with the news that my uncle had died of a heart attack, alone, in a hospital in New York. He was a few days shy of turning 45. My parents flew immediately to the

city; my sister stayed home with friends, while my brother and I followed our parents the next day by train. As we arrived in Grand Central Station late in the afternoon, we could see our father waving to us on the platform with my uncle's two daughters. We greeted one another with hugs and kisses, and then, holding hands, walked along the platform to the crowded, main lobby. My father stopped at a newsstand, where he bought the *New York Times*. A loud voice announced the arrival and departure of other trains. Among a thousand strangers, we gathered around my father by the information kiosk in the center of the enormous lobby as he opened the newspaper to the obituary page, which he scanned.

"There," he said to our cousins, pointing to a one-column story near the center of the page. "There, girls, there's your father." Leaning with one hand on my shoulder, hard, he brushed away tears with the other, and we walked from the station without speaking.

I've told my children many of these stories. Maren, living at home while she finishes college, usually just listens, or she'll remind me sometimes that what I've started to say she's heard before. I've told her about my friend who shot himself, the motel he checked into after the holidays when we were in college, the incredibly sad visit I made to see his parents afterwards. I've told her about another childhood friend whose father died suddenly of a heart attack just a few weeks before we started high school. I've told her, too, about the widow of a civil rights martyr I met in Mississippi, how her home was firebombed by the Klu Klux Klan one night and her husband's last word before he died was his wife's name. I've told her about a Native American woman I first met when I was a teenager, doing volunteer work in North Dakota, and how this woman's home and those of many of her friends were taken by the government when she was a child and flooded as part of a project to build a huge dam on the Missouri River.

One night after talking at dinner, I drove to Northampton, where I thought I'd see if a café a friend runs was open, but I got there too late. I kept driving and parked my car in a lot behind Main Street, with the radio on. The local NPR jazz program hosted by my friend Tom Reney was having a Miles Davis night. As I sat in my parked car for a moment and listened to the end of *So What*, I became aware of a woman in what must have been the back of an apartment closing the blinds in her room. I watched as the light in another window went dark. Then I locked my car and walked through an alleyway to Main Street, which I crossed, and then continued walking around the corner of an office building adjacent to City Hall and stopped finally by the first-floor office where my mother once worked part-time for the city's Council on Aging, retiring—in her 80s—not long before she moved to the apartment in Bronxville, and, then, Maine. The office is on the side of the building that looks out on a small park toward an old theater where Anna used to dance in the *Nutcracker* every Christmas. Maren was also in the production one year as a reindeer. I used to meet my mother for movies there, too.

I walked back toward my car, decided on impulse to see if the Iron Horse was open, walked toward it in the dark and knew as I neared it from the quiet outside its entrance that it was closed. I kept walking anyway and stopped, finally, at the huge window behind its stage, remembering how I'd stood at this very spot waiting in line to get into the club the first night I'd come to hear Wynton play.

I peered into the window, looking and listening, as if by some mysterious mental alchemy I could bring back the past, not permanently and certainly not all of it but selected moments: a dinner my mother invited us to at her apartment after one of Christian's soccer games—this must have been in October when he was in fourth or fifth grade, when he played on a Northampton team that the father of one his school friends coached, and the game would have started around four in the afternoon, so it would have been dark by the time it was over and we got to my mother's, where she had set the table festively, even putting out candles, and Christian must have helped her in the kitchen while Anna drew pictures on the floor and Bonnie nursed Maren, who was still a baby. It would have been so warm from the oven in my mother's small apartment that she opened the door to the front patio where she got her mail and liked to sit on nice days, reading and listening to music from the stereo she could hear through an open window.

Now, at Tanglewood, after the rehearsal and a very brief, backstage meeting with the exhausted conductor—once a neighbor of my parents, early in his career, when he held the same post as my godfather before eventually moving west—I walk across the immense lawn, stopping at the old mansion that was formerly the main house of the estate from which Tanglewood was created. I remember a picnic Anna and I shared near the porch, Anna not yet ten years old, wearing a dress because she was going to meet Seiji Ozawa after the concert. I leave the house, walk back across the lawn and find my car and leave the grounds, taking a right that brings me to Hawthorne Street, where I take another right and pass a small cottage that is a replica of the building in which Hawthorne once lived, and with a nod to Nathaniel and his buddy

Herman, who wrote *Moby Dick* in a house not ten miles away, I look for a new place to park, but the entrance to the lot—really a large field—by the cottage has been blocked off. Continuing a little farther, I come to a four corners, across from which, to the left, I know I can leave my car and then cut back, on foot, through a field and around some woods until I reach a meadow that lies between the lot that was closed and the lake—called Stockbridge Bowl—below.

Soon, through the meadow I walk, down past trees that line the dirt and gravel driveway that becomes a path through the woods just before it reaches the little beach the symphony owns, where I must first have been taken swimming by my parents when I was two years old. Probably, my father swam there when he was still living in the Berkshires as a young man, before the war.

I remember again the waist-high water of the nearby Green River, talking with my dad the summer we were together at the house his friends the Homers gave us, and one day we hiked up the mountain where a decade later we would scatter his ashes. After my mother died I returned there and looked for the spot but wasn't sure I'd found it until I came upon an outcropping on which a young couple sat picnicking. I apologized for interrupting them and they said no, it was fine, would I like something to eat.

"No, but thanks," I said. "Where are you from?"

"The Connecticut shore," one of them answered. "We've been here before. There's something about this particular place—the air, the sky."

"Yes," I said. "I know."

And now the beach, the old bathhouse that still stands with its well worn steps.

No one else is here.

I walk down to the water, out onto the small dock.

Shedding my clothes, I dive into the lake

When I surface, I hear the waves lapping, hear my own body moving through the water. And I hear music, this time in my head, as if each of the people in my life was or is a note.

More than a year ago at the iconic Mobil station in South Deerfield, where I used to get our car fixed, I'd asked after Mrs.

Moro, the longtime, beatific bookkeeper whose son Frank, a su-premely cheerful, diffident man in his late 60s, was the proprietor, his older brother Don having retired. Frank, who I learned later was dying of diabetes, told me in a frail but proud voice that his mother, too, had finally stopped working but was in good health.

"I'm so happy to hear that," I'd said. "I can still see her sitting there at the wooden desk, behind the sliding glass window above the counter. How old is she?"

"Ninety-six," Frank had replied, straining both to stand and to speak.

Before I left South Deerfield that day, I'd poked my head into a couple of my other old haunts, the dry cleaners with the black and white photo of its Polish founder by the front door, and the spiffy new office building of our former tax accountant. His agency used to be in the building adjacent to the one-time pharmacy with a lunch counter, where the cigarette smoke mixed with grease and you could get a prescription filled without the prescription if you knew the pharmacist, who eventually went to jail for this, a bum rap I always thought. Finally, I'd continued to my original destina-tion, the kielbasa kingdom of Pekarski Sausage, a place we used to frequent, still run by one of the sons of the same Polish family who once sold sides of beef, too, which we also bought. They raised livestock on a farm where the barn burned one night. A friend called to tell me, and I drove over in the dark and filed a story about it for the *Recorder*, my first front-page byline, though not the last about arson—there would be many more around the time of the Bicentennial, many it turned out started by volunteer firemen.

Tredding water now, I hear in my head my old Amherst Col-lege custodian friend Stanley Dlugozima, see him now and then in town, he always wears a coat and tie when he takes the bus from his Easthampton home each day, long retired, still an ardent Yan-kees fan, told me he once got a double off Art Ditmar in Legion ball, the same Art Ditmar who would go on to play for the Yan-kees, "I was sixteen," Stanley said, "and I doubled off Ditmar, that was in 1946," and he always reminds me to drink red wine for a long life, told me his wife died 25 years ago, said he was "too old now for the ladies," said maybe I'll hit the jackpot someday, and I didn't think to say I already had, meeting him again.

Swimming toward the shore, I hear notes that could be the feeling of someone's hand backstage or the peepers for the first time in April, the wind at night as I come up over the hill at the golf course, the smell of my dad's cigar smoke when I came home late...skating with Maren at the Amherst College rink, skating with my son at Deerfield...cleaning manure in the barn at the farm where I worked that fall in Conway...wading into Cranberry Pond years ago next to some other naked people I did not know...helping to gather hay bales on a hot June afternoon in the field by our farmhouse...hiking to the secret apple orchard that formed part of the boundary between the Harris farm and Archie's...pitching Little League batting practice...hitting a 5-wood on the blind tee shot of the sixth hole at the Ashfield golf course where you put your greens fee of five dollars in a little slot of the one-tiny-room clubhouse that was rarely open...skiing on a spring day with my young son in Vermont the first time he beat me to the bottom, or Stowe where we went *en famille* several times when I was on a magazine assignment, once it was so cold the lifts didn't run, another visit we had dinner at a restaurant on the mountain and then skied down afterwards under the lights, Christian, Anna, and I; another, earlier time, pre-children, Bonnie and I skied there with our friend John, who lives now on the Maine coast in the house where I stayed overnight after I'd called Wynton about the sword, and it was so cold they gave us blankets at the bottom of the lift; yet another trip we were at Smugglers Notch, on the other side of the mountain, a place we have been often, in the winter with the summit road closed you have to drive around the mountain to reach it, though you used to be able to trek across a frozen lake and ski Stowe if you were at Smugglers, which we once did and I wrote about that, kept that column for many years, long after I'd stopped seeing movies in Greenfield's old Showplace or Garden Theater and then walked next door to the darkened *Recorder* building to write my review, or another time in the early evening, getting something to eat at Carl's Charcoal Broiled that was run by the Greek uncle of my friend Tom, whose wife taught kindergarten at the Conway elementary school and one fall when I was his assistant we built a chimney for someone in Leyden, a town to Conway's north, almost in Vermont, and the chilly mornings there, eating an apple, and then home late in the day for dinner and time to write; if there were indeed a secret to the universe I was certain I was finding it each day in the sound of that milking machine coming on from the milk room or Ed Baxter's greeting at the Shell station, "hey, young feller," and the time after his wife died that he invited me next door, the little house by his station, for a C&C, which we drank as we toasted the memory of Mrs. Baxter, and Ed lit another Winston and offered me one, and how I loved the feeling of the air on my face as I came outside afterwards and could hear the brook that ran behind the station, same stream that went through town, under that bridge where I helped Ray the fire chief pick up those nails that had spilled the morning after the party at the Sportsmen's Club and then turned north, the South River did, and followed the road, or rather the road followed its route, out past the Harris farm and then farther past the sawmill that was now a house and on, beyond the Herzig farm where I also knew the family, cheerful Mr. Herzig who later became the transfer station attendant and whose son Barry who took over the farm and died of cancer before his father and whose sister Gail was married to the superintendent of buildings and grounds at Deerfield Academy and ran the daycare that Christian first went to, and there was a secret swimming spot beyond the woods by one of the Herzig fields and then further north the other farm that Mr. Harris used to own where today there is a miso operation and a CSA farm but back then he sold it to a Connecticut doctor whose kids hung out one summer, one of their friends was my mermaid dressing in the flower fragrant air of early evening, and one night a fuse blew and they used a penny to substitute and the old house with wide boards burned and the doctor sold the place to two brothers who did not remain business partners but one of whom still runs the business…and Jimmy Weeks, the late owner of the Conway luncheonette, who smoked Luckies and you had to watch out that Jimmy didn't drop any ashes on your order if you bought a donut that his hard working wife Marie made, each such temptation weighing half a pound because she used so much lard...what a great day it was in my Conway life when I was welcome to drink coffee and read the *Globe* at one of the tables they had by the old penny-candy counter; I used to eat lunch there sometimes, too; once Jim scolded me for pumping gas with bare feet and a few days later Jim was sitting at the four-stool bar at Fred & Jean's Doghouse, up the road from where we first lived at the Harris farm, a fortress-like restaurant where Jean gave us provisions our first night in town when I came in thinking it was a store...I was sitting in the backroom by the pinball machine eating my favorite steak grinder, and Jean brought me a second beer I hadn't ordered—they served only Budweiser, in mugs that were frosted in a freezer used for no other purpose—and I said, "What is this?" and Jean said, "It is from Jimmy, he says he's sorry he got angry."

Reaching the shore, I climb naked onto the dock and stand there, letting the sun dry me off. Staring at the blue expanse of water, with small waves in the lake lapping on the little beach behind me, I see again the water surrounding the same city where my road life began, where I last flew on a spring morning and rode past homes on the highway with their roofs gone, stopped briefly at a university where the main courtyard was grown over with weeds, the entire campus empty, abandoned cars piled up on a nearby road more than half a year since the day the levees broke and in the lower Ninth Ward where a friend took me that evening saw whole blocks of homes gone, saw houses unmoored from their foundations, saw an uprooted tree in someone's living room, saw a boat in someone else's front yard, saw a weeping woman walking by another destroyed house as if she were looking in her grief for something which she would never find in this city where already tourists were back in the old quarter drinking Margaritas and eating oysters and watching topless dancing girls in clubs along Bourbon Street, drove with another friend the next morning to his mother's home near the city's largest park to her brick ranch on an oak-lined street of single-story homes and every house was empty, windows blown out, doorways boarded up, refuse along the walks, and not a single person on the street nor the next, and then in east New Orleans whole neighborhoods gone, an entire shopping mall boarded up and empty stores closed, gas stations closed, sidewalks piled high with people's possessions, and that afternoon we went back to the old quarter in the Treme section and there was a parade, men in golden shirts carrying golden parasols leading a second line of musicians from the Salvation Army and a kid who played the trumpet and several older musicians and hundreds of other people, old people young people black people white people male people female people following, filling the sidewalks, filling the streets, turning the corner finally onto North Rampart Street to a police escort, and the musicians playing "When the Saints Go Marching In" and they marched into Armstrong Park onto a stage next to the site of Congo Square, the only place in pre-Civil War America where slaves were allowed to sing and dance on Sunday afternoons, and the musicians sang "Peace in the Morning" and people in the audience, most of them standing in front of the raised stage, danced in place—feet tapping, hips swaying, heads moving—to the complicated rhythms within the shadow of the old city's long, often tragic and yet triumphant history.

With a planned visit to see an old friend, I take the long way home from Tanglewood, stopping first in the center of Lenox at a café frequented, I've been told, by James Taylor, who lives nearby. I met him, briefly, backstage during intermission at a Tanglewood concert in which Wynton opened for the evening's apparent main draw, Natalie Cole. It was an odd pairing, I thought, Wynton and Natalie, and almost unheard of for Wynton at that point in his career to open for someone else, but no one including Wynton seemed bothered. I remember fumbling for the title of one of his songs as I introduced myself to James—what everyone in the room called him—but he helped me when I quoted part of the evocative lyric, "the last time I saw Alice."

Enough to Be On Your Way.

No James today, though I know he just performed again at Tanglewood, something he did to astoundingly large crowds every year, and then he and his wife, Caroline—I remember her as Kim, when she used to work for the orchestra—make an annual gift that supports one of the BSO's Tanglewood concerts. In the kind of minor coincidence I can hear Wynton telling me means nothing, as in it was just by chance, I once saw Kim at nearby Canyon Ranch, a trendy spa set within an old estate, where I'd met a friend for a picnic lunch before a concert. Everything, I would say to Wynton, has meaning, but you have to create that meaning, I would add, paraphrasing what he had said to me in Colorado about playing the trumpet.

Walking with my coffee to my car, which I left unlocked by a yarn shop in back of a deli where I once bought a corkscrew—the things we remember—I drive slowly past what used to be the fabled Curtis Hotel, where I hang a left toward the highway that will take me north toward Pittsfield, once a thriving manufacturing center until GE under the ballyhooed leadership of Jack Welch closed many of its now empty facilities. Also the site of Wahconah Park, an historic baseball diamond about which I wrote in my first piece for a glossy magazine, Pittsfield was a frequent stopping place en route to Tanglewood when we lived in Conway and came over via the route I am taking today in reverse, with a detour in Ashfield, where my friend and his wife of many years have restored a Colonial era house.

Even before I reach bucolic Ashfield, thirty or so miles to the east of Pittsfield along a winding, hilly state highway that follows or crosses several brooks and rivers, I'm certain I will detour again, after my visit, and cut over slightly to the north, to Conway. I'm curious to see what's happened at the Harris farm since Jack and I took our last trip. Sometimes it seems to me the place has become a kind of pole star, drawing me towards it through the magnetic power of some strange mnemonic force. Something else may be prompting me as well, something I can't name but can certainly hear.

Initially after we had moved I could not bring myself to return. During my first forays with Wynton, I might have mentioned the farmhouse we had sold but never talked about the practical reasons that had necessitated a decision I can still, twenty years later, second guess. Little by little, however, the town began to pull me back. My children, especially Maren, wanted to see where they had lived when they were little. A couple we know hosted a party every Fourth of July, and we were always invited. There was no place to swim where we had moved, and one hot day I headed up into the hills with Maren and pulled off the road at a tractor crossing over the South River that I remembered from when we had lived at the Harrises.' Later, I came again to the same place with Jack. One time I drove up with a friend who wanted me to take him by Archie's, which I'd heard was often vacant, though his granddaughter still lived in the house she and her husband had built nearby and friends of theirs had bought his sister's place that, I believe, had been inherited by his surviving son (when his other son had died, he called me and asked if I would place an obituary in the *Recorder*, which he dictated, and after it was published he wrote to thank me). On another outing I found his gravestone in a small cemetery, on the other side of the South River, beyond Mr. Harris's cornfields and through some woods, where on a solitary hike years earlier I'd come upon an old man placing flowers by the grave of his wife. A more recent visit was prompted by an ad in the Northampton newspaper that announced the new sale of our farmhouse, and I called the realtor and arranged to see it, likening my request to that of a divorced person who is contemplating remarriage to his or her former spouse. But I was mostly interested in testing myself. How would I react, I wondered, though by then I was already pretty certain I knew. The life we'd lived in that house on the hill wasn't *there*.

But where has "it" gone, I wonder again, as I make the familiar turn a mile north of the town center, the same turn around which Bonnie and I first came on the early August day we rented the apartment. It is late in the afternoon, but the summer sun shines brightly on the fields by the river where Jack and I last walked. Driving past the house, I turn around in the driveway that used to separate a tobacco barn, still standing, and the dairy barn, now just a foundation covered with debris, with small trees and weeds already growing near the spot where the barnyard door once was, and only the shambles of the milk room still standing. Coming back toward the house, I turn up the steep driveway and park where I always did when we lived there, in a space by Mr. Harris's former garden, itself a sea of weeds and brambles.

I don't stay long. From my car, I can see that the picture window of our apartment, which looked out on the garden, is almost completely obscured by the growth of some kind of vine that has been left untrimmed. Other growth behind the house would make passage in a car impossible, but it's an easy walk, on grass that someone has mowed, by a stone retaining wall over which the outdoor fireplace still remains, hidden however by more weeds and bushes. The picnic table is long gone, as, around the corner, is Mrs. Harris's clothesline, though the wooden posts that held it aloft still stand. By that side of the house I come close to the kitchen windows and peer into a ghostly, decrepit emptiness, but can see near the door that the woodstove remains.

On an earlier visit, I was reminded by the Harrises's older son John, who still lives near the turn in the road, that his parents are both buried in the town's main cemetery, which I passed coming from the center of town. I have not been there since the burial of Fred Parker, from whose family we bought our farmhouse. At Fred's funeral service, held in the same Congregational Church across Pumpkin Hollow from our farmhouse where Archie's maternal grandfather had been the pastor—thus his original connection to Conway—the congregation had been invited to speak, Quaker style, and I had stood and remembered aloud how, upon waking, I would look out the kitchen window of the farmhouse across our front lawn, past the pear trees, and then across the adjacent mowing to the house where Fred and his wife Violet lived, and no matter how early I might be up, the light in their kitchen window was already on. Violet, the longtime clerk to the board of Conway selectmen, died of cancer while middle-aged, but Fred hung on for many more years, though he moved to a smaller, new house. Raising cattle and working for the town, he still plowed our driveway sometimes after a big storm, and I would see him sometimes in the backroom at Ed's Shell station, where with Raymond Boyden and my Buffalo friend Jamie Bryce we would all drink Heineken while watching Monday night football on the tiny black and white TV. After Fred's service, a cortege was formed behind the bucket loader he used to drive, the bucket filled to overflowing with flowers, and we followed it to the cemetery where he is buried next to Violet.

I'm standing now by their shared stone. It's on the high edge of the cemetery's main hillside, directly across from which, on a smaller hill, are the oldest gravestones, some dating back to the lives of men who fought in the Revolutionary War and the women who often survived them unless they had died in childbirth. The engraving on those stones is hard to make out, as it is on a few of the newer stones, including that of Lawrence and Dorothy Harris, where some of the lettering is already moss covered. Near their stone, with flowers planted in front of it and a flowering bush to one side, is a stone for Lawrence's father, John, dead more than half a century, whose farm, divided after his death between his two sons, once encompassed more than a thousand acres here in this hilltown river valley.

Looking out, in the direction of the old homestead, I can see the tops of trees at what must have been the northern border of his land holdings, near my old skinny dipping spot. Past there, though hidden from my view, is another hill where Lawrence's good friend Andy Hart used to farm. Andy's stone, shared with his wife Sophie, is on the next little knoll, maybe a hundred feet from where I am standing. I remember when Lawrence made the extraordinary gesture of introducing his hippyish, college-educated tenant to Andy, with whom he went hunting for bear every fall in Vermont, at Stratton Mountain, before the development of the ski area that I still visit at least once every winter. Andy invited me into his kitchen, where he proudly showed me his hunting rifle, on the barrel of which, just like in the movies, were notches for every bear he had killed. I haven't been by there recently, but I know that the Hart farm, before the Sportsmen's Club, has been fixed up by someone new who moved into town.

Near the stone for the Harts is another marked Staelens. It includes the name of a young man who was my student in the grammar school when I was a substitute; only a couple of years ago, driving a tractor trailer on I-91, he was killed in an accident. The name of his grandfather, Ernie, is the first under the surname, dear old Ernie who was our near neighbor in his Pumpkin Hollow house, a brick mason like his son Dick and also a trapper. Ernie grew blueberries behind his house, and I remember stopping to buy some and he, like Andy Hart, invited me into the kitchen, where his wife was baking blueberry pies in an oven across the room from a sink in which Ernie was in the midst of skinning a raccoon.

If I don't leave soon for the half hour drive to Amherst I'm going to be late for dinner. Lingering still, here on this ridge, surrounded by other stones—Ed Baxter's and his wife Anne's close to the top boundary of the property; lower down on the hill, Jean Rhood's, whose Fred & Jean's Doghouse, long closed, was just around the corner from the cemetery entrance, toward the Harris farm; farther down, Raymond Boyden, gone now for a quarter of a century, and we still have in our Amherst kitchen a fire extinguisher, certified by Ray as fire chief and purchased after we moved into our farmhouse—I walk among them a final time, looking for but not finding the marker for a young woman, another former grammar school student, also killed in an accident, I believe on the state highway between Williamstown and Greenfield. Her parents have opened a restaurant on the road leading east out of town. It serves dinner on weekends and is named after their daughter. Someday I must go there and pay my respects to Holly's memory.

With or without a stone, here or elsewhere, tomorrow or twenty years from now, my name, too, will be among these dead and all those others, living and dead, whose paths, as if in a secret symphony of grace given and gratefully received, cross today in the breathless present of this July breeze and the sun, the rustle of green leaves and fragrance of mown grass, sound of birdsong, iridescence of sky. Whatever these beings that comprise ourselves, our bodies, our souls, we are alive in the moment, seeking an echo of our happiness, the recollection of someone's touch, his or her voice, their eyes. Music gives us back that love and then gives it again, what we know, what we hear, the hidden harmony of our being, a sense of owning an instant that feels, long after the music ends, like forever.

Thank You...

...to all the people in this book, especially my family and the extended family of friends, many of whom like Wynton and my father are musicians; and to Christopher Vyce at the Brattle Agency; Steve Strimer at Levellers Press; Wayne S. Kabak; Stephanie Bradford, Denis Laflamme, Stuart Schoffman, Kim Townsend, and David Tripp; Edward C. Arrendell II, President, The Management Ark, and Isobel Floyd-Allen, Genevieve Stewart, and Larry Williamson at Wynton Marsalis Enterprises; Vincent Gardner, Victor Goines, Ryan Kisor, Andre Hayward, Ted Nash, Marcus Printup, and Joe Temperly in the Jazz at Lincoln Center Orchestra; Erika Floreska, Susan John, and Christa Teter at Jazz at Lincoln Center; Katherine Drohan, Bernadette Horgan, James Levine, and Taryn Lott at the Boston Symphony Orchestra; Art Clifford, Marcie Savoie, Norman Sims, and Bruce Wilcox, and Sanford Appell, Lisa Malecha, Molly Quinn, Mandy Russell, and my other students, past and present, in "The Writing Life" at the University of Massachusetts at Amherst; Anne Woodhull, Gordon Thorne, Hans, Casey, and Missy at Bramble Hill Farm; Richard McAdoo and Ellen Zale; Jack Arena, Thom Dumm, Stanley Rabinowitz, and the late Benjamin DeMott, Marshall Schell, and Douglas C. Wilson at Amherst College; Ann Maggs and the Frost Library at Amherst College; the Hampshire College Library; Gordon and Cindy Palley, Jack Shea, David Twohig, and the late Ed Twohig Sr. at the Amherst Golf Club; Donald J. Allison, David Foster, Karen Franklin, William E. Hart, Peter Ickes, Phil Kass, Betsy March, Davina Miller, and the Rev. Robert L. Polk; Joe Bills, Ronnie Carbo, Ed Cole, Vernon Dahmer Jr., Deryle Daniels, Colin Faith, Abbie Gulliver, Shana Kuhn-Siegel, Steven Lee, Karen Moraghan, Kimberly Wang, and Rae-Ann Wentworth; the late William Alfred, Joan Benham, Robert Coles, Stanley Crouch, Lolis Elie, Ann Godoff, Thom Haxo, Hilary Hinzmann, Tracy Kidder, Hana Lane, Cammie McGovern, Charles McGrath, Larry Pruner, Andrea Schulz, Richard Todd, Nick Trautwein, Geoffrey Ward, and William Whitworth; Rob Gibson, Tom Guralnick, Kurt Masur, Neal Robinson, Dawn Singh, Eric Suher, and Michael Tilson Thomas; Marilyn Laverty and Paula Witt at Shore Fire; Gwen Brier, Justine Holdsworth, Katya Magee, and Harriet Rogers; the gang at Rao's Café; Rebecca at Woodstar; Kristina Ashton, Madeline Burke-Vigeland, and Lauren Vigeland; Dave and Patty Barbosa, Rebecca Bolton, Myra Foster, Imani Gonzalez, Deb Gorlin and Alex Gorlin-Crenshaw, John and Agnes Gormley, Jennifer Jade Ledesna, Bonnie MacPherson, the Honorable Christopher Muse, and Barbara Thomke; Annie, Caleb, Faith, Gregory, Jen, Leigh, Matt, Nancy, Stephen, and Tom at Collective Copies Amherst.

The Breathless Present:
A Memoir in Four Movements

was designed and printed
by Steve Strimer of Levellers Press

The paper is Mohawk Vellum
The type is Caslon

5231